PHENOMENOLOGICAL PERSPECTIVES

PHAENOMENOLOGICA

COLLECTION FONDÉE PAR H. L. VAN BREDA ET PUBLIÉE SOUS
LE PATRONAGE DES CENTRES D'ARCHIVES-HUSSERL

62

PHENOMENOLOGICAL PERSPECTIVES

HISTORICAL AND SYSTEMATIC

ESSAYS IN HONOR OF HERBERT SPIEGELBERG

PHENOMENOLOGICAL PERSPECTIVES

HISTORICAL AND SYSTEMATIC
ESSAYS IN HONOR OF
HERBERT SPIEGELBERG

MARTINUS NIJHOFF / THE HAGUE / 1975

ISBN 90 247 1701 9

PRINTED IN THE NETHERLANDS

PREFACE

Professor H. L. Van Breda had hoped to write this preface, but his recent, unexpected and untimely death has left that task in my hands. Although my remarks will not be as eloquent and insightful as his surely would have been, some few words are clearly in order here; for the phenomenological community has not only lost the leadership of Fr. Van Breda these last years, but also the scholarship and leadership of Aron Gurwitsch and Alden Fisher – both contributors to this volume – as well as that of Dorion Cairns and John Wild. Our leaders are fewer now but Herbert Spiegelberg is still very obviously one of them.

This volume thus presents the work of some of the past and presently recognized leaders in phenomenology – e.g. Gurwitsch, Straus, and Fisher – but, more important perhaps, it also presents the work of some of those who are sure to be future leaders of our community of phenomenological philosophers, if in fact they have not already achieved this status. Most, if not all, of the contributors to this volume are in some way or another indebted to Herbert Spiegelberg and his work in phenomenology. The debt takes many forms and is owed by many more than just those represented here; and it is a debt that I believe one of the contributors, Waltraut Stein, has captured very well in her opening remarks:

"He who sings a true song joins in an antiphony and finds that his own voice does not simply die with his own last tones. To understand and to be understood, to love and to be loved, to create and to be the catalyst of creation – if these are the basic chords of life, then Herbert Spiegelberg is indeed singing a true song and this volume may be considered as part of his antiphony."

The original editor of this volume encountered numerous problems which resulted in repeated delays and which make this volume some five years overdue. Since taking over this task myself
about a year ago, my work has been considerably eased by the
cooperation and encouragement of Fr. Van Breda, Prof. Tami-
niaux, and Heinz Leonardy of the Husserl-Archiv in Louvain, This
volume is thus very much a joint effort of the contributors, several
editors and readers, and a publisher – all of whom extend their
best wishes to its recipient, Herbert Spiegelberg.

Philip J. Bossert
Kaneohe, Hawaii
January 10, 1975

TABLE OF CONTENTS

PART I

HISTORICAL PERSPECTIVES

ARON GURWITSCH
New School for Social Research

COMPOSSIBILITY AND INCOMPOSSIBILITY IN LEIBNIZ

In a previous article we endeavored to deal with a paradox which seems to arise in Leibnizian philosophy.[1] Substances or monads are conceived by Leibniz to be totally self-contained and self-sufficient: they cannot act upon one another nor receive any influence from without. Every monad is confined to living in its own states which, all of them, árise only and exclusively from its own grounds. On the other hand, the Leibnizian philosophy contains a great many statements concerning the totality of monads. Every monad represents the entire universe from its particular "point of view." Hence the states and modifications of all monads or substances stand in the ideal relation of mutual correlation and correspondence. Between all substances and monads prevails the principle of the "universal harmony" which manifests itself in the just mentioned thoroughgoing correspondence.

The paradox in question arises from the fact that the monadological doctrine is established by a human mind, one monad among others, subject to the general monadic condition of self-containment and self-sufficiency and that, furthermore, the monadological philosophy is supposed to be understood and eventually accepted by other human minds, equally subject to the same general monadic condition. Under those circumstances, how can the philosopher come to know that there are other monads besides the one he is himself, that all of them represent the same universe, that his mental states, to which he is confined, are coordinated with, and correspond to the states of other monads

---

[1] A. Gurwitsch, "An Apparent Paradox in Leibnizianism," *Social Research* XXXIII, 1966.

and so on? If the monadological philosophy is correct, it is hard to see how it can be conceived; the truth of its doctrinal content seems to be at variance with the very fact of its formulation.

To be sure, Leibniz ascribes to the human mind a distinction and a privilege over all other monads, in the first place the souls of animals, namely the capacity of self-consciousness and reflection upon itself.[2] By this means the human mind may become explicitly aware of its windowless self-containment and of all its states as originating within itself. But self-consciousness and reflective analysis, however far carried out, do not lead beyond the confines of the reflecting monad. It seems that no avenue of access to other monads and their states can thus be opened up. Hence it seems to be impossible to account for the mere conception of a correlation between the reflecting monad's states and those of other monads.

To dissolve that paradox we proposed a working hypothesis according to which every monad and all of its states contain as inherent and essentially determining features references to all other monads of the same universe and to the respective states of those monads. While remaining within its own confines, the reflecting human mind may, by analyzing its own states, discover and disclose the mentioned references which, to stress it again, are part and parcel of the states under reflective scrutiny, since they are inscribed in them as immanent features and thus qualify them and make them to be what they are. Such disclosure, of course, is not tantamount to a detailed and accurate knowledge concerning the other monads and their states nor of the law of coordination obtaining between the states of the several monads. Rather the knowledge in question is indistinct, vague, and highly unspecified.[3] No more is in question than a general and abstract knowledge that there are other monads and that the states of all monads correspond to one another, while the law of that corre-

---

[2] Cf., among other texts, *Considérations sur les Principes de Vie, et sur les Natures Plastiques* (*Die philosophischen Schriften von Gottfried Wilhelm Leibniz*, ed. by C. I. Gerhardt (henceforth referred to as *P*) VII 542); *Essais de Théodicée* III 250 (*P*. VI 265 f); *Principes de la Nature et de la Grâce, fondés en Raison* 4 f. (*P*. VI 600 f); Monadologie 29 (*P*. VI 611).

[3] The difference between those two kinds of knowledge is formulated by Leibniz as that between "rem comprehendere, hoc est quicquid in ea latet in potestate habere" and merely "scire aliquid de re," *Animadversiones in partem generalem Principiorum Cartesianorum* I 26 (*P* IV 360).

lation and correspondence remains unknown as to its specific content. Still, that knowledge seems to provide a sufficient basis for the conception of the monadological philosophy in its general outlines.

Our working hypothesis rests on the assumption that the particular monads cannot be accounted for in their own terms. It is not the case that every particular substance or monad has its being and its nature in its own right and possesses its properties and qualities independently of other monads, such that "ready made" substances, so to speak, are subsequently united into a system (the universe), which might require their equally subsequent adjustment to one another. On the contrary, the particular monad can be accounted for only within the context of the monadic system to which it belongs and as a member of that system. Its membership in that system makes the particular monad to be what it is. All substances pertaining to the system in question mutually determine and qualify one another, such that any given monad has its specific nature and properties on account of all members of the same system possessing theirs. In this sense, all monads can be said to be contained and to be present in one another, that is to say in any given monad. *We interpret the principle of the universal harmony to the effect that every particular monad is essentially oriented with regard to all other monads of the universe, that orientation being a constitutive element of its nature.* Our interpretation derives support and substantiation from Leibniz's insistence upon the unity of the universe, to which we shall presently return.

Methodologically speaking, our procedure purports departing from the traditional approach to Leibnizian philosophy, namely starting from the particular monad and then trying to find the transition to the monadic system.[4] Rather we take our departure from the system of the substances and endeavor to understand the particular monad under the perspective of the systematic context within which it has its place. Since our methodological procedure seems to have proved fruitful in the case of the men-

---

[4] L. Brunschvicg, *Les Étapes de la Philosophie Mathématique* (Paris 1942) ch. XI, who follows the traditional approach, has shown the almost insuperable difficulties by which it is beset.

tioned paradox, we propose to apply it also to the interpretation of the concepts of compossibility and incompossibility.

Leibniz defines possibility by absence of contradiction. By compossibility is meant compatibility of some entity, notion or substance, with other entities while incompossibility denotes incompatibility of entities with one another, each one of which is in itself possible, that is to say free from internal contradictions.[5] Though the terms in question occur frequently in his writings, Leibniz has hardly ever presented an explicit conceptual discussion of the grounds of compossibility in incompossibility. Occasionally he makes the pessimistic remark that incompossibility has thus far remained unexplainable to man, because all primitive notions of which the complex ones are composed, seem perfectly compatible with one another.[6] Still, the use which Leibniz makes of those concepts in the discussion of a few examples strongly motivates and suggests their interpretation with reference to the unity of the universe.

On the strength of the Principle of Continuity it is not only permitted but even required to conceive of species of living creatures between those that actually exist, such that a continuous transition be made possible from one actually existing species to another, which as far as our experience shows us, are separated from one another by discontinuous jumps. However, those intermediary creatures ("créatures mitoyennes entre celles qui sont éloignées") are not encountered in the real world, because not every form or species fits into every order ("toute forme ou espèce n'est pas de tout ordre").[7] They are absent from the universe on account of their incompatibility, as Leibniz expresses it, with the sequence of creatures and things.[8] We furthermore

[5] We say "notion of substance" in view of Leibniz's doctrine that every individual substance has a complete notion (*Discours de Métaphysique* 8 *Leibniz, Discours de Métaphysique et Correspondance avec Arnauld*, ed. by George Le Roy (Paris 1957, henceforth referred to as *Le Roy*), p. 43 f). In this doctrine appears the Leibnizian panlogism, that is to say the conception of reality as an incarnation of logic. The individual substance proves the ontological equivalent of its complete notion, and concepts which have logical meaning and refer to notions may also be applied to the corresponding substances.

[6] "Illud tamen adhuc hominibus ignotum est, unde oriatur incompossibilitas diversorum, seu qui fieri possit ut diversae essentiae invicem pugnent, cum omnes termini pure positive videantur esse compatibiles inter se," *P.* VII 195.

[7] *Nouveaux Essais sur l'Entendement* III, VI & 12 (*P.* V 286).

[8] *Ibid.* ". . . toutes les espèces possibles ne sont point com-possibles dans l'univers tout grand qu'il est, et cela non seulement par rapport aux choses, qui sont ensemble

refer to another text, complementary to the one just mentioned, insofar as the point at issue is not the absence but the presence of a certain creature, in this case a human individual. At the end of the *Essais de Théodicée*, Theodorus is shown in a dream a plurality of possible worlds which, all of them, contain a Sextus Tarquinius, more correctly a certain variety of Sextus Tarquinius.[9] Each "Sextus Tarquinius" takes a certain course of action and has a fate consonant with his course of action. All the courses of action and all the fates differ from one another as well as from those of the Sextus Tarquinius of the real world, the last king of Rome, who because of his crime was deposed and expelled from the city. In other words, any possible world as well as the real world, which, of course, is also a possible world, admits of only one specific variety of Sextus Tarquinius, and of no other. To every variety of Sextus Tarquinius corresponds a specific world.

Compossibility and incompossibility have meaning only with reference to the world or the universe to which the substance in question belongs. At this point the problem arises concerning the manner in which the structure of a world at large and especially its unity is to be conceived. If by world is meant the sum total of existing individual substances and if, accordingly, its unity has the sense of a mere agglomeration, no more is possible than simply to ascertain the presence or the absence of a certain being or substance. Denoting the presence as compossibility and the absence as incompossibility amounts to no more than stating the problem of the reasons of the presence and absence. Not only does that problem seem insolvable, but it also appears impossible to indicate in a general way the grounds on which compossibility and incompossibility obtain. Hence no definition of those concepts can be given.

As his discussion with Arnauld shows, Leibniz does not endorse

---

en même temps, mais même par rapport à toute la suite des choses ... il y a nécessairement des espèces qui n'ont jamais été et ne seront jamais, n'étant pas compatibles avec cette suite des créatures que Dieu a choisie." Cf. also *Essais de Théodicée* II 201: "... comme tous les possibles ne sont point compatibles entr'eux dans une même suite d'univers, c'est pour cela même que tous les possibles ne sauraient être produits ..." *P.* VI 236).

[9] *Essais de Théodicée* III 414 ff (*P.* VI 362 ff). See also the discussion of a plurality of "possible Adams" in *Letter to Landgraf Ernst von Hessen-Rheinfels*, April 12, 1686; *Remarques sur la lettre de M. Arnauld;* and *Letter to Arnauld*, July 4 (14) 1686 (*Le Roy* pp. 88, 108, 119 f).

the just sketched conception of the unity of the world. Arnauld takes exception to Leibniz's thesis that the complete notion of every person contains ("enferme") once for ever whatever will happen to that person as well as in the whole universe.[10] According to Arnauld, Leibniz's thesis entails the consequence that God was free to create Adam or not to create him. Once, however, Adam was created, no room is left any longer for the freedom of God, since all events concerning both Adam and his posterity, i.e. the whole human race, derive with strict necessity ("par une nécessité plus que fatale") from the creation of Adam and the complete notion pertaining to him.[11] Leibniz rejects both alternatives which underlie Arnauld's reasoning, the other alternative being that in order to preserve the divine freedom, a plurality of free decrees or decisions which God takes on, the appropriate occasions must be admitted. From this admission it would follow that the divine decrees or volitions are disjoined and disconnected from one another. God, however, unlike man, does not make his decisions from one occasion to the next, according to circumstances ("selon les occurrences").[12] Strictly speaking, God does not have particular volitions nor issue particular decrees apart and detached from His general will and general decree.[13] His will is all-comprehensive and concerns first of all the universe as a whole which He penetrates by a single glance ("d'une seule vue"),[14] and only secondarily or, more correctly, in a derivative manner the particular substances and persons pertaining to the

[10] *Discours de Métaphysique 8 and Sommaire 13* (Le Roy p. 43 f and 81). It was only the Sommaire, and not the integral text of the *Discours de Métaphysique* that Leibniz had sent to Arnauld through the intermediary of Landgraf Ernst von Hessen-Rheinfels.

[11] Arnauld's *Letter to Landgraf Ernst von Hessen-Rheinfels*, March 13, 1686 and his *Letter to Leibniz*, May 13, 1686 (*Le Roy* p. 83 and 95 f).

[12] Leibniz's *Letter to Landgraf Ernst von Hessen-Rheinfels*, April 12, 1686 (*Le Roy* p. 87 f.).

[13] "Si ... voluntas particularis est, ... quae in nullam generalem potest resolvi, puto nullam Dei voluntatem esse particularem, cum omnia a Deo secundum generales quasdam leges fiant," Bodemann, *Die Leibniz Handschriften der Kgl. Öffentlichen Bibliothek zu Hannover* (Hannover and Leipzig 1895) p. 106; *Essais de Théodicée* III 337: "Dieu ne saurait jamais avoir une volonté particulière primitive, c'est à dire indépendante des Lois ou des volontés générales ..." (*P.* VI 315); cf. also *ibid.* II 196 (*P.* VI 233) and *Letter to Clarke* V 66 and 68 (*P.* VII 407). In this respect Leibniz's position is in agreement with, and has, perhaps, been stimulated by, the views of Malebranche, *Recherche de la Vérité*, XV. Éclaircissement: *Traité de la Nature et de la Grâce*, I. Éclaircissement XV; *Méditations Chrétiennes et Métaphysiques* XI, XIII ff (*Oeuvres de Malebranche* III 215 ff, V 165 f, X 120 ff (Paris 1958, 1959, 1964).

[14] *Letter to Landgraf Ernst von Hessen-Rheinfels*, April 12, 1686 (*Le Roy* p. 87).

universe. That is to say, *in creating Adam*, or, as Leibniz often prefers to express it, *in admitting Adam to existence, God*, so to speak, *did not have in view Adam in particular nor any member of his posterity in particular but rather the entire universe comprising both Adam and his whole posterity as well as all other beings*.[15] Therefore, the question is not as to whether Adam is destined to sin, but rather as to whether Adam, who on account of his complete notion is going to sin, is to be admitted to existence.[16] If, with respect to particular beings and substances of the universe, one wishes to speak of particular decrees, one may legitimately do so, provided the particular decrees are understood as being contained in the general decree and deriving from it as consequences.[17] Leibniz goes as far as to maintain that the particular decrees differ from the general one much like the aspect under which a city appears when approached from a certain direction, differs from its "plan géométral." All particular decrees express the entire universe as every aspect under which the city presents itself expresses the city.[18] In this sense, the universe as a whole has priority over all its particular beings, substances, and monads. Its unity manifests itself in this priority.

The unity of the universe rests upon, and is founded by, a general decree. Leibniz also uses expressions like principal plans ("desseins principaux"), purposes or ends ("fins"), principal or primitive notion ("notion principale ou primitive").[19] These expressions apply not only to the real world which has been admitted

---

[15] *Remarques sur la lettre de M. Arnauld*: "... ce n'est pas tant à cause que Dieu a résolu de créer cet Adam qu'il a résolu tout le reste, mais ... tant la résolution qu'il prend à l'égard d'Adam, que celle qu'il prend à l'égard d'autres choses particulières, est une suite de la résolution qu'il prend à l'égard de tout l'univers ..." (*Le Roy* p. 108); see also *Letter to Arnauld*, July 4 (14), 1686 (*Le Roy* p. 117).

[16] *Specimen inventorum de admirandis naturae generalis arcanis*: "... intelligi ... potest Deum non decernere, utrum Adamus peccare debeat, sed utrum illa series rerum, cui inest Adamus, cujus perfecta notio individualis peccatum involvit, sit aliis nihilominus praeferenda" (*P.* VII 311 f). To speak exactly, one should not say "Deum ... decernere, ut Petrus peccat, aut Judas damnatur, sed decernere tantum ut prae aliis possibilibus Petrus ... peccaturus, et Judas damnationem passurus ad existentiam perveniant," *Opuscules et Fragments inédits de Leibniz*, ed. by Couturat, (Paris 1803), p. 520.

[17] *Essais de Théodicée* I 84: "... tous les decrets de Dieu ... sont simultanes, non seulement par rapport au temps, ... mais encore in *signo rationis*, ou dans l'ordre de la nature ... un seul decrets total, qui est celui de créer un tel monde, ... comprend également tous les decrets particuliers ..." (*P.* VI 147 f).

[18] *Letter to Landgraf Ernst von Hessen-Rheinfels*, April 12, 1686 (*Le Roy* p. 87 f).

[19] *Remarques sur la lettre de M. Arnauld* and *Letter to Arnauld*, July 4 (14), 1686 (*Le Roy* p. 107 f and 116).

to existence, but to all possible worlds as well. Every possible
world corresponds to certain designs or ends which God might
entertain; to every possible world belongs a determinate principal
notion and laws of general order ("lois de l'ordre général") specific
to it.[20] Russell interprets Leibniz's doctrine in a strictly teleological sense,[21] and this interpretation is certainly supported by quite
a few formulations of Leibniz. Yet, according to Lovejoy, Russell
has overemphasized the teleological element, the doctrine in
question, which is closely connected with the principle of sufficient
reason, admitting of a purely logical interpretation, which,
Lovejoy maintains, expresses more adequately the intentions of
Leibniz.[22] At any event, the principal or primitive notion, or,
as we may say, the fundamental notion of a universe, whether
actual or merely possible, strictly determines what may have a
place and happen within that universe, down to the last details,
e.g., that Spinoza died in the Hague, and not in Leiden, since
every circumstance, however insignificant apparently, is connected with the whole order and sequence of the universe in
question.[23] If a single occurrence were different from what it
actually is, the entire universe and all its parts would be different
from the very beginning.[24] Because of the limitations of the finite
human mind, we know only in a general and abstract way that
there is a fundamental notion to every universe, but we do not
know in the sense of "comprehendere"[25] the fundamental notion

---

[20] *Letter to Arnauld*, July 4 (14), 1686 (*Le Roy* p. 116 f); *Remarques sur la lettre de
M. Arnauld:* "... comme il y a une infinité de mondes possibles, il y a aussi une
infinité de lois, les unes propres à l'un, les autres à l'autre, et chaque individu possible
de quelque monde enferme dans sa notion les lois de son monde" (*Le Roy* p. 107);
Specimen inventorum de admirandis naturae generalis arcanis: "... unaquaeque series
universi possibilis certis quibusdam decretis liberis primariis sibi propriis sub possi-
bilitatis ratione sumtis innititur" (*P.* VII 312); "Nimirum Deus videt sese infinitis
modis posse res creare aliamque atque aliam prodituram seriem rerum, prout alias
leges seriei seu alia decreta sua primitiva eliget," *Opuscules et Fragments inédits de
Leibniz* p. 23.
[21] Russell, *A Critical Exposition of the Philosophy of Leibniz* (London 1949), chap.
III 14 f.
[22] A. O. Lovejoy, *The Great Chain of Being* (New York 1965), p. 146. It may be
noted that, according to Couturat, *La Logique de Leibniz* (Paris 1901), p. 221, the
principle of sufficient reason has originally merely logical meaning and is only subsequently given metaphysical and theological significance. Within the present context, the problem of the relation between logic and teleology in Leibniz cannot be
touched upon.
[23] *Essais de Théodicée* II 174 (*P.* VI 218).
[24] *Remarques sur la lettre de M. Arnauld* (*Le Roy* p. 109).
[25] See above p. 4 note 5.

of any universe, not even of the actual one. For this reason, we are not in the position to derive conceptually, i.e. to prove a priori any proposition concerning facts and events in the real or a possible world; in the former case we have to rely on experience.

In the light of the conception of the unity of the universe as founded by its fundamental notion and the strict determinism which that conception entails, an interpretation of the concepts of compossibility and incompossibility may be attempted. Both concepts can be understood in two senses. *Compossibility can be taken as denoting either the relation of a certain substance and its complete notion to the fundamental notion of the universe in question, that is to say the requiredness of the former by the latter; or the relation which obtains between the substance under consideration and all other substances of the same universe on the basis of their common origin from the same fundamental notion.* Understood in the second sense, compossibility means that all the substances of a universe mutually demand, require, and hence, as stated above,[26] determine and qualify one another. This sense underlies Leibniz's definition of a universe, actual or possible, as a collection of compossible entities.[27] Correspondingly, *the incompossibility of a certain substance means its being incompatible with the other substances of the universe in question and, therefore, its being excluded from that universe. Incompatibility and exclusion can have no other ground or reason than the complete notion of the substance in question being at variance with the fundamental notion of the universe under consideration.* Because of the just mentioned human ignorance concerning the concrete and detailed content of any fundamental notion, no more is possible than to define compossibility and incompossibility in a general and abstract manner. As humans we are not able to account for either compossibility or incompossibility in any concrete case. This might explain Leibniz's pessimistic statement concerning incompossibility, which has been quoted before.[28]

In the proposed interpretation, compossibility is understood

---

[26] P. 5 f.

[27] *To Bourguet*, Dec. 1714: "... l'univers n'est que la collection d'une certaine façon de compossibles ... comme il y a de differentes combinaisons des possibles, ... il y a plusieurs univers possibles, chaque collection de compossibles en faisant un" (*P*. III 573).

[28] P. 8 note 11.

as necessity under the fundamental notion of a certain universe or, if one may say so, as co-necessity obtaining between all the substances of that universe, while incompossibility rests on the principle of contradiction. Leibniz's distinction between necessary and contingent truth seems to be disregarded in our interpretation. Such is not the case, however. Necessary truths depend, according to Leibniz, upon the principle of contradiction or, which amounts to the same, the principle of identity and are valid in and for all possible worlds.[29] Compossibility and incompossibility, on the other hand, essentially refer to a certain possible universe and its fundamental notion which, as must be most strongly emphasized, is one among many, even infinitely many others, all equally possible. A certain compossibility obtaining in one possible universe does not have to obtain in a different one, can even not obtain in it on account of the strict determinism which holds for every possible world as a context systematically unified by virtue of its fundamental notion. Leibniz's doctrine of the plurality of possible worlds as here interpreted bears resemblance to the idea of alternative geometries, as developed since the XIXth century.

Far from being dismissed, the distinction between necessary and contingent truths is reaffirmed in our interpretation. With respect to contingent truths, Leibniz uses the expression necessity by hypothesis ("ex hypothesi") and, so to speak, by accident ("par accident").[30] We take the term hypothesis to refer to the fundamental notion of the universe within which the contingent truth in question holds, and we, furthermore, see in the *fundamental notion* the *ultimate sufficient reason* for whatever pertains to, and happens in, that universe. This explains the preeminent importance of the principle of sufficient reason ("principium reddendae rationis") for contingent truths.[31] Contingency, we submit, has

---

[29] "... Aeternae veritates (read instead of veritatis) nec tamen obtinebunt, dum stabit mundus, sed etiam obtinuissent, si Deus alia ratione mundum creasset," *Opuscules et Fragments inédits de Leibniz*, P. 18. R. Kauppi, *Über die Leibnizsche Logik* (Acta Philosophica Fennica XII, Helsinki 1960), p. 247, points out that Leibniz does not maintain the converse, namely that a truth which is valid in every possible world is by that very token a necessary one. That is to say, the definition of necessary truth does not require the conception of possible worlds.

[30] *Discours de Métaphysique* 13 (Le Roy p. 48).

[31] In some texts Leibniz maintains that the principle of sufficient reason applies to all truths and to all sciences (*P.* VII 200); *Introductio ad Encyclopaediam arcanam* (*Opuscules et Fragments inédits de Leibniz* p. 514); *Essais de Théodicée* App. III 14 (*P.*

with Leibniz two senses. In his critique of Leibniz, Russell recognizes as contingent such propositions only which have an existential import, that is to say, assert existence, and he rejects Leibniz's definition, according to which a contingent truth is one that happens to hold, but whose opposite is also thinkable and conceivable, i.e. could be true, since it involves no contradiction.[32] Abiding by Leibniz's definition, we may say that a true contingent proposition refers to a state of affairs which happens to subsist, but in whose place a different state of affairs might subsist as well. Considering the intrinsic connection which on account of the strict determinism obtains between every single state of affairs and the universe in which it subsists, *the concept of contingency extends to the whole universe in question and its fundamental notion, precisely because it is one among others, equally possible.* Besides the existential sense of contingency, there is the other sense deriving from the idea of a plurality of possible worlds. Our interpretation is supported by a text in which Leibniz explicitly distinguishes two decrees from one another: one being involved in the notion of the series of things and whatever enters into that series, the other actualizing the former and admitting the corresponding series to existence.[33] Hence the actually existing world is affected by contingency in both senses.

Within the context of the present discussion, those matters cannot be pursued any further; it must suffice to indicate the new problems which appear on its horizon.

VI 414); *Monadologie* 36 (*P.* VI 612); in others he confines that principle to contingent truths and to sciences like physics and mechanics, *G. W. Leibniz, Textes inédits*, ed. by G. Grua (Paris 1948), p. 287; *Specimen inventorum de admirandis naturae generalis arcanis* and *Second Letter to Clarke* (*P.* VII 309 and 355 f). For the different and partly controversial interpretations to which that discrepancy has given rise cf. Couturat, *La Logique de Leibniz*, chap. VI & XX; Kauppi, *Über die Leibnizsche Logik*, p. 91 ff; G. Martin, *Leibniz, Logik und Metaphysik* (Köln 1960), p. 29 f; Y. Belaval, *Leibniz Critique de Descartes* (Paris 1960), p. 387 f.

[32] Russell, *A Critical Exposition of the Philosophy of Leibniz*, chap. II 12 and chap. III 13.

[33] "... aliud esse decretum possibile in seriei ac rerum seriem ingredientium notione involutum, quod decernit reddere actuale; aliud esse decretum quo decretum illud possibile decernit reddere actuale," *Opuscules et Fragments inédits de Leibniz*, p. 24.

RICHARD M. ZANER
Southern Methodist University

HUME AND THE DISCIPLINE OF PHENOMENOLOGY: AN HISTORICAL PERSPECTIVE

I

Determining the place of phenomenology in the spectrum of philosophical persuasions and styles has been a peculiarly difficult question to resolve. A not inconsiderable amount of effort has been devoted to it, as well as the correlative issue concerning the meaning of phenomenology itself. Certainly, these issues form part of the motive for Husserl's repeated efforts to "introduce" phenomenology; and practically every philosopher working within the field has at some point felt compelled to address himself to them.

Herbert Spiegelberg's major study, *The Phenomenological Movement*,[1] makes it quite plain that an even more complex question, however, concerns the historical placement of phenomenology. "Less than any other philosophy did phenomenology enter the scene out of nowhere," he argues,[2] and proceeds to display the brambled path one must take if he would grapple directly with the problem. In order to put the question manageably, it is imperative to delineate the forbiddingly diverse uses of the term itself, and the varieties of "phenomenologies" issuing from them. It is likewise necessary to undertake the job of establishing acceptable criteria for inclusion and exclusion of thinkers as regards the "movement."

A further complication, Spiegelberg rightly stresses, is that

---

[1] Herbert Spiegelberg, *The Phenomenological Movement* (The Hague, Martinus Nijhoff, 1966).
[2] *Ibid.*, p. xxv.

"not only is phenomenology itself still history in the making; even its historiography is still in its formative stages."[3] In one sense this indicates that phenomenology, as conceived by Husserl, is essentially an historically communal task involving an ever-increasing body of phenomenological co-workers. In another sense, it signifies both that the sense of phenomenology is itself a phenomenological issue, and that its historical placement is a cardinal theme precisely because unraveling its sense necessitates the historical thematic.

Indeed, as with any communal undertaking, the sense and history of phenomenology reciprocally shape one another. It is true, as Spiegelberg reminds us, that phenomenology exceeds the work of Husserl, or of any single member of the community. Just so, the work of later thinkers, like subsequent explorers of a newly discovered land, builds upon but also comes to modify and enlarge the scope, meaning, and directions of previous scholars. There thus develops a progressive accumulation of knowledge, and this fact influences the meaning of the undertaking itself. On the other hand, new light is thereby also shed on the work of earlier thinkers, revealing aspects and directions which are implicit and unnoticed in their labors. Reciprocally, that recovery of past efforts has its inevitable impact on the sense and directions of the present, from the stance of which the past is viewed in the first place.

The progressive recovery of phenomenology's past, in short, is a prime theme for phenomenology. The demand of this recovery is at once for a continual re-study of previous philosophy, and the uncovery of the sense of phenomenology as an already nascent theme in it. It is as if ongoing phenomenological study provided the major tools for the uncovering of their own historical sources; as if their historiographical use were a major tool for further determining the sense and place of the tools themselves. In a way, I am suggesting, what Husserl accomplished (among other things) was the explication and grounding of a theme already implicit in much previous philosophy. Making it explicit permits the closer appreciation of the latter's inherent directions; and that very uncovery reciprocally discloses new dimensions of the explicated theme, and hence of present-day phenomenological philosophy –

[3] *Ibid.*, pp. xxviii-xxix.

and so on indefinitely. Spiegelberg's point concerning phenomenology's history and historiography must thus be modified: not
only are these "still in the making," it could not be otherwise.
Being in process is essential to phenomenology, hence to its
historiography and its history.

II

To bring such assertions down to earth it is enough to turn to
a prominent case in point. One of the more intriguing passages
in Husserl's work is found in the first volume of *Ideas*, where he
sets out "the distinctive peculiarity of phenomenology" and then,
in a maddeningly brief but nevertheless suggestive place, he
points to Descartes, Locke, Hume and Kant as exhibiting, in
Husserl's well-known phrase, a "secret longing" for phenomenology. The passage is worth quoting in full:

I have just made use of the term "dogmatist." We shall see that no merely
analogical use of that word is here intended, but that an affinity with the
Theory of Knowledge is implied in the very nature of the case. There is
good reason at this point for thinking of the epistemological opposition
between dogmatism and criticism, and for designating as *dogmatic* all the
sciences which yield to the reduction. For it is clear from essential sources
that the sciences which are bracketed are really just those and all those
which stand in need of "criticism," and indeed of a criticism which they
are not able on principle to supply themselves, and that, on the other hand,
the science which has the unique function of criticizing all the others and
itself at the same time is none other than phenomenology. To put it more
precisely: It is the distinctive peculiarity of phenomenology to include all
sciences and all forms of knowledge in the scope of its eidetic universality,
and indeed in respect of all that which is *immediately transparent* in them,
or at least would be so, if they were genuine forms of knowledge ... As
applied, phenomenology supplies the definitive criticism of every fundamentally distinct science, and in particular there with the final determination of the sense in which their objects can be said to "be." It also clarifies
their methodology in the light of first principles. It is therefore not surprising that phenomenology is as it were the secret longing of the whole
philosophy of modern times. The fundamental thought of Descartes in its
wonderful profundity is already pressing towards it; Hume again, a
psychological philosopher of the school of Locke, almost enters its domain,
but his eyes are dazzled. The first to perceive it truly is Kant, whose
greatest intuitions first become quite clear to us after we have brought
the distinctive features of the phenomenological field into the focus of
full consciousness.[4]

[4] Edmund Husserl, *Ideas: General Introduction to Pure Phenomenology*, tr. W. R.
Boyce-Gibson (London, Macmillan Co., 1931) sec. 62. Husserl was later to modify this,

Three things stand out here. First, phenomenology is most properly conceived as "criticism"; second, its main historical pre-
cedents are Descartes, Hume (and Locke, as seems implied here
and elsewhere) and Kant; third, what is said of Kant in the last
sentence applies to all the others as well – and, reciprocally, the
more clearly are the "greatest intuitions" of past thinkers brought
out, the more clearly do the "distinctive features" of phenomenology come into focus. Postponing the first point until later, I
want to turn to the second, as a way of demonstrating the third.

The references to Descartes and Kant seem obvious enough,
although Descartes especially seems to me in need of thorough
re-study in the light of Husserl's many comments on him. Even
Locke's place can be made plain. Locke, after all, with Husserl
and in opposition to Kant, argued that the mind and its activities
can be directly apprehended without the mediation of those
curious epistemological entrepreneurs, "ideas." Indeed, the mind
is able to be grasped *immediately*, albeit with considerable difficulty. And, the necessary step for accomplishing this is what
Locke calls "distancing":

The understanding, like the eye, whilst it makes us see and perceive all
other things, takes no notice of itself; and it requires art and pains to set
it at a distance, and make it its own object.[5]

Such distancing, it could be argued, while perhaps not carried
out with the strictness of Husserl's epoches and reductions, is
nonetheless not at all dissimilar. In any case, Descartes, Kant
and Locke can be readily appreciated as genuine precursors of
Husserl's phenomenology.

The curious figure in this regard is Hume, for his skepticism
is surely the great arch-enemy of every effort to philosophize
with the ideal of giving apodictic foundations to knowledge.
Beyond this, Hume's version of the theory of ideas, his conception
of mind and perception, and his theory of abstraction have been
prime targets of phenomenological criticism. His "empiricism"
is commonly regarded as anathema in phenomenological circles.

---

for he began to see that Hume had really first posed the fundamental problem of
transcendental philosophy.

    [5] Locke, *An Essay Concerning Human Understanding*, A. C. Fraser (ed.) (London,
Oxford University at the Clarendon Press, 1894), Vol. I, p. 1.

And with Kant, Husserl doubtless believed that Hume's skepticism must be definitively refuted if the idea and ideal of philosophy is to be secured – not to mention science of every type.[6]

Hume's eyes, Husserl argues, are dazzled by his "sensualism"; nevertheless Hume came as close as any to becoming the "founder of a truly 'positive' theory of reason," Husserl later emphasized. Indeed, he went on to remark,

All the problems that move him so passionately in the *Treatise* and drive him from confusion to confusion, problems that because of his attitude he can in no way formulate suitably and purely – all these problems belong entirely to the area dominated by phenomenology.[7]

Behind Hume's skepticism Husserl discerns an entirely new kind of "world-riddle" (*Welträtsel*), namely, "the riddle of a world whose being is a *being produced from subjectivity* ... that and nothing else is Hume's problem."[8] Understanding in what sense Hume was tending toward phenomenology requires unraveling this "riddle."

III

The obscurities and infelicities of his *Treatise*[9] are notorious; so, too, are its minutiae, paradoxes, complicated arguments, and the profusion of issues encountered in it. All the same, the work is a *tour de force*, not only in its detailed undercutting of causal metaphysics but also in its frequently brilliant posing of crucial issues. For all his confusions, however, Hume is unmistakably clear about his aims. Noting the sorry state of knowledge in his day (p. xviii), Hume embarks upon "the only expedient, from which we can hope for success in our philosophical researches," which is to quit the tedious and contentious clamor, the busy bustle of debates over at best marginal issues, and

---

[6] Edmund Husserl, *Phenomenology and the Crisis of Philosophy*, Quentin Lauer (ed.) (New York, Harper & Row, Torchbooks, 1965), pp. 113–15.

[7] *Ibid.*, pp. 113–14.

[8] Edmund Husserl, *Die Krisis der europäischen Wissenschaften und die transzendentale Phänomenologie* (Den Haag, Martinus Nijhoff, 1962), p. 100.

[9] Hume, *A Treatise of Human Nature*, L. A. Selby-Bigge (ed.) (London, Oxford University at the Clarendon Press, 1888). All quotations from this are cited textually.

Instead of taking now and then a castle or village on the frontier, to march up directly to the capital or center of these sciences [logic, morals, criticism and politics], to human nature itself (p. xx).

Despite his aversion to making such claims, Hume is utterly convinced that all the sciences are dependent on what he calls the science of man. This science, the "capital city" of all knowledge, must first be won before any mere village or province can be conquered. Again, he is quite unequivocal:

In pretending therefore to explain the principles of human nature, we in effect propose a complete system of the sciences, built on a foundation almost entirely new, and the only one upon which they can stand with any security (p. xx).

Although he is here completely at one with Descartes, Hume's understanding of this "solid foundation" does apparently distinguish the two thinkers rather substantially. For Hume, this foundation can only be "experience and observation." Beyond these we simply cannot go. Only what appears to us in experience can be strictly relied upon; there is no 'substance' whatever 'behind' appearances (pp. 139, 187–211, 638). What Hume proposes, then, in his march on the capital, is the search for the foundations of all knowledge, one which he regards as lying self-evidently in man himself, discoverable only by the "science of man." In this, of course, he is in fundamental agreement with Descartes and Kant, both as to aim and to the place where the foundations will alone be found.

But the science of man is to be based strictly on experience and observation. What is problematic here is the meaning of these notions: (A) what does the appeal to "experience" entail, and what is to be understood by "observation"? (B) How can and does experience, whatever it might mean, serve as the foundation for the science of man, which in turn is to function as the foundation of all the sciences?

A. The question concerning experience is quite complicated. In fact, Hume's appeal involves two different conceptions, which he tends to conflate uncritically. On the one hand, "experience" can be taken in what has become the usual sense: referring to sense perception in Hume's sense, the appeal is then understood to mean that all knowledge derives from and is based on impres-

sions and ideas. No knowledge of 'ultimate causes' is at all possible. Hume's philosophy is then seen as an empiricism, with all
its usual trappings and antitheses to rationalism – an interpretation having Hume's apparently full endorsement (e.g. pp. xxi-
xxii, 82, 87, 139, 157).

Such an interpretation, however, invariably creates the curious
and irreconcilable anomalies pointed out by many phenomenological critics – not so much in the villages on the frontier but in
the capital city itself.[10] First, if Hume's appeal to experience is
taken to mean that all knowledge is strictly sensory in origin (even
"relations of ideas" have their source in perception) and thus
never *in principle* capable of certainties, then his frequent claims
to "undoubted truth," certainties "beyond question," and other
"unquestioned principles" are mere rhetorical devices designed
perhaps to persuade but with no proper place in his philosophical
arguments. Either that, or they are utter nonsense, since no
appeal to principles is even possible, *including the thesis that no
certainties are "in principle" possible.* And this would mean, quite
obviously, that Hume's unequivocally expressed aims in his
Treatise are *at the outset* either rhetorical or nonsense: the very
idea of the "science of man" being the "foundation" of all the
other sciences would have to be eidetically impossible on the
grounds of the theory itself, and thus his "proposal" would have
to be self-defeating.

Second, such an interpretation (however much Hume seems
to support it) would render his philosophical assertions radically
unaccountable and unintelligible, his *caveat* against what he calls
the infelicities of language notwithstanding. The thesis that perception consists of "impressions and ideas," that ideas become
connected by means of the "associative principles," and similar
theses he maintains about the mind, knowledge, and the like,
are neither mere matters of fact nor relations of ideas. The
knowledge that knowledge is either the one or the other cannot
itself be either the one or the other. However difficult it is, as he
says, "to talk of the operations of the mind with perfect pro-
priety and exactness" (p. 105), these difficulties cannot be confused with the modality-character of epistemic claims, on pains

---

[10] See, e.g., Aron Gurwitsch's essays collected in his *Studies in Phenomenology and
Psychology* (Evanston, Northwestern University Press, 1968).

of vitiating the grounds of the enterprise he undertakes. Such an interpretation of experience, in other words, does a gross injustice to Hume's conception (and in many ways, the execution) of his proposal – and this suggests that the interpretation itself, and not just Hume, has gone awry. Are there any grounds for entertaining this suggestion in Hume's work?

I think that there are such grounds, although they are admittedly rarely as explicit as one is led to expect from a philosopher who proposes to construct a "compleat system of the sciences" in order to demonstrate that the grounds of knowledge are to be found in man himself. In fact, Hume's actual practice of his "science" suggests just such a broader interpretation of experience. He proposes to "observe" experience, seeking to apply "experimental philosophy to moral subjects." Noting that there are differences between experiments in natural, as opposed to moral, philosophy,[11] he writes:

We must therefore clean up our experiments in [moral] science from a cautious observation of human life, and take them as they appear in the common course of the world, by man's behavior in company, in affairs, and in the pleasures. Where experiments of this kind are judiciously collected and compared, we may hope to establish on them a science, which will not be inferior in certainty, and will be much superior in utility to any other of human comprehension (p. xxiii).

What is meant by this "collecting and comparing" of "experiments"? To discover the powers and qualities of the mind, Hume's express aim in Book I, he must conduct "careful and exact experiments" which permit the "observation of those particular effects, which result from [the mind's] different circumstances and situations" (p. xxi). This method, one to which he is unusually faithful (although he rarely explicitly deliberates on it as such), seems to have three basic ingredients.

(1) It is clear from his actual analyses that "to observe" the mind in its operations can only be *to reflect* on them – although, again Hume does not explicitly focus on reflection itself as his

---

[11] Hume is by no means consistent in his understanding of the relations between moral and natural science. Indeed, at times he says they are opposed, at others that they are much the same. I would argue that the inconsistency is intolerable, and that the most consistent view, in Hume, is the one which holds that the two sciences are opposed (as asserted in the quotation in the text) – fundamentally, the contrast is between empirical (natural) and philosophical (moral) science.

philosophical method. Instead, he variously uses such expressions as "consider," "find," "reason," "argue," "observe," as well as "reflect." But it is quite clear that for him, or any philosopher, to observe anything at all about "the mind" and its operations, he must necessarily have something which is to be "considered" and on which to base his observation and subsequent arguments. (It must especially be true of a good Humean to recognize that there is no such entity as "the mind" in the abstract.) If he wants to observe "the" mind, he must willy-nilly observe "his" own mind – however subjectivistic and solipsistic that may seem (indeed, I rather suspect that his skepticism is partly tied to this point). However that may be, the principal difficulty with his analysis here is that he rarely distinguishes between the "operations" of the mind *as observed* by him, and the "operations" which *he himself engages in as a philosopher* concerned to discover the former. He continually confuses, in other words, *what is reflected upon* (observed or considered), with *the reflecting itself* – so much so, in fact, that the two are easily collapsed. It is nevertheless clear that when he speaks of "experiments" he is speaking of something done by the philosopher, as distinguished from that on which the philosopher reflects. What he both proposes and in fact carries out (despite himself, it would seem) are reflections on his own mind as set in a variety of circumstances and situations; and from there he moves to conclusions concerning the mind as such.

(2) His experimental method consists of a kind of *inventory* or geography (as he calls it in his *Enquiry*) of the mind and its ingredients. To be sure, his effort to take stock of the minds is frequently mixed in with critical discussion of other views, both philosophical and "vulgar." But at every point his aim is unmistakable: he "pretends" (supposes, claims) to "explain the principles of Human nature" (p. xx), and this pretension is carried out by tracing "up the human understanding to its first principles ..." (p. 266). That he thinks he winds up in "the most deplorable condition imaginable, inviron'd with the deepest darkness ..." (p. 269), is irrelevant here. What is relevant is the kind of philosophical task projected in his "experiments": namely, reflectively to consider the mind in as many and various circumstances as possible, in order to determine its true character and

limits. This reflection is a matter of making an accurate inventory of the mind's operations, ingredients, and the multiple connections among them. The geography purports to be nothing less than the theory of mind which will ground the theory of man, and thus all the other sciences. Such an effort, philosophically to observe the mind in as many different situations as possible, it seems patently clear, is already well on the road to what Husserl describes as a prime method of phenomenological explication – namely, "free variation." Thus, although Hume would doubtless be somewhat disturbed by this way of characterizing his procedure and aims, he is in truth embarked on an inquiry to delineate the *essential features and principles* of consciousness, and thus is already on the brink of phenomenology.

(3) His method involves, moreover, an *appeal to others* to reflect or observe along with him in order to see for themselves whether or not he is correct in his claims. Although he is by no means as explicit as was Descartes in this demand, he is enormously confident (most of the time) that his findings will indeed be confirmed by everyone (e.g. p. 23), but he expressly enters his well-known caveat against the interpretation of this confidence as implying a dogmatism or "conceited idea of my own judgment" (p. 274). Indeed, it seems no extravagance at all to suggest that his railing against the rationalists, and against the faintest suspicion that he himself might have indulged himself in an absolutist word or two, is in truth more negative than positive in import. It seems more an earnest desire to *avoid dogmatism* or conceit, than it is a disclaimer of the possibility of discovering principles which can also be found by others, if they but take the effort to go and see for themselves. And here, too, Hume is already tending toward phenomenology.

The appeal to experience must therefore be understood in broader terms than is usual. If, in fine, Hume's method necessarily involves reflection on his own mental life, and drawing conclusions about "the" mind and its operations in respect of their essential features, and thus also involves an appeal to others; and if, as Hume argues, all knowledge is derived from experience; then "experience" must necessarily include that kind of experience the philosopher has when he engages in his reflective observings, arguings, considerings, and the like.

It would thus appear that "experience" is not only a *thesis* invoking sense experience, but it is also a *methodological injunction* to "experiment and observe" in an effort to determine the "nature of mind" itself. It is therefore crucial to Hume's proposal that one keep in mind that experience not only points to sense perceiving, but as well to the "experiments" the philosopher must perform in order to make experience in the first sense at all stand out as such. What the philosopher finds must moreover always be submitted to criticism, and this invitation to others to follow him in his analysis (cf., e.g.,ₚp. 273) is an essential ingredient in the appeal to experience. In his methods and its requirements, Hume has given several of the prime themes of phenomenology, and thus exhibits very much the same conception of criticism which Husserl is later to emphasize.

B. The second question – how can and does experience serve as the foundation for the science of man? – can be treated more briefly. Keeping in mind the discussion of experience, the crucial distinction, without which Hume's effort is a shambles, is between experience *as reflected upon* (or, as disclosed in reflective observation) and experience *as reflection* (experiment, in Hume's usage). Now, whether or not one agrees with Hume's specific conclusions, it is patently clear that he is indeed embarked on a project seeking to disclose the "solid foundations" of all science, and that he claims that these must be found in the mind itself, if at all. The search is thus for the principles (or essences) of human nature (or mind).

That Hume's *Treatise* (and, the *Enquiry*) literally abounds in such principles is thus not surprising at all. In his own terms, "experience is a principle which instructs me in the several conjunctions of objects for the past. Habit is another principle, which determines me to expect the same for the future" (p. 265). That both habit and experience are founded on the "imagination" is also a principle, however "inconstant" the imagination is. Beyond these are the principles of the division of perception (pp. 1–2), of the association of ideas (pp. 10–11, 92–93), of belief (pp. 96–97, 624), of the connection of cause and effect and the inferences one may legitimately draw therefrom (p. 139), of custom (pp. 102–03, 134–35), and so on.

IV

Despite Hume's militancy regarding the 'impossibility' of our ever reaching "ultimate principles" (pp. xx-xxii, 263–73), it seems clear that his major emphasis here is against those who would indulge their fancy in easy eloquence about matters metaphysical, than it is against the possibility of our being able to learn, through cautious experiments, the principles of human life. Despite his splenetic feeling (p. 270) that "we have, therefore, no choice left but betwixt a false reason and none at all" (p. 268), Hume does in fact make numerous claims of truth concerning the nature, operations and principles of the mind. Whether he regards these claims with skepticism is beside the point. The point is that he makes the claims, and these are expressly seen by him as in need of critical assessment; indeed, he readily admits the possibility of his having been mistaken in his analysis (pp. 105, 623) – even, one must presume, as regards his skepticism.

In short, his skepticism is in its philosophical status an epistemic claim supposedly issuing from his study of man, and thus is a specific philosophical stance, a conclusion supposedly reached *after* his systematic inventory of the mind – or, as we shall say, after criticism. His skepticism has the same status as any other metaphysical stance, in short, and thus presupposes the accurate and adequate inventory which alone is capable of yielding such a conclusion.

And from this emerges one of the most intriguing features of his philosophy – one he does not, unhappily, pursue or even see as such. If he had, he would have found himself even more in the midst of phenomenology than Husserl supposed. Since the point is important, it must be made as explicit as possible. Hume writes:

When we trace up the human understanding to its first principles, we find it to lead us into such sentiments, as seem to turn into ridicule all our past pains and industry, and to discourage us from future enquiries ... We would not willingly stop before we are acquainted with that energy in the cause, by which it operates on its effect; that tie, which connects them together; and that efficacious quality, on which the tie depends. This is the aim in all our studies and reflections: And how must we be disappointed, when we learn this connexion, tie, or energy *lies merely in ourselves, and is nothing but that determination of the mind, which is acquir'd by custom,* and causes us to make a transition from an object to its usual attendant, and from the impression of one to the lively idea of the other (p. 266; my emphasis).

Hume's own response to this (one with which one may of course quarrel) is that a "total skepticism" must follow. For if objects and their connections are products of subjective operations and tendencies (belief arising from custom and habit), and on the other hand, the subject is "nothing but a heap or collection of different perceptions" (p. 207; also p. 635) which do not themselves form any self-identical whole, then radical skepticism is inevitable.

Nevertheless, Hume is saved from his skepticism, for, remarkably, the peculiar thing is that *it matters not in the least to us in our daily lives anyway!* "Carelessness and in-attention alone can afford us any remedy" (p. 218). The "natural propensity" inherent in our daily lives is to go right on about our business as if things really were as we believe them to be. Philosophical analysis shows them to be otherwise; they are merely consequences of habit and custom. It seems, says Hume, that we must either reason not at all, or else reason falsely. What happens, however, as Hume puts it, is that "this difficulty is seldom or never thought of; and even where it has once been present to the mind, is quickly forgot, and leaves but a small impression behind it" (p. 268). While we *as philosophers* are forced to skepticism, then, the *prime fact of human life* is that "if we believe, that fire warms, water refreshes, 'tis only because it costs us too much pains to think otherwise" (p. 270).

Precisely "what is commonly done," however, proves to be the happiest magic for Hume; but he strangely ignores it with almost magnificent oversight. The inadvertence which so easily resolves the excruciating dilemma of skepticism, precisely because of this potent but wholly unaccounted ability of common sense to resolve the skepticism, is exactly what requires exploration – and just this, Hume utterly fails to do. What is it, after all, which "lies merely in ourselves" to account for the lucky legerdemain, the carelessness and inattention, of our common life?

Hume's response is at once evasive and yet strangely compelling: "belief." Although we know, philosophically, and with genuine certainty for him, that ideas are not really connected, we come to believe in connections and really existent objects as a consequence of the effects of the associative principles (pp. 93, 96–97, 102).

We find from common experience, in our actions as well as reasonings, that a constant perseverance in any course of life produces a strong inclination and tendency to continue for the future ... This habit or determination to transfer the past to the future is full and perfect; and consequently the first impulse of the imagination in this species of reasoning is endow'd with the same qualities (pp. 133–34).

This turn to common experience yields the insight that a "secret operation" (p. 104) is at work to produce this strong belief in a connected, continuing objective world and subjective self. But what precisely is this operation and how does it work? And, if it is so potent for common sense life, why is it not equally significant for philosophers?

V

Hume verges on discovering that rudimentary and enormously significant phenomenon which Husserl termed the "general thesis of the natural attitude," and his turn to common experience is likewise on the verge of that central theme in Husserl's later works, the lifeworld. What Hume utterly fails to see, however, is the sense of his own analysis, its cardinal direction. He brings us to the brink of a discovery of immense significance for his own express aims, and then leaves us dangling. What is crucial here is that while he does see clearly that "what lies in ourselves" is that which accounts for connection and regularity, he yet denigrates this very fact ("how must we be disappointed ...") and thereby fails to push his inquiry into that region of belief and custom – *and just that region is precisely what must be examined, on Hume's own terms, as essential to "human nature."* Just this will answer to his effort to "push our enquiries, till we arrive at the more original and ultimate principle" (p. 266). But Hume fails to do just that "more" which his own conception of his task necessarily commits him to do. Just that "strong inclination" is responsible for the belief in the world and in ourselves, and Hume confessedly takes this for granted (p. 218).

Yet, Husserl is clearly correct, I believe, to discern behind Hume's skepticism and its radical formulation of the problem of accounting for objectivity as well as the mind, an entirely new kind of "world-riddle" – as we saw, the riddle of a world whose being is itself produced from subjective sources – specifically, belief and custom.

> Hume's greatness (a greatness still unrecognized in this, its more important aspect) lies in the fact that ... he was the first to grasp the universal *concrete problem* of transcendental philosophy ... The real world and the categories of reality, which are its fundamental forms, became for him a problem in a new fashion. He was the first to *treat seriously Cartesian focusing purely on what lies inside* ...[12]

With Descartes, Hume saw that the nature of knowledge is such that it requires *foundations*, that all science must be securely anchored in those foundations, and that they are to be found only in "what lies inside" – i.e., in the knower, the mind or subjectivity – a fact which, to be sure, drove Hume to despair, since he unfortunately saw in this nothing but reasons for skepticism. In any case, however mistaken he may be and, I think, was in this, for him the "science of man" is the foundational inquiry, and that part of this science which focuses on the mind is the most basic. His method, intended to make it possible to observe consciousness in a variety of common circumstances, is then supposed to enable the philosopher to grasp those features of mind which are invariant throughout these careful and judicious variations. The "principles" of human nature which he seeks are precisely those invariancies found in methodic "experimentation." It is only by attending to human life as it appears "in the common course of the world" that these principles will at all stand out. In all these respects, Husserl emphasizes, Hume

> began by freeing the soul radically from everything that gives it the significance of a reality in the world, and then presupposed the soul purely as a field of "perceptions" ... Within this "phenomenological" realm, he outlined for the first time what he called "constitutional" problems; for he recognized the necessity of making it possible to understand how it happens that, purely within this phenomenologically reduced subjectivity and its immanent genesis, this same subjectivity can find, in a supposed "experience," transcendent objectivities – realities with the ontological forms (space, time, continuum, physical thing, personality) that we already take for granted.[13]

---

[12] Edmund Husserl, *Formal and Transcendental Logic*, tr. Dorion Cairns (The Hague, Martinus Nijhoff, 1969), p. 256.
[13] *Ibid.*, pp. 256–257.

It is nevertheless true not only that Hume failed to appreciate the sense and direction of his own thought, but also that he "completely *overlooked the fundamental essential property of mental life,*"[14] namely, intentiveness. And although his procedure and aims require that methodological shift involved in the epoché and reduction, Hume by no means practiced this consciously. Still, by focusing the central problem of transcendental philosophy, Hume's accomplishment was manifestly profound and consequential for the advancement of the discipline of criticism – which, Husserl consistently urged, is the prime feature of phenomenology.

‹ VI

A brief final point should be made, returning to the quotation already given from Husserl's *Ideas*, in particular to the first part. All the sciences stand in need of "criticism"; that unique science which has this as its task, and which is alone capable of criticizing itself as well, is phenomenology. In other places, Husserl characterizes this discipline as "presuppositionless" in the sense that it seeks to make all presuppositions explicit, leaving none naively taken for granted. It is clear that these are equivalent expressions, for to criticize, as Husserl understands it, *is* to explicate all presuppositions – radically, that is, to the foundations.

As Hume had seen with remarkable, if still naive, insight, "belief" is the core phenomenon of consciousness; or, as Husserl says, consciousness is acceptive or doxic in its foundational thrust. Since every scientific doing involves beliefs (specifically, that mode called epistemic claiming), the criticism of science necessarily requires the turn to consciousness, to "what lies inside", as the source of every believing. More generally, every human engagement whatever – religion, art, science, practical affairs – is necessarily doxic in some modality, and this doxic stratum is the foundational one (as both Hume and Husserl argue). Hence, each is in need of criticism, not only in respect of its doxic modalities, but its non-doxic as well (valuational, emotive, volitional).

Hence, Husserl insists that criticism must no longer be left as

---

[14] *Ibid.*, p. 257.

something done now and then, but must be developed as *an autonomous discipline in its own right*. It has three major levels (two of which were foreshadowed by Hume). First, it is concerned with the foundations of every human engagement (phenomenology of art, religion, etc.). Second, it must focus on the foundations of "belief," that is, on consciousness or subjectivity in all its strata. Finally, since a theory of criticism is necessary to criticism, the discipline must be established with *completeness*, systematically capable of self-criticism – which Hume seems not to have seen. In different terms, phenomenology must be completed by transcendental phenomenology.

Precisely because phenomenology is the discipline of criticism, it comprises a field of issues peculiar to itself – those, namely, having to do with foundations. In this sense, it is deeply mistaken to identify it as merely one more metaphysical stance alongside other, equally possible ones.

Just such a discipline, I have argued, was at the heart of Hume's effort. To paraphrase Husserl,[15] this characterization of Hume is itself made possible by the development of phenomenology as the autonomous discipline of criticism; but the analysis of Hume's work, on the other hand, reciprocally advances the understanding of phenomenology as the fruition of Hume's signal intuition.

---

[15] *Ibid.*

DAVID GOICOECHEA
Brock University

ROYCE AND THE REDUCTIONS

Herbert Spiegelberg has pointed out how Husserl was interested in Royce. There were many reasons for this, not least among which is Royce's method of achieving philosophical certitude or truth. As can be seen in his Gifford Lectures, Royce arrived at truth through what might be called three reductions. What is the reductive method of Royce?

When treating the problem of Ethics in *The Religious Aspect of Philosophy* and when treating the problem of metaphysics in the first volume of *The World and The Individual*, Royce makes a similar methodological move which we might call his method of reduction. Even though this methodological procedure has a very important role in his philosophy he does not speculate on its nature and necessity. Thus in determining the role of reduction in his method we shall not be able to rely upon his analysis of his method but rather we ourselves shall have to analyze how he develops his philosophical argument.

The central argument of the first volume of *The World and The Individual* is a very detailed application of this method of reduction. In fact, the very subtitle points to this method. For if one considers the significance of the subtitle, *The Four Historical Conceptions of Being*, one sees that Royce reduces all conceptions of Being to four basic conceptions. The book is an attempt to make this reduction and an examination of the implications of it. Thus to understand Royce's philosophical method it is necessary to examine this reduction. To accomplish this we might answer two questions: (1) What is the purpose of the reduction? (2) How does he make the reduction?

What is the Purpose of the Reduction?

The purpose of the reduction is to so classify and yet respect the uniqueness of the opinions concerning a problem that in this act one sets up a disjunctive argument, which through a critical and yet ecumenical process logically proves one's thesis concerning that problem.

Consider the task that is before Royce. In his Gifford Lectures he wants to develop a theory of Being that will adequately ground his theory of religion. At the level of both metaphysics and religion he wants to consider all relevant opinions. He wants to show their advantages and disadvantages and from them to construct a theory that keeps the advantages of all and avoids the disadvantages of all. But he is faced with a swarm of opinions each claiming to be the truth. What is he to do with this almost infinite variety? He begins by trying to reduce the many to the one or differences to identity first at the level of metaphysics. He must perform this reduction in order to overcome the infinite variety, in order to so simplify his task that he can at least perform it. His task is to get one theory of Being, so he first reduces the many to four and then the four to one.

Thus the first aspect of Royce's reduction is one of classification. He is not one who thinks he can arrive at philosophical truth through mere conceptual analysis or logical reasoning independent of the history of philosophy. Royce is very much an historian of philosophy and develops his own philosophical theory out of this history. Thus he must make the move from the history of philosophy to his philosophy. He does this by first classifying the theories of Being into their most basic genera and then by moving from the basic genera to one all-encompassing genus.

But this process of reduction by classification is not just a haphazard grouping for the mere sake of simplification. It also aims at grounding Royce's critical analysis. In fact the simplification is for the sake of criticism and criticism is for the sake of further simplification.

The path toward truth or the philosophical path is one of criticism for Royce. He always begins his philosophizing by a consideration of opinions and through a criticism of these opinions he moves towards his own theory. But the criterion of this critical process is rooted in the simplification movement from the many toward the one. For Royce criticism asks the twofold question after consistency and adequacy.

Both the consistency test and the adequacy test are made workable because of the simplification that Royce achieves through the classificational aspect of his reduction. If he were to question the consistency and adequacy of realism or of Platonism or of Plato's realism in the *Parmenides* he would in each case have to prepare for his criticism by way of simplification. He would have to reduce the statements of the realists or the Platonists or of Plato's *Parmenides* to some common denominator before he could see if they were consistent or adequate. Only through a process of classificational reduction can he arrive at a theory to criticize.

But notice, the very classificational process depends upon criticism. How does he find the simplest common denominator? He does this by the criteria of consistency and adequacy. If he wants to classify a group of philosophers as realists there has to be a common trait in their theories. There has to be an agreement among them. They have to be consistent with one another. Their theories have to be adequate to qualify them to be grouped as one.

Thus Royce's simplification is for the sake of criticism and his criticism is for the sake of simplification. But, this is not merely talking in circles, for there are distinctly different moments of simplification and criticism. The first phase of criticism looks toward the consistency among the many and the adequacy of the many to be reduced to basic groups. Once this phase of criticism has led Royce to his basic groups then he applies the test of consistency and adequacy to each basic group and thus moves to the simplicity of his own theory. Hence, in Royce's reductive method there are two essentially different interconnected phases of classification and criticism. There is the test for consistency among the many which reveals a basic class, *e.g.*, he discovers the core of realism by critically viewing what is essentially common to the realists. Then there is the test for consistency within the idea of realism itself. If realism fails this test he moves toward greater simplicity by eliminating one basic theory.

Thus, Royce's reductive method enables him to classify opinions

in such a way that he can meaningfully criticize them and thus
move beyond them. But this is only the negative side of Royce's
reduction. There is also the positive side which we might call his
respect for the individual and his ecumenism. Balancing his
critical classification is his ecumenical respect for the individual.

Royce is aided in his search for truth not only by his method
of classification but also by his method of respect for individuality.
If we consider again the task Royce has before him we shall see
why this is also the case. In *The World and The Individual* Royce
is searching for a theory of Being to ground a theory of Religion.
He considers the opinions concerning Being in both their disadvantages and their advantages. Yes, Royce really means that.
He thinks that each theory must have certain advantages and
these he seeks to preserve. Even though Royce seeks for truth
by finding the common denominator in the swarm he at the same
time searches for that same truth in the "individual" itself. Royce
is committed to the truth of both the many and the one and thus
he seeks to cancel the many into the one and yet to preserve the
individuality of each of the many.

Now apart from metaphysical or religious reasons there is a
purely methodological reason for Royce's doing this, and that
reason can be seen in the very nature of his reductive method.
The negative phases of his reductive method will not work without the positive phases. The very dynamism of his critical classification would be halted without his respect for the factor of
"individuality."

As we have already begun to see Royce's method is dynamic
and not static. There is a constant movement from "individual"
to class and from class to individual and then to another class.
He doesn't reach truth by a once-and-for-all one phase classification. Rather by analyzing the "individual" in a critical process
he arrives at a genus. But then he finds this basic genus inadequate and moves on to another until he finally reaches the all-
encompassing genus. After that there is still the task of interpreting even this basic theory in light of the infinite "individual"
cases of its application. Thus the very two-way movement from
classification to criticism and from criticism to classification is
always by way of the individual.

To be more specific, it is easy to see that Royce's move of

classification or simplification to basics is always at the same time a move of individuation or complexification. To turn to Realism again, Royce argues that Parmenides, Plato, Aristotle, Thomas, Descartes and Kant were realists. This very move is from the class of realism as such to the individuals in it. But then in his very next chapter he also argues that Plato and Thomas were mystics. And then when dealing with the third basic genus of theories of Being he also argues that Plato, Aristotle, Thomas and Kant were critical rationalists. All of these theories are really basically distinct. But that does not mean that it is contradictory for one man to be classified under all of them. In one aspect of his theory he could be a realist, in another aspect a mystic and in still another a critical rationalist. Thus Royce pays so much attention to the individual differences that he makes a continual effort to avoid oversimplification. He respects the many. And yet he knows that only theorizing and criticism will be groundless without classification. He respects the one.

The dynamic aspect of Royce's reduction can be better understood if we also examine the other positive side of his method. As respect for the "individual" balances classification so ecumenism balances criticism and it is in this very balancing that philosophy gets its perpetual motion. By the ecumenism of Royce's method I mean that character of his method whereby he seeks to unite essentially different theories. His ecumenism is not mere eclecticism and thus he avoids both skepticism and a static method. Let us see what this means.

So far we have seen that Royce by a reductive process arrives at a basic theory such as realism. Now this very classification so respects the individual differences of the philosophers whom Royce has classified as realists that he also classifies them as mystics and critical rationalists. Then we have seen how Royce eliminates these classes through critical reduction. So far these three phases of his method are clear. But now comes the fourth phase. Royce does not merely start afresh in his treatment of mysticism or critical rationalism. But rather he goes to them through his critique of realism and his critique of skepticism. And, in fact, he eventually incorporates within his own theory the advantages of all the theories he has refuted. This incorporation of other rejected theories is something more than mere criticism. It is what I call ecumenism.

But Royce's ecumenism is not eclecticism. It is a harmonizing of opposed theories but not by merely placing them side by side externally and statically together. Rather it is a dynamic and internal uniting such that a new being comes from the united members which is truly both but different from either. Royce achieves this ecumenism by constantly going beyond eclecticism through skepticism.

Skepticism and yet going beyond skepticism appears at every moment of Royce's method. Royce looks at the swarm of opinion and it implies either skepticism or classification. He looks at skepticism and he finds it self-refuting and he moves to his first classification. But he came to the first classification through skepticism. He looks at the first classification and it is contradictory. It implies either skepticism or another classification. Skepticism is, of course, out, so mysticism is established. But mysticism is contradictory and so the process continues. But some would say if the process continued forever Royce would in effect be caught up in skepticism. Thus Royce has to establish his theory of the infinite process that doesn't imply skepticism. His theory has to account for all that it has refuted and the skepticism which kept him questioning even beyond skepticism. If Royce were only an eclectic he wouldn't worry about the relation of skepticism to other theories and the relation between the other theories. If he didn't really believe in the advantages of opposed opinions he would fall into the once and for all trap of the static dogmatists.

Thus the purpose of Royce's fourfold reductive method in general terms is very much the same as any philosopher's purpose. He hopes to attain truth by avoiding extreme dogmatism and extreme skepticism. But before we go on to make this much more specific let us pay attention to one final summary note that has emerged out of our analysis of why Royce uses the reductive method.

In our summary statement at the beginning of this section we referred to the reductive aspect of Royce's method as a disjunctive argument by which he logically proves his own thesis. As we have seen it isn't merely a static disjunction. He doesn't just set up either A or B or C or D and then knock out, A, B and C and thus establish D. Rather he sets up B out of A or

skepticism and C out of A or skepticism. Then he knocks out B
and C. Next he gets D out of C. He claims that there are no other
possibilities and he even treats skepticism so as to include it in
D. Then he reviews how D includes the advantages of A, B and
C. That is good logic and it is a fine example of disjunctive reasoning.

Such in general terms is what Royce hopes to achieve by his
reductive method. But more specifically now –

How Does He Make the Reduction?

I am one of these who hold that when you ask the question: What is an
idea? and: How can ideas stand in any true relation to reality? You
attack the World-Knot in the way that Promises most for the untying
of its meshes. (p. 17)

When Royce approaches the question of Being he does it
from this special point of view. He doesn't begin by just asking
about Being or reality but about the relation between Being and
idea. His reductive method is a way of studying this relationship.
He begins with the realistic theory of the relation between Being
and idea.

The first move which Royce makes is the one of classification.
He begins by defining realism and his definition of realism is a
reduction of all forms of realism to their lowest common denominator. However, in performing this reduction Royce does not first
look at the history of philosophy in order to see how many forms
of realism there are and then abstract the essence from the many.
Rather with a process which is much like Husserlian free imaginative variation he focuses on the notion of the independence of idea
and reality as the core of realism. Through conceptual analysis
he sees that independence cannot mean that reality is "outside
the mind" or "other than the mind." (pp. 91–97)

Notice the twofold negativity of this definitional moment of
the classification process. The first negation is the limiting of the
term "realism" according to its extention. By focusing on the
notion of "independence" Royce excludes from the class of realists
those who do not see idea and being as independent. The second
negation is the limiting of the term "realism" according to its
comprehension. By contrasting "independence" with the charac-

teristics "outside of the mind" and "other than the mind" he eliminates the latter from the concept of independence.

It is only at the second step of his classificational movement that Royce turns seriously to the history of philosophy and this is in order to confirm his definition. He elucidates and justifies his reduction of realism to the notion of independence by showing how for the Eleatics, Protagoras, Plato, Aristotle, Descartes, Locke and the Sankhya that is precisely what their realism consisted of. So, having reduced all instances of realism to that basic notion of independence by his twofold negative way of defining, Royce now takes that positive step out toward the many with his historical confirmation. Thus in his simplification down to the basics there is still the respect for the individual differences. In fact there is even a twofold positivity bringing perfect balance. There is an extension of realism to all the philosophers mentioned and by implication to many more. But also there is a picking out of certain key figures like Locke and the Sankhya and by a kind of free imaginative variation in reverse Royce shows how these greatly different individuals are realists. (pp. 97–106)

Having performed the classificational reduction of realism to the notion of independence, Royce immediately proceeds to the critical reduction of realism to the absurd. He begins by asking if the abstract sundering of the what and the that can be consistently carried out. He suggests that pluralistic realism (there are many independent realities) becomes isolationistic and must postulate hopeless complex relating mechanisms. Monistic realism (there is only one independent reality – Parmenides) becomes absurd when faced with the real fact of false opinion. (pp. 107–112)

As is characteristic of his method he continues to define realism until this negative process becomes critical. In other words, the negative side of his classifying reduction flows right into the negative side of his critical reduction. In arriving at his basic essence of realism he saw that to interpret independence as "outside the mind" or "other than the mind" was contradictory. Now he carries this further and shows that no matter how you interpret independence it is contradictory. At root his objection is this. If reality is independent of the idea then there is a gap between them which can never be bridged. That means that

the idea makes no difference to reality and reality makes no difference to the idea. But if reality makes no difference to the idea
then there is no legitimate criterion for saying an idea is false.
But there are false ideas according to the realist. Therefore,
reality must make a difference to ideas. After many exemplifications of this two-pronged attack – the realist cannot bridge the
gap he defines into existence, nor can he explain false opinion.
Royce sums up his criticism with the comment – according to
the realist his theory (an idea) has nothing to do with the world
(its object).

Notice the relation between Royce's classificational reduction
and his critical reduction. When setting up his basic genus he
eliminates certain interpretations of independence as being contradictory. He says "outside of the mind" and "other than the
mind" is not what realists mean because it would be obviously
contradictory. But when eliminating the genus he interprets independence as "makes no difference." He finds this to be contradictory and concludes that realism is false. Now, why at the level
of classificational reduction does he eliminate the interpretation
in light of the genus, and why at the level of critical reduction
does he eliminate the genus in light of the interpretation? The
difference between these two negative moves is to be found in
the positive aspect of respect for the individual or in the historical
confirmation. Royce could not show that all realists meant "outside the mind" by independence but he could show that all realists
meant "having nothing to do with" by independence. Thus Royce
eliminates an interpretation that would not have been held
historically in order to set up his genus. He eliminates the genus
by an interpretation that would have been held historically. The
interpretation "makes no difference" would not be held explicitly
but implicitly by the realists of history. Royce refutes them by
making this tenet explicit.

Also the two reductions are further related in that the critical
reduction always contains within it the classificational reduction.
Royce is able to critically eliminate realism as the theory that
says "the idea makes no difference to the object" – "the object
makes no difference to the idea" because he has definitionally
reduced "independence from" to "makes no difference to."

Royce could stop right here with the failure of realism and

accept the consequences that there is no relation between the idea
and reality. He could say the world-knot cannot be untied. In
short, he could accept skepticism. But he knows that skepticism
is self-refuting and thus he moves on to try another solution. If
the idea and reality are not independent are they identical? That
is the solution of the mystic; it is the second historical conception
of Being.

Royce's method in treating mysticism is the same as it was in
treating realism. He begins by defining Being according to the
mystic as that which when immediate to man satisfies all of his
desires both intellectual and bodily. Again he clarifies his definition, this time by answering the objections of the Protagorian
skeptic, the realist and the worldly critic. Royce shows that the
mystic is not inconsistent when he is concerned with the finite
because he is on his way. (pp. 144–148) He further clarifies the
definition by treating only the predicate and not the subject of
mysticism. He eliminates any concern over what the absolute of
the different mystics might be and chooses to treat only immediacy. By his definition, his answer to the objections against it and
his distinction between the mystical subject and predicate, Royce
again performs the negative side of his classificational reduction.

Then he mentions that the mystics come to this immediacy
because of the inadequacy of the finite in fulfilling their needs.
At the theoretical level the mystic says "no" to realism's contradictions. At the practical level he says "no" by following the as-
cetic way. Royce thinks that all mysticism began in the Upanis-
hads and spread from there into the West through Plotinus. He
sees the entire history of mysticism as taking this twofold path
toward immediacy with the absolute. (pp. 154–156) Here we
again see the positive side of Royce's classification where he extends the limited definition to all mystics. Interestingly enough
in this case, and it is the only case, Royce thinks that the mystic
class is one through historical dependence and not only through
conceptual unity.

As in his treatment of realism Royce next makes his transition
from classification to criticism. His first step of the transition is
to further clarify the notion of immediacy by contrasting mysticism with eleatic realism. He points out how the Eleatics, even
though they held that all Being is one, still had a Knower-Known

dualism. The Upanishadic mystics very explicitly avoid this dualism by their interior approach wherein they discover that they are the One. The famous refrain – "That Art Thou, O Shvetaketu" is a constant of mysticism. Hence immediacy means that I am Being and Being is me. (pp. 156–165)

Royce continues this path of clarification by looking at the implications of immediacy until he reduces the notion to contradiction. The steps through which he goes are as follows: (1) Immediacy is equivalent to unconscious union, for consciousness implies dualism which is absurd. Royce points out historically, especially with the dreamless sleep analogy and the lesson of Yajnavalkya to Maitreyi, that the true self is unconsciousness. (2) Next, Royce shows how the mystic reaches immediacy by the neti neti or the nescio nescio. The Absolute is expressed by contrasting it with the finite. Royce again appeals to the case of Bernard, Yajnavalkya and Browning. (3) However, the mystic does not want to say that his absolute is mere nothing for it is the source of all satisfaction. It is the final truth. Again Royce argues how the intent of the Via Negativa is to express fullness of perfection. (4) However, the mystic does hold that the finite is mere nothing. The many is illusion. Only the One really is. (5) From this arises the contradiction. Royce argues that it is contradictory to say that the finite is mere nothing but that the absolute isn't mere nothing. For one expresses the being of the absolute only in contrast to the finite. And if you reduce the finite to nothing you cannot by way of contrast establish anything more than nothing for the absolute. Thus, in affirming nothing of the finite and not nothing of the absolute, mysticism falls into contradiction. (pp. 186–195)

Thus Royce reduces mysticism to contradiction. He has now knocked out the two extreme possibilities of untying the world-knot – the idea and reality are independent, the idea and reality are immediately identical. Again he is faced with the contradiction of skepticism. He must push on. So he goes back to realism to see if there is any hint of another path between realism and mysticism and he finds moderate realism. One version of this theory would say that the primary sense qualities are independent while the secondary depend on the mind. But for the primary qualities this still has the contradiction of realism and thus realism must not be merely modified but radically transformed. (pp. 195–202) Such is Royce's transition to the third conception of Being, that of critical rationalism.

Upon defining Being as that which gives validity to our ideas (pp. 202–204), Royce does not clarify the definition by contrasting validity with what it is not. Perhaps he finds the negative limiting of the concept unnecessary because this theory of Being is so well-known, being the dominant theory of the 19th century. (pp. 204–207) Instead he moves right in to a twofold positive phase of the reduction by showing the grounds for seeing Being as validity in common sense exemplification and in the history of philosophy.

Conventional entities such as prices, ranks, partnerships are thought of by common sense not as independent realities in themselves. However, they are also seen not as mere facts of private consciousness. They are dependent upon the mind and yet they have a binding force upon the mind. The same is true of moral examples such as justice and charity even though many philosophers would claim these to be less conventional than the former examples. Thus popular speech reflects the Platonic Tradition that culminates in "omne ens est verum." (pp. 207–211) Mathematical entities are of this type. They too are not independent entities and yet they are not merely like six-winged fairies. The mathematician can posit their Being only when he discovers their validity. (pp. 212–220) Thus Royce first gives evidence for the critical rationalist's concept of Being by confirming their theory in a certain segment of everyday thinking. He points out the popular opinion as it were, which supports Being as validity.

But then he also confirms his classification by going to philosophical opinion. In a very interesting interpretation of Lotze's Plato, Aristotle's *Ens in Potentia* as real, Augustine's view of Being as Veritas that looked back to Neo-Platonism and forward to Anselm's ontological Argument, and Aquinas' theory of God knowing all possibilities in knowing Himself, Royce shows that Being as possibility which grounds ideas as true has long been thought. (pp. 227–233) Finally he shows how present-day critical rationalism emerged with Kant who lifted Being as possible experience out of the context of realism. For Kant the *Ding an sich* is a realistic Being independent of the idea. But the phenomena

are the objects of possible experience or the validity of ideas.
Being is that which is experienced and then validates our idea
of it. Spencer, J. S. Mill, Wundt and Avenarius follow Kant in
his interpretation of science and the meaning of Being. (pp. 233–
239)

Thus far Royce has merely established his classification of critical rationalism. But now he begins to question Being as validity
and thus to perform the critical phase of his reduction. The lines
of his criticism which he at first merely hints at by questions are:
(1) if Being is interpreted as those possibilities which validate
our ideas must we not say that those very valid possibilities must
be grounded in other possibilities that are not now experienced
as valid? In other words, if something is not experienced as valid
but is possible to be experienced as valid, isn't it Being also? (2)
if only the universals are real what is the place of individuality?
(3) critical rationalism involves a confidence in reasoning, but is
reasoning identical with experience? (pp. 239–262)

After these preliminary questions, which are Royce's transition
to his critical reduction of Being as validity, Royce goes on to the
chapter on *The Internal and External Meaning of Ideas*. Here by
critically analyzing meaning he finds critical rationalism to be
inadequate and, by saying what is adequate, moves into his
fourth conception of Being. Notice that he does not find the third
conception of Being contradictory but only inadequate. His critical reduction in this case is not to the absurd but to the inadequate.

In his analysis of Being as validity or Being as truth Royce
distinguishes two kinds of truth – the truth of the object and the
truth of correspondence. In analyzing the truth of the object he
discovers two inadequacies of critical rationalism. The first inadequacy reveals itself when one analyzes a judgment. Royce
argues that each hypothetical judgment points indirectly to some
existent object – or, the internal meaning of a hypothetical judgment always intends to an external object – or, the internal
meaning implies an external meaning. He then shows how the
four kinds of categorical judgment can be reduced to the hypothetical judgment and that they also at least indirectly have an
external meaning. Then he shows how the disjunctive judgment
also has external meaning. Now it is just this external meaning

that critical rationalism overlooks. The third conception of Being
is that internal meaning is enough to account for validity or reality. Royce claims that the internal meaning of judgments about
objects implies an external meaning in the object. The truth or
validity of a judgment doesn't lie merely in the inner structure
of the judgment but also in the external meaning of the object.
(pp. 270–290)

In his next analysis Royce shows that the individual alone is
adequate as the object of truth and that the critical rationalist
does not go far enough in postulation of the universal or particular as the object of truth or validity. Royce agrees with the Kantian that we never experience the individual. He thinks that the
form of universality is so telling that every experience is influenced
by it. But he thinks that metaphorically we know of the existence
of the individual and that this individual, which is not the object
of experience but of our love and belief, is the ultimate test of
validity. He argues that in seeking the validity of an idea we seek
to move from vagueness to determinacy. But the full determinate is not the universal or particular of experience but the
individual. Therefore, even though the idea as finite can never be
fully determined it is always seeking that which is to be found
only in individuals. Thus if there is to be validity there must be
individuals. If this is not the case then we again fall into skepticism which, of course, is self-contradictory. Thus Royce makes
another concession to the empiricist. Just as in his analysis of the
judgment he agreed the crushing power of facts had to be respected as well as the stubborn enduringness of ideas so now he
argues that there must be individual facts to ground validity
even though we cannot experience them as such. (pp. 290–300)

Next, in his analysis of truth as correspondence Royce establishes the voluntary side of his idealism by finding the mere
rationalism of the Kantian inadequate. So far he has shown that
an idea goes beyond itself from internal meaning to external
meaning and from its universality to the objective individuals.
He has shown that finite ideas have an ideal which as finite they
can never attain but toward which they must always strive. Finite
ideas are seen as striving. Now he clarifies this notion of striving
in terms of voluntarism.

Correspondence, as Royce shows, is of many kinds. There is

numerical correspondence wherein symbols correspond to things according to a kind of amount. There is cartological correspondence wherein maps correspond accurately. Science seeks pictorial correspondence. The purpose of the idea determines the kind of correspondence sought. Thus, not mere agreement but intended agreement, constitutes truth. Every idea is as much a volitional process as it is an intellectual process. (pp. 300–311)

Objects are not the causes of ideas as the seal is the cause of the impression in wax. How could future or past or distant events imprint their impression upon the wax of present ideas? (pp. 311–316) Rather, there is a twofold predetermination of objects by ideas. The idea selects its object and the aspect of the object in which it is interested. Thus, correspondence implies that the idea predetermines which object it will correspond to and the kind of correspondence it will have. But, with the problem of error and the truth of empiricism in mind, Royce is quick to point out that the finite idea does not predetermine if it shall succeed in attaining entire agreement with the object. (pp. 316–320)

After thus uncovering the attentive selectivity implied by correspondence, Royce now clarifies even further the voluntarism of ideas by attending to the antinomy he has hit upon. The thesis is that: the object seems predetermined by the purpose and internal meaning of the idea. The antithesis is that: no finite idea predetermines in its object exactly the character which when present in the object, gives the idea its truth. Error is possible. (pp. 320–324)

Having reached this antinomy, Royce's notion of Being is now clarified in its essential structures. Being has an extended authority over ideas and yet it is idea selected. What this means can be seen by looking at the implications of the classificational and critical reductions. 1) Since the realistic definition of Being falls into contradiction, Being must be mind-related. 2) However, since mysticism falls into contradiction, Being must be distinct from mind. Here already we have a vague statement of the antinomy. Being is mind-related and yet distinct from mind. The implications which arise from Royce's criticism of critical rationalism further clarify this antinomy. 3) Because ideas have internal as well as external features, there could never be validity unless there were an external criterion which grounds a judgment. Being has an external authority over ideas. 4) But not only that, this Being must be an individual whole self. For the idea is always seeking to move from vagueness to determinacy. Only an individual can fully determine an idea. Now the finite idea always knows under the rubric of universality. But there can be a metaphorical way of knowing the individual through faith, hope, love, desire, work, etc. These metaphorical ways of knowing the individual lead the finite knower on toward a full knowledge of the individual. The external authority which is distinct from idea is an individual. 5) But still, Being is mind selected; it is not merely external to the mind. When we know, we always select our object and the aspect of the object which we know. All finite ideas have this two-fold selective activity owing to their figures on the background structure. Points one and five point to the mind-relatedness of Being and points two, three and four indicate the distinctness of Being from mind.

Already by seeing how Royce uses implication, we can get a glimpse of what we might call his implicational reduction. Just as he drew implications from the first three views of Being in order to arrive at his fourth concept of Being, so will he now draw implications from this concept of Being in order to approach theological, epistemological, cosmological, psychological and ethical problems. To analyze this implicational reduction is work for another day. Let it suffice to say that it is a clarificational process whereby Royce will extend the field of his absolute certain truth that he has reached with the first two reductions.

So Royce's method proceeds according to three reductions. By the first two he reaches absolute and indubitable truth. He has satisfied his philosophical quest to get beyond opinion. But the Being which he has defined is still vague. It needs to be further clarified. By his implicational reduction, he seeks to extend the horizon of his truth.

It is no wonder that Husserl was interested in Royce! I can only wonder if Heidegger knows anything of Royce's treatment of Being. Of course in the second volume of *The World and the Individual*, time arises as a central concept which relates finite man to Being.

Don Ihde

State University of New York at Stony Brook

WITTGENSTEIN'S "PHENOMENOLOGICAL REDUCTION"

In recent years there has been a proliferation of studies and articles comparing the methods of linguistic analysis and phenomenology. Herbert Spiegelberg's "'Linguistic Phenomenology' John L. Austin and Alexander Pfänder,"[1] was among the early contributions to this literature. But until recently most such comparative studies have dealt with structural similarities and differences apart from historical connections. Paul Ricoeur's recent demonstration of the parallel internal developments of theory in Wittgenstein and Husserl from an early "abstract" to a latter "concrete" emphasis is a good example of possible parallel evolution.

However, Spiegelberg's noteworthy sense of the historical and even personal connections between philosophers has raised a new set of questions. His article, "The Puzzle of Ludwig Wittgenstein's *Phänomenologie* (1929–?)"[2] suddenly re-opened for me a question left dangling some years ago. I was struck when I first read the *Philosophical Investigations* by passages which seemed to be almost intimate arguments with Husserlian phenomenology, but yet couched in emphases which seemed to fit all too neatly the curves of theories once more closely related. I had argued in class, but never in print, that there seemed to be some sort of "phenomenology" but with an inverted emphasis in Wittgenstein and at the time I thought the key was to be found in Husserl's evaluation

---

[1] H. Spiegelberg, "'Linguistic Phenomenology' John L. Austin and Alexander Pfänder," *Memorias del XIII Congreso de Filosofia, Comunicaciones Libres*, Vol. IX, pp. 509–517.

[2] H. Spiegelberg, "The Puzzle of Ludwig Wittgenstein's *Phänomenologie* (1929–?)," *American Philosophical Quarterly*, Vol. 5, No. 4, October 1968, pp. 244–256.

of imaginative variations in contrast to Wittgenstein's deliberate
exclusion of them in favor of using concrete objects (bits of
paper colored red, words on cards, etc.).

Spiegelberg's enticing discovery of a short-lived use of a generalized phenomenological vocabulary, presumably begun in 1929
just upon Wittgenstein's return to Cambridge, to its submergence
at the latest in the 1933 *Bluebook* coupled to the hint of an anti-
Husserl question suddenly jelled what had been missing in my
earlier suspicions. And although I wish to be cautious and admit
that the limited thesis argued here remains speculative and based
upon the same limitations Spiegelberg suffered in having no access
to unpublished Wittgenstein texts, I am now willing to offer a
hypothesis: *Wittgenstein was influenced by a generalized phenomenological method which provided in part a basis for the turn to ordinary language. But at the same time the peculiar use of a "phenomenological reduction" takes a turn inverse to Husserl and towards
the isolation and description of linguistic phenomena over a phenomenology of experience.* This hypothesis remains speculative to the
degree that more comprehensive textual evidence is still wanting
for more thorough confirmation of historical connections. But if
the thesis does turn out to be plausible its potential challenge to
the now "orthodox" interpretations of Wittgenstein, dominated
by an "Anglican" scorn for things European and the primarily
neo-positivist empathies of North America, is worth the risk.

I have here chosen to open the question of a phenomenological
reduction by way of the *Blue Book*. According to Spiegelberg's
chronology and evidenced by the text, the phenomenological
vocabulary as such has been submerged. But the investigations
of Spiegelberg have provided clues about how and where this
vocabulary leaves a trace of bubbles. There are some substantial
textual hints. Two of these need initial note: (a) In the short
period of its use, the term phenomenology is clearly linked to
the increasing emergent use of grammar. A grammar, or phenomenology, is the descriptive laying out of structural possibilities of
the phenomena in question. "'Thus *phenomenology would be the
grammar* for the description of those facts upon which physics
erects its theories ... Is the theory of harmony at least in part
phenomenology, hence grammar?"[3]

[3] *Ibid.*, (Spiegelberg's translations, italics mine), p. 254.

The *Blue Book* begins a study which frequently distinguishes a grammatical (hence phenomenological) study as one apart from both physics and psychology. Here, perhaps, lies one reason for the parallel set of problems Wittgenstein addresses himself to, problems which have been major themes in phenomenology as well: solipsism and privacy, a way between realism and idealism, a rejection of the Cartesian tradition of mind and matter, etc.

(b) If grammar is a phenomenology its method must be essentially descriptive. This parallelism, often enough noted, must be more precisely developed. Phenomenologists point out over and over again that a descriptive method is one which seeks to avoid certain types of *reductive* (explanatory) tactics.[4] Rather than reduce all phenomena to some single basic substratum the task is to display the multiplicity and multi-dimensioned aspects of the phenomenon in question. The way to do this is to horizontalize (bracket out) the usual assumptions about the phenomenon. Wittgenstein in the *Philosophische Bemerkungen* points out that one must, in "inspecting the phenomena which we want to describe . . . [try] to understand logical multiplicity."[5] The *Blue Book*, and later the *Philosophical Investigations*, takes this even more rigorously. "I want to say here that it can never be our job to reduce anything to anything, or to explain anything. Philosophy really *is* 'purely descriptive.'"[6]

The grammatical, descriptive method which Wittgenstein begins to work out in the *Blue Book*, I shall argue here, is a submerged and inverted "phenomenological reduction" addressed to phenomena in such a way that *language* becomes the world-theme of this "phenomenology."

But it is now time to enter the problem from the bottom up. Grammars, essential structural characteristics of linguistic phenomena, are what we must understand. But first comes the question of how one arrives at the essences. I may pose this question

---

[4] There is a persistent confusion in this terminology. Reduction in the "bad" sense is used in phenomenological literature to mean a reduction to explanation whereas a phenomenological reduction is a reduction in the "good" sense as description.

[5] *Ibid.*, p. 247.

[6] Ludwig Wittgenstein, *The Blue Book*, (Harper Torchbooks, 1958), p. 18. And if by grammar, Wittgenstein means phenomenology, here still in its earlier sense of a science of possibilities, then is it any wonder Moore can't understand what use Wittgenstein is making of "grammar"? Note Moore's perplexity in his report of Wittgenstein's lectures from 1930–33.

in a hypothetical way: if Wittgenstein was using some type of
phenomenology what must the ingredients be? The answers form
the argument for a viable parallelism with the suggested inversion
at the point of reductions proper.

   1. The first radical step of a phenomenology, *epoché*, functions
as the conversion of a point of view. Whether epoché is understood as the bracketing of certain assumptions about the real
existence of things, or the asserting of an initial set of systematic
values which will create the focus of the method, or as a vehicle
by which certain traditional or "natural" prejudices are to be
overcome, the result is a change in perspective upon the phenomena in question. In Husserl's case all these aspects of epoché
were directed against the "natural attitude" which was to be
suspended and be replaced by a "phenomenological attitude."
Epoché, at one and the same time, seeks to bracket the judgments
which obscure the appearance of phenomena and to open the field
of phenomena for description. In Husserl's case, however, this
methodological device and an implicit metaphysical decision
cross.[7] The field is understood (interpreted) to be the field of
transcendental experience and thus from the first gives a weighted
primacy to the question of the subject and his experiences.

   But what if one employs the same method and applies it to a
different set of questions? In this case the field to be inquired
into, apparently at first more narrowly, is the field of expressions.
It is here that we find the Wittgenstein of the *Blue Book* and of
the whole transitional period leading to the *Investigations*. The
conversion of a point of view, "epoché," is quite systematically
described. (I grant that more than a purely methodological question is involved here. Wittgenstein is obviously arguing with
himself in relation to his earlier period and with Russell and Moore
as well. But the later-to-be-shown implications for a primacy of
language over experience is too strong for me to believe these are
the only figures in the debate.) What needs to be called into
question is the long held traditional philosophic view of language.
This linguistic "natural attitude," perhaps better termed the
"logicist attitude," is what must be overturned and replaced with
a descriptive or grammatical "attitude." I shall not here elaborate

---

   [7] See especially Ricoeur's critique in "Kant and Husserl," *Husserl*, (Northwestern
University Press, 1967).

fully the constitution of a "logicist" prejudice which must be "bracketed" other than to indicate that it is at base precisely the tendency to view all expressions as if they contained or were at bottom some kind of logic (or calculus as Wittgenstein puts it). A "logicist attitude" is from the start reductive in the bad sense as an explanation which lies behind or below the phenomena as they are actually "used."

To avoid this deeply held prejudice reductive assumptions must be purposely bracketed and replaced with a set of concepts in keeping with a descriptive approach. The *Blue Book* announces this program in its attempt to avoid what Wittgenstein calls "a craving for generality." He lists four aspects to this bracketing process which fall into two groups:

(a) The first group attacks what I am calling here the "logicist's attitude" which Wittgenstein wishes to avoid. There is a tendency, he claims, to look for a common property to all things included under a general term. But this is a first step in an exclusionary reduction. Instead, Wittgenstein proposes to use the concept of "family resemblances" in which likenesses may "overlap" without there being a common property throughout. Secondly, this tendency of craving generality is linked to what Wittgenstein calls our preoccupation with the methods of science which is throughout reductive in the sense of being an analysis which reduces everything to the smallest number of primitive laws and unifies them by means of generalization. This tendency must be staunchly resisted. It is "the real source of metaphysics, and leads the philosopher into complete darkness."[8] (Husserl and Heidegger locate the trouble at this point as well.) Rather, a careful study of particular cases should just as well reveal the complexities of grammar as the too easy generalization which overlooks this richness.

This first group of assumptions to be set aside, apart from the fact that some Wittgensteinians seem not to have heeded the call to a non-reductive description, is less interesting than the second set of "logicist prejudices" which center on the role of experience and which open the way for the inversion of (Husserlian) phenomenology. Wittgenstein strongly insists that in relation to general terms one must not suppose that there is a general mental picture

[8] Wittgenstein, *Blue Book*, p. 18.

which corresponds to the term. Like Berkeley, Wittgenstein holds that there can be no general idea *as an image* before the mind. But the reason for this, he claims, is the tendency to believe that "the meaning of a word is an image."[9] To so believe relates back to the deeply held notion that for every substantive there must be an "object." The inversion to be introduced will attempt to show this is not the case.

In the case of meaning-as-image Wittgenstein may perhaps be seen to be arguing more with Empiricism than phenomenology and it does remain the case that a theory of experience much more clearly empiricist than phenomenological remains a ghost haunting Wittgenstein. But the attempt to bracket certain beliefs about experience goes further in the second step of this group. Wittgenstein claims that there is a persistent "confusion between a mental state, meaning a state of a hypothetical mental mechanism, and a mental state meaning a state of consciousness (toothache, etc.)"[10] Here the swords will clash and the implied question is one which revolves around intentionality.

Spiegelberg notes that Wittgenstein does not seem to have utilized or grasped the implications of intentionality. To that may be added that Wittgenstein in no way seems to utilize a *reflective* method. Thus intentionality as a structure of consciousness without a reflective method must remain a "hypothetical mental mechanism" and will fall under Wittgenstein's version of "phenomenological reduction." I shall indicate below where intentionality does indeed function and give reason for its different placement by the absence of, or refusal to, accept a reflective method.

In short, Wittgenstein deliberately employs a conversion of a point of view to clear the field of expressions for descriptive investigation. The attempt to understand grammars remains in line with the earlier actual use of a phenomenological vocabulary in the *Philosophische Bemerkungen*. But the transition to a descriptive stance is complex because there are at least two issues involved in Wittgenstein's own change of mind. The early Wittgenstein had sought for answers to his philosophical confusions in some form of ideal or artificial language. But in the transition

9 *Ibid.*, p. 9.
10 *Ibid.*, p. 18.

which we see taking place from the *Bemerkungen* to the *Blue Book* it becomes apparent that the concept of primitive languages must change. A more modest goal is differentiating what is essential from what is not and that through the use of a variational method becomes the goal. We begin to see the introduction of "free variations" to accomplish this task.

As of now, phenomenological language or "primary language," as I have called it, does not appeal to me as a goal; now I no longer consider it necessary. All that is possible and necessary is to separate what is essential to *our* language from its unessentials.

That is to say: if one describes, as it were, the class of languages which satisfy their purpose, then one has shown what is essential to them and thus *presented immediate experience immediately*. [italics mine].

Each time I say that this or that presentation could also be replaced by this different one, we take another step toward the goal of seizing the essence of what is presented.[11]

Note preliminarily that the class of languages which satisfy their purposes – later to be designated as types of satisfactions in terms of different language games – *presents immediate experience immediately*. Experience will be read through expressions. In the later terminology of the *Blue Book* to have uncovered the grammar is to have thus presented experience. This point, extremely important for the inversion which occurs in Wittgenstein's use of a reduction, tends to give a weighted value to language over experience and eventually (but unsuccessfully in my opinion) to attempt to collapse experience into language.

Secondly, the variations by which the essential is to be described do not necessarily arrive at a pure primary language. By the time of the *Blue Book* a version of "inexact essences" has already appeared in the notions of concepts with "blurred edges" and "inexact usages."

But the radicalness of a Wittgensteinian epoché remains transitional and the past still plagues Wittgenstein in the form of (a) an analytic version of preferring to build up the complex from the simple (as in the understanding of language games); (b) a narrow view of experience which remains limited to a largely Empiricist view; and (c) a lurking logicism which is never quite overcome.[12]

---

[11] Spiegelberg, *op. cit.*, p. 255.

[12] Similar criticisms may be made of Husserl in relation to the problems which

The change of goal, from primitivity as a possible ideal language
to the primitivity of the essential, begins to take shape in the
Blue Book. The specific use of a phenomenological vocabulary
has disappeared but its trace remains. Compare this description
of "language games" with the notions of PB:

> I shall in the future again and again call your attention to what I shall
> call language games. These are ways of using signs simpler than those
> in which we use the signs in our highly complicated everyday language.
> Language games are the forms of language with which a child begins to
> make use of words. The study of language games is the study of *primitive
> forms of language or primitive languages* [italics mine].13

Language games, to become the concept around which variations
may be played, are the multivocal equivalents of the earlier
univocal calculus of languages.

"Epoché" as a conversion of a point of view in relation to a
"logicist attitude" must be thoroughly rigorous in its rejection
of any single hidden calculus of language. But beyond epoché lie
the "phenomenological reductions."

2. The "reductions" employed by Wittgenstein *invert* the
emphasis of Husserlian phenomenology. Where Husserl reduced
things to transcendental experience; Wittgenstein reduces things
to linguistic usages – *the meaning is the use*. What must be seen
here is that this "reduction" is one which wants to get back to
the structures of language. This grammar must be displayed.
Hence the "reductions" become the series of variations which
successively uncover the grammar of expressions.

(a) The first step in the "reduction" is to remove the notion
that words have necessary objects. In response to such questions
as, "what is meaning?" Wittgenstein notes, "We are up against
one of the great sources of philosophical bewilderment" a substantive makes us look for a thing that corresponds to it."14 But
for our purposes one way in which an "object" is supposed is of
particular interest. (b) It is a case of supposing that some group
of mental processes are the objects of meaning.

---

plagued his turn to phenomenology. There seems to exist an isomorphism between
these two 20th century philosophies in the sense that the places within their theories
where difficulties occur are functionally the same.

13 Wittgenstein, *Blue Book*, p. 17.
14 *Ibid.*, p. 1.

It seems that there are *certain definite* mental processes bound up with the working of language, processes through which alone language can function. I mean the processes of understanding and meaning ... We are tempted to think that the action of language consists of two parts; an inorganic part, the handling signs, and an organic part, which we may call understanding these signs, meaning them, interpreting them, thinking.[15]

At just this point the phenomenologist may take heed. Is the "mental process" of which Wittgenstein speaks intentionality? And although I think it clear that the phenomenological sense of intentionality would undoubtably be regarded a hypothesis regarding a mental process by Wittgenstein there seems to be lacking any clear concept of intentionality here at all. But its *function* does occur within language itself.

But a second look at what type of mental process Wittgenstein wishes to get rid of should also cause a second pause for the phenomenologist. Wittgenstein is clearly attacking what may be called a "Cartesian" linguistic dualism. On the one side is a mechanical inorganic operation of signs; on the other an organic "soul" which understands. In rejecting this dualism Wittgenstein is asserting, perhaps inadvertently, that *there is no disembodied thought*.

(c) The exorcism of a disembodied mental process takes the shape of a series of ingenious free variations (mental experiments?). The first of these is one which brackets the imagination as an *imaging* ability. Wittgenstein suggests that we replace all mental images with concrete objects.

There is one way of avoiding at least partly the occult appearance of the processes of thinking, and it is, to replace in these processes any working of the imagination by acts of looking at real objects ... We could perfectly well ... replace every process of imagining by a process of looking at an object or by painting, drawing, or modelling; and every process of speaking to oneself by speaking aloud or by writing.[16]

This *public* embodiment of the linguistic act is presumed to remove the mystery of the (private) image. "In fact, as soon as you think of replacing the mental image by, say, a painted one, and as soon as the image thereby loses its occult character, it ceases to seem to import any life to the sentence at all."[17]

[15] *Ibid.*, p. 3.
[16] *Ibid.*, p. 4.
[17] *Ibid.*, p. 5.

Note here that while Wittgenstein nowhere denies that "mental processes" may in fact accompany thinking – which is now on its way towards being a type of linguistic performance – they are not *necessary* for meaning. The variation has a quite narrow point to make: images are not necessary for meaning as such.

(d) Nor is thinking a translation of some pre-language into language. "The phrase 'to express an idea which is before our mind' suggests that what we are trying to express in words is already expressed only in a different language; that this expression is before our mind's eye; and that what we do is to translate from the mental into the verbal language."[18] But this is not the case, either, Wittgenstein argues. By a series of further exercises he hopes to show that thinking itself is a kind of linguistic performance. Note two of these: In the first we are asked to substitute any "thought" for its expression. "If you are puzzled about the nature of thought, belief, knowledge, and the like, substitute for the thought the expression of the thought, etc. The difficulty which lies in this substitution, and at the same time the whole point of it, is this: the expression of belief, thought, etc., is just a sentence."[19] Thinking, in the narrower sense which develops in the *Blue Book*, *is* a linguistic operation.

In the second set of variations the opposite side is tried. As a counter we are first asked whether we may speak without "thinking" in a kind of automatic behavior. The implied answer is yes. But then,

Speaking a sentence without thinking consists in switching on speech and switching off certain accompaniments of speech. Now ask yourself: Does thinking the sentence without speaking it consist in turning over the switch ... that is: does thinking the sentence without speaking it now simply consist in keeping on what accompanied the words but leaving out the words? Try to think the thoughts of a sentence without the sentence and see whether this is what happens.[20]

The implied answer is clearly *no*.

What Wittgenstein is trying to show is the necessity of what I have called embodied thought. Thinking is at least a linguistic performance, an "operating with signs." Again, Wittgenstein does not deny that other mental accompaniments may be co-

18 *Ibid.*, p. 41.
19 *Ibid.*, p. 42.
20 *Ibid.*, p. 43.

present with language, but he does want to establish the *primacy* of language in thought.

I have been trying in all this to remove the temptation to think that there *"must* be" what is called a mental process of thinking, hoping, wishing, believing, etc., *independent* of the process of expressing a thought, a hope, a wish, etc. [last italic mine].[21]

Rather thinking, the operation with signs, is the basic stratum to which may be affixed other mental occurrences.

[This variation] ... rids us of the temptation to look for a peculiar act of thinking, independent of the act of expressing our thoughts, and stowed away in some peculiar medium. We are no longer prevented by the established forms of expression from recognizing that the experience of thinking *may* be just the experience of saying, or it may consist of this experience plus others which accompany it.[22]

For our purposes here the inversion is now complete. If linguistic performance (thinking now in the narrower of Wittgenstein's senses) is the base, then all the other accompaniments are related secondarily to the question of meaning. Embodied thought whether an "inner" or "outer" performance is an operation with signs. Or, another way of saying it, operating with signs now *contains* what in the "Cartesian" model was a separated organic process. Thought, embodied in such a way, grammatically breaks down the distinctions between "inner" and "outer" so far as any metaphysical solipsism would have it. Its result, oddly enough, is not too far from what could have been said by Merleau-Ponty as well: "We may say that thinking is essentially the activity of operating with signs. This activity is performed by the hand, when we think by writing; by the mouth and larynx, when we think by speaking ..."[23] Only the vestige from a sense-data view of experience is excluded, "and if we think by imagining signs or pictures, I can give you no agency that thinks."[24]

Thinking is a concrete activity, operating with signs. All other experiences as accompaniments relate secondarily to language in operation so far as meaning is concerned. Thus in a way perhaps more literal than a Heidegger would put it, Wittgenstein intimates that "language speaks."

[21] *Ibid.*, p. 41.
[22] *Ibid.*, p. 43.
[23] *Ibid.*, p. 6.
[24] *Ibid.*, p. 6.

3. This leaves us with two dangling problems so far as any Wittgensteinian "phenomenological reduction" is concerned. First, what happens to the notion of intentionality, the central structure of consciousness in the Husserlian context? And second what of the subject? The answer to both these questions is intimately tied to the total absence of a reflective method in Wittgenstein's thought.

For Husserl all structures of consciousness are not arrived at introspectively or directly, but reflectively and indirectly. The world of phenomena is first read on the object (noematically) prior to any description of necessary reflected structures (noetically). Intentionality is not first, but last in the order of progress. It is the goal of a phenomenology of experience.

But Wittgenstein from the beginning had another goal in mind, one which in many ways radically precisely brackets the fullness of experience. The goal is an understanding of *grammar*, the structure of language. An inversion, though, may retain a certain isomorphism with that from which it is inverted. I believe this is the case with Wittgenstein. Thus if the structure of language replaces the structure of experience in this "phenomenology" one can expect the *functions* of intentionality to be found *within language*.

And that is precisely the case. The "intentionality" of Wittgenstein is to be found in the concept, "the meaning is the use." The *life* of meaning is collapsed into language itself. The "meaning is the use" provides the structural key to all language. "But if we had to name anything which is the life of the sign, we should have to say that it was its *use*."[25] This, whatever the size of the unit. "The sign (the sentence) gets its significance from the system of signs, from the language to which it belongs. Roughly: understanding a sentence means understanding a language."[26] To be able to correctly use a sentence implies the larger operation. "As a part of the system of language, one may say, the sentence has life."[27] Language, as it were, contains its own "life."

Further, the operations which Wittgenstein has in mind are of a particular type. They are immanent *within* language. He

[25] *Ibid.*, p. 4.
[26] *Ibid.*, p. 5.
[27] *Ibid.*, p. 5.

early distinguishes between "what one might call 'a process being *in accordance with* a rule,' and, 'a process involving a rule.'"[28] It is clear that it is the latter kind which is involved with meaning as use – "the symbol of the rule forms part of the calculation . . . A rule, so far as it interests us, does not act at a distance."[29]

All of this is understood by Wittgenstein as an *essential notion* regarding language. And here we reach one standard criticism of the Wittgensteinian enterprise. While avoiding general concepts in the initial "epoché" as I have called it, Wittgenstein does employ one general concept, meaning as use. But in this interpretation its circularity with the original attack is not perfect. Instead, the generality here described, if understood as the linguistic correlate of intentionality, raises the level of the debate to what might be called a "linguistic ontology."

But is it an ontology without a subject? The answer must remain ambiguous in Wittgenstein's case. That there is no disembodied subject as a unique mental object is clear. And at points it appears that Wittgenstein is re-fighting the same battles fought earlier by Hume. But on the other hand there is a hint, already in the *Blue Book*, of what for a phenomenologist on the other side of the inversion sounds like making room for an implicit subject. But the implicit subject, even in answer to the question of *"who* operates with signs?" remains more "transcendental" than Husserl's ego. Nevertheless, Wittgenstein does produce some *grammatical* parallels to the "subject" and "object" concepts of the person. He notes, for example, that there are different cases of use involving "I," one of which is the use as "object," the other as "subject." In the cases of "My arm is broken," "I have grown six inches," etc., possibilities of error, designation of a body or a particular person is involved. But in the "subject "use, "I think it will rain," "I have a toothache," etc. there is no provision for error – but this also implies that "To say, I have pain is no more a statement about a particular person than moaning is."[30] And here comes the particular rejection of any possible reflective procedure. Wittgenstein *denies* just what phenomenologists assert: "It would be wrong to say that when someone points to the sun

---

[28] *Ibid.*, p. 13.
[29] *Ibid.*, pp. 13–14.
[30] *Ibid.*, p. 66.

with his hand, he is pointing both to the sun and himself because it is *he* who points . . . " But with a small reservation, "on the other hand, he may by pointing attract attention both to the sun and to himself."[31] What Wittgenstein calls attracting attention both to the sun and oneself is precisely what is referred to in a phenomenological reflexivity. I am known to myself – but via the otherness of the world and other egos because all subjectivity is already intersubjectivity. The turn to language ought, above all, to make this apparent.

[31] *Ibid.*, p. 67.

FRED KERSTEN
University of Wisconsin - Green Bay

THE OCCASION AND NOVELTY OF HUSSERL'S PHENOMENOLOGY OF ESSENCE

The primary purpose of this essay is to elaborate in broad out-line the fundamental significance of Husserl's analysis and doctrine of essence both as regards the occasion of its formulation and the novelty it contains. This is obviously a complex task, and to provide a manageable focus for discussion we shall confine ourselves to considering but one aspect or dimension of Husserl's analysis of essence, namely its so-called "Platonism" and the peculiar shape it takes in Husserl's thought. A secondary purpose is to locate within this framework various insights into essence by other phenomenologists, particularly those of Roman Ingarden, which supplement and perchance correct Husserl's phenomenology of essence.

§ 1. The External Occasion of Husserl's View of Essence

At least since publication of the first volume of *Ideen zu einer reinen Phänomenologie und phänomenologischen Philosophie* in 1913, if not before, "Platonism" has been a common charge brought against phenomenology – be it that of Husserl himself or of those who shared his interest in the investigation of essences.[1] The validity of that charge was as frequently denied in ways and connections too diverse to rehearse here. But no matter how decisive the denial, the charge continuously seemed to prove an

---

[1] In addition to Roman Ingarden, I refer principally to Jean Hering, Wilhelm Schapp and Fritz Kaufmann. Max Scheler, Hedwig Conrad-Martius and Adolf Reinach are equally important, though their work cannot be reviewed here. In this connection, see Herbert Spiegelberg, *The Phenomenological Movement. An Historical Introduction* (The Hague, 1960), Vol. I, Chapter IV.

embarrassment to phenomenology. Indeed, the fact that "Platonism" should be both a charge and an embarrassment already bespeaks a common, though tacit, ground shared by critics no less than adherents of phenomenology. This common ground nevertheless appears as a stumbling block to further investigations and development of an account of essence.[2] Perhaps one of the reasons, though by no means the only one, lies in the nature of the occasion of Husserl's setting of the phenomenological problem of essence in the first volume of *Ideen* – a setting not fully transcendent in the rest of the writings published during his lifetime. This setting and its occasion can be stated in the following way.

With the first volume of the *Ideen* and the second edition of the *Logische Untersuchungen* (1913 ff.) Husserl was chiefly interested in offering an account of essences such as, but not only, generic and specific universals, and formal-mathematical universals, in what can be regarded as a novel way: namely an account which advances the view that ideal existents such as universals can be seen and grasped in a manner generically alike *but specifically different* from the way in which individuals, such as real things of perception, can be seen and grasped. However, the occasion for advancing this view may have hindered, even concealed, rather than emphasized its novelty. At least part of the occasion consists in the fact that Husserl, following up his thorough-going critique of psychologism in the first volume of the *Logische Untersuchungen*, presented his view in opposition to the then current empiricistic theories that denied universals and

---

[2] To be sure, Husserl continued to develop his own view up through his posthumously published *Erfahrung und Urteil* (1939). Of recent writers dealing with the phenomenology of essences, perhaps the most original approach is that of Aron Gurwitsch using the (philosophically reformulated) results of Gestalt psychology, e.g., "Gelb-Goldstein's Concept of 'Concrete' and 'Categorial' Attitude and the Phenomenology of Ideation," *Studies in Phenomenology and Psychology* (Evanston, 1966), pp. 359ff., and in his *The Field of Consciousness* (Pittsburgh, 1964), pp. 390f. See also Alfred Schutz, "Type and Eidos in Husserl's Late Philosophy," *Collected Papers* (The Hague, 1966), Vol. III, edited by I. Schutz, pp. 99ff. In this connection, see the present writer's "Phenomenology, History and Myth," *Phenomenology and Social Reality* (The Hague, 1970), edited by M. Natanson, pp. 221ff. It seems to me, however, that the last systematic attempt to fully develop a phenomenology of essence was Herbert Spiegelberg's "Über das Wesen der Idee. Eine Ontologische Untersuchung," *Jahrbuch für Philosophie und phänomenologische Forschung*, XI (1930). It is unfortunate that this lucidly written work has not been given the attention it deserves in the literature of phenomenology.

held that there are names which are general in their functions by being generally representative of real individuals. Clearly those who held that there were no universals also held that there was no consciousness of universals, that if universals do not exist they cannot be seen and grasped.[3]

This occasion is rendered complex by the fact that Husserl, at the same time, was concerned to develop his view in opposition to the then equally current neo-Kantian theory that universals, essences, not only exist but are a necessary part of the experienced world – even though they are not objects of possible seeings and graspings, or "intuitions" in the neo-Kantian sense.[4] Instead

[3] This whole situation is reviewed by Husserl himself in the posthumously published "Entwurf einer 'Vorrede' zu den 'Logische Untersuchungen' (1913)," edited by Eugen Fink and published in *Tijdschrift voor Philosophie*, I (1939), §§ 1 ff., 8; see below, § 12. These reflections bring up to date, i.e., 1913, a polemical line of thought initiated with his Habilitationsschritt of 1887, see *ibid.*, pp. 125 ff. A good picture of what Husserl believed himself up against in advancing this view, aside from his interest in Bolzano but above all in Lotze, can be found in his "Bericht über deutsche Schriften zur Logik in den Jahren 1895–1899," *Archiv für systematische Philosophie*, 9 (1903) and 10 (1904); see for example, Vol. 9, pp. 399 f., 540 ff.

[4] This part of the occasion is made explicit by Husserl himself in a famous passage in *Ideen*, I, § 62: "Somit liegen in der Phänomenologie alle eidetischen (also unbedingt allgemein gültigen) Erkenntnisse beschlossen, mit denen sich die auf beliebig vorzugebende Erkenntnisse und Wissenschaften bezogenen Radikalprobleme der 'Möglichkeit' beantworten." And the first to see this was Kant "dessen größte Intuitionen uns erst ganz verständlich werden, wenn wir uns das Eigentümliche des phänomenologischen Gebietes zur vollbewußten Klarheit erarbeitet haben." The multiple and varied philosophical dimensions of this aspect of the occasion are admirably and painstakingly spelled out by Iso Kern in his *Husserl und Kant. Eine Untersuchung über Husserls Verhältnis zu Kant und zum Neukantianismus* (Den Haag, 1964). Even a cursory look at Husserl's lecture notes and letters from 1907 onwards shows his careful study of neo-Kantians such as Rickert, Cohn, but especially Natorp. Examination of both published and unpublished writings of Husserl suggests that it is indeed Natorp with whom Husserl is most sympathetic in the light of the many great differences between them. With important exceptions, Natorp represents the neo-Kantian view against which Husserl advances his own. For example, with specific reference to Natorp's review of the first volume of the *Logische Untersuchungen* in the *Kant-Studien* (1901), Husserl takes the opportunity to point out in his "Entwurf einer 'Vorrede'" (pp. 111, 113 f., 114) that the critique of psychologism led to the necessity of the analysis of purely logical idealities and the essential relations among them. In addition to Kern's penetrating summary of the relationship between Natorp and Husserl, *op. cit.*, pp. 32 f., and §§ 30 f., especially pp. 335 ff., see Natorp, *Platos Ideenlehre* (Leipzig, 1921²), pp. 419 ff. (In connection with the discussion of the *Meno*, Natorp introduces the concept of "*passive Doxa*" – a possible source for Husserl's use of the term.) and *Die logischen Grundlagen der exakten Wissenschaften* (Leipzig, 1910), §§ 9 ff., especially pp. 95 f. – According to Kern, pp. 432 f., both of these works, among others, were carefully studied by Husserl. Strangely enough, Cohen's *Kants Theorie der Erfahrung*, on which Natorp often heavily relies, was scarcely read by Husserl (apparently only a few paragraphs of the first chapter). For a general summary of neo-Kantian views, see Jules Vuillemin, *L'Héritage Kantien* (Paris, 1954), pp. 133 ff., especially pp. 164 ff., 173 ff.

they are inferred as necessary conditions for the possibility of an experienceable world for natural and (later with Cassirer) cultural science. On this view only space and time, and only real individuals existing in time or in space-time, can be seen and grasped, "intuited." The reason why this view renders complex the occasion for that advanced by Husserl is that it is equally a criticism of Husserl's view, but on *Platonic grounds*. This is seen especially as regards Natorp who, in fact, develops the criticism in his review of the first volume of *Ideen*.[5] By briefly rehearsing this review as regards Husserl's account of essence we can, albeit retrospectively, make transparent the occasion for that doctrine precisely in terms of the *Ideen* and, by extension, the second edition of the *Logische Untersuchungen*.

Discussing the "Einleitung" to the *Ideen*, Natorp resets Husserl's account of essence in Kantian terms when he observes that essences such as mathematical axioms in no way contain the "co-positing of the facts of experience" and thus cannot be conceived as being grounded by those facts.[6] Accordingly, if knowledge of essences is not grounded by experience, what, then, is the foundation of certainty of that knowledge? Just this line of thought will call into question Husserl's view that the seeing of essences and the seeing of the "facts of experience" are generically alike but specifically different.

Natorp acknowledges in this regard the Platonism which he finds in Husserl's account; indeed, the very term "intuition" employed by Husserl is seen to evoke the Platonic tradition of postulating an analogy between seeing Ideas and seeing things.[7] But what legitimates this analogy? Certainly what one sees *is*; what is seen must be there before one's eyes, must be at hand. But must it be there beforehand? For Natorp this is the crux of the matter. Kant's observation is relevant here, namely that we

---

[5] Paul Natorp, "Husserl's 'Ideen zu einer reinen Phänomenologie'," *Logos*, VII (1917/18), pp. 224–246.

[6] Natorp makes this statement specifically with regard to *Ideen*, I, § 25. He cites in this connection § 6 of Kant's 1770 Dissertation (*De mundi sensibilis atque intelligibilis forma et principiis*), where Kant says of the positing activity of pure thinking that while it abstracts, it is not abstracted from sensuous experience.

[7] Natorp, *op. cit.*, *loc. cit.*, p. 228. As we shall suggest in the next section and later on, Husserl does not have an analogy in mind here; essences as well as material things, idealities and realities, are presented as "they themselves" in clearly discernible acts of consciousness of them.

can discriminate an original acquisition of what had not been there before, that in the final analysis there is no Being given to thinking which is not itself posited by thinking, that Being is always defined, determined Being. Is this the sense, then, of what it signifies to speak of an "act of knowing essences," of the "giving" of essences – the acquisition of what was not there be-fore? Or do we mean nothing more by "giving" than what Kant means when he speaks of something exhibited in intuition and related to experience? (*Kritik der reinen Vernunft*, Bl 95.) If Husserl is speaking in these terms then there is no objection to his speaking of the "giving" of essences.

There may be, however, more to the matter than first appears. Even Plato was aware of the fact that the seeing of essences, of Ideas, had to be grounded, justified and demonstrated. Kant likewise saw this:

> For if, in dealing with synthetic propositions, we are to recognize them as possessing unconditioned validity, independently of deduction, on the evidence merely of their own claims, then no matter how evident they may be, all critique of understanding is given up. And since there is no lack of audacious pretensions, and these are supported by common belief (though there is no credential of their truth), the understanding lies open to every fancy, and is in no position to withhold approval of those assertions which, though illegitimate, yet press upon us, in the same confident tone, their claims to be accepted as actual axioms.[8]

One way to overcome the problem raised by Kant is to substitute a connexus of intuitions which mutually mediate, condition, each other, for a single intuition claiming unconditioned validity. But this directly refers us back to a *continuity*, a movement of thought, a successive and demonstrable ordering of thought. Indeed only within that ordering can we speak at all of a claim to truth made by a single intuition; at first isolated, the single intuition is grounded by and in virtue of the continuity of thought. As a con-sequence, the fixed and isolated insight into essence must be cancelled out, overcome in the movement of thought.

This has serious consequences for Husserl's notion of "given-ness" since it suggests that essences, for example, are neither given all at once nor once and for all; the "givenness" of essence is not a "tout-fait," be it *a priori* or empirical:

[8] Kant, *Critique of Pure Reason* (London, 1953), translated by Norman Kemp Smith, p. 251 (B 285). Natorp cites this passage on p. 229.

the so-called "fixed stars" of thinking are to be known as the "moving stars of a higher order"; the presumed *fixed* point of thinking must be dissolved, made to flow in the *continuity* of thought-processes. Thus nothing *is*, but instead only *becomes* "given."[9]

The upshot is that the "intuitus," the intuition or insight into essence proves to be an insight into the original continuity of thinking in and out of which thinking in its positive and acquisitive character first emerges. Natorp finally draws the typical neo-Kantian conclusion that "ground," as it pertains to the grounding of the seeing and grasping of essences, must be conceived in Cohen's sense of "origin" where being grounded in itself signifies and can only signify "being in process."

Historical reflection discloses that precisely this had already been hinted at by the Pythagoreans who defined the finite by the "non-finite" in the sense of being beyond the finite – the "un" of "un-limited," "un-ending," beyond the limit or end: "un-ending" in the sense of "pre-determined." This view gets its full formulation in Plato's discovery of the *Kinesis* of *Eidé*. For Natorp it was to the discredit of Aristotle and Aristotelianism that it took over Platonic rationalism only as regards the notion of truth and, characteristic of late Hellenism, shrunk back from the "un-limited," the "infinite." Aristotelian finitism was finally overcome by the cosmology and mechanics of Copernicus and Galileo who found in the method of the infinitesimal a rigorous scientific fronting with the infinite. Ultimately we find this at the basis of Kant's reaffirmation of the synthetic character of genuine knowledge and, Natorp adds, "we are only now at work developing it in full rigor and purity."

From this historical perspective Natorp measures Husserl's account of seeing and grasping essences. It turns out that Husserl has approached the view Natorp sketches following Cohen and Kant, but nonetheless remains embedded in the Platonic tradition:

as things stand it would seem that Husserl, more particularly, has pushed forward to Plato's *Eidos*, but only to the *first stage* of Platonism which remains with the fixed, immobile *Eidé* "subsisting in Being"; he has not taken along with it Plato's last step which was the greatest and most authentic step of all: to bring the *Eidé* into *motion*, to make them flow in the ultimate *continuity* of thought.[10]

[9] Natorp, p. 230. The translation is mine.
[10] *Ibid.*, p. 236. The translation is mine. This view is more fully developed in *Die logischen Grundlagen der exakten Wissenschaften*, §§ 4 f.

The charge of "Platonism" here is not only made on Platonic grounds but it is really the charge of *not enough* "Platonism"– Husserl's account of essence stops at Being and does not go on to comprise Being *and Becoming*. As a result essences cannot be concrete with experience, the intuition of essences cannot be grounded and "lies open to every fancy."

This controversy about "too little" or "too much" Platonism, i.e., about "Kant" and "Hume," finally about "idealism" and "realism," forms the occasion for the view of essence advanced by Husserl. As we shall try to show in the following sections, the novelty of Husserl's view vitiates that controversy in the shape it has at the time of the *Ideen* and the second edition of the *Logische Untersuchungen*. The novelty, however, is not simply another view among others, but rightfully purports to arise out of the very situation which any account whatever must clarify to ground the seeing and grasping of essences.

§ 2. The Novelty of Husserl's Account of Seeing and Grasping Essences

In its novelty, Husserl's view is perhaps most succinctly expressed in the second edition of the *Logische Untersuchungen*:

phenomenology is not descriptive psychology: its peculiar "pure" description, its contemplation of pure essences on a basis of exemplary individual intuitions of experiences (often freely imagined ones), and its descriptive fixation of the contemplated essences into pure concepts, is no empirical scientific description. It rather excludes the natural performance of all empirical (naturalistic) apperceptions and positings. Statements of descriptive psychology regarding "perceptions," "judgments," "feelings," "volitions," etc., use such names to refer to the real states of animal organisms in a real natural order, just as descriptive statements concerning physical states deal with happenings in a nature not imagined but real. All general statements have here a character of empirical generality: they hold for *this* nature. Phenomenology, however, does not discuss states of animal organisms ... but perceptions, judgments, feelings *as such*, and what pertains to them *a priori* with unlimited generality, as *pure* instances of *pure* species, of what may be seen through a purely intuitive apprehension of essence, whether generic or specific.[11]

---

[11] Husserl, *Logische Untersuchungen* (Halle, 1913), II, 1, pp. 17 ff. The English translation is by J. N. Findlay (London, 1970), Vol. I, p. 261. For what follows, see also *ibid.*, § 52 of the Sixth Investigation (English translation, pp. 800 f.); *Ideen*, I, § 23, and *Erfahrung und Urteil*, pp. 434 ff.

Here and in the continuation of this passage Husserl makes the following four points concerning the seeing and grasping of essences:

1. The seeing of an essence, consciousness of an essence, is founded on actual or even imagined perceiving of individual exemplifications. Indeed, the founding stratum can be as much an actual as an imagined perceiving, as it can be a recollecting of a perceiving. This signifies, for instance, that I do not have to see any particular colors to see and grasp the universal Color, but I do have to imagine the perceiving of colors.

2. There is no analogue in perceiving for the structure manifested in the seeing and grasping of essences, hence there is no "empirical, scientific description" of them.

3. In the case of perception, the perceived is something real, something in space and time. In contrast, space and time are utterly unimportant for the seeing and grasping of essences. The clear recollecting of an essence, for instance, as previously seen and grasped is forthwith a clear seeing and grasping of that essence with as much originality as before. Thus even though we can speak of a consciousness of essences, that need not signify that we must also speak of an original acquisition of essences – anymore than the generic likeness and specific difference of seeing essences and real individual things signifies that we must also speak of an analogy between those seeings.

4. Finally, as regards perception there is a clear-cut distinction between actually seeing something, for example, and imaginatively or fictively seeing something. This signifies that I can speak of possible actual and imaginary real individuals. In contrast, this distinction is unimportant for seeing and grasping essences.[12]

As Husserl suggests, all of the differences important for perception are not only unimportant but also are absent in the case of seeing and grasping essences. The only important difference among essences is that obtaining between those which have actual and possible individual exemplifications and those that do not.[13]

These four points cannot be further elaborated without re-

---

[12] The situation may not be quite so unambiguous, as suggested by Oskar Becker, "Zur Logik der Modalitäten," *Jahrbuch für Philosophie und phänomenologische Forschung*, XI (1930), pp. 538 ff.

[13] See below, §§ 6 ff.

ferring directly to the situation Husserl's view purports to clarify. In making that reference we also elicit a systematic *rather than merely* an "occasional" basis for the inquiry into essence.

§ 3. The Situation to be Clarified by an Account of Seeing and Grasping Essences

The on-going course of daily life gears us into and confronts us with a world of changing things, affairs and events under perchance similar but varying conditions, from varying and variable perspectives. But the presented world and things, affairs and events in it are not, as such, chaos: in the midst or at the margin of that course of life certain "non-changes" with definite-indefinite limits are also co-presented. To be sure, the changes, variations, alterations, the factual contingencies may be expressed by the laws of functional regularity, by belief in the uniformity of nature or in the permanent possibility of "sensations" and the like. Yet such laws and beliefs are external to the matters of fact experienced and thought about; they do not express the essence or "inner What" of the things, affairs and events encountered.[14] A given thing or set of things change; this or those things change; a thing or some things or such a thing change. There is accordingly a limit to change, to "becoming." Indeed, there is no more "pure" becoming than there is "pure" contingent factuality. The correlative of contingent change is, then, *necessity*. Individual matters of fact are not meant merely or only in their individuality, but also *as* individuals, as instances of specific and generic essences.

The foregoing is a brief statement of the situation Husserl wishes to clarify with his view of essence, and the novelty of his view is rooted in that very situation. In the first volume of the *Ideen* he expresses it in the following words:

If we say that every factuality can, "according to the essence peculiar to it," be otherwise, we have already said, then, that *it belongs to the sense of that contingency precisely to have an essence and hence an Eidos which can be purely apprehended, falling under truths of essences at different levels of universality.*[15]

---

[14] See Harmon Chapman, "Realism and Phenomenology," *Essays in Phenomenology* (The Hague, 1965), edited by Maurice Natanson, pp. 94 f.
[15] *Ideen*, I, p. 9. The translation is mine.

An important aspect of this situation is that it is not, of course, the prerogative of the philosopher to enjoy that situation or see it with original insight:

> The truth is that everyone sees "ideas," "essences," and sees them, so to speak, continuously; they operate with them in their thinking and they also make judgments about them. It is only that, from their theoretical "standpoint," people interpret them away.[16]

Thus regardless of the occasion for advancing a view of essence, the chief philosophical problem at hand is to analyze, clarify and explain what in truth everyone, philosopher and non-philosopher, neo-Kantian or empiricist, sees in confronting a matter-of-fact world. As it were, the novelty of Husserl's account of essence emerges in consequence of placing ourselves at the highly ambiguous point of view of a consciousness unaware of the disputes among philosophers, thus a "standpoint" which does not interpret any thing away. Indeed only then do the disputes take on significance and themselves become an occasion for elaborating a philosophical view.[17]

§ 4. Examples Elaborating Husserl's Account of Essences

Certainly the view which Husserl advances and which is expressed in the preceding quotations from the *Ideen* and *Logische Untersuchungen* is not without its difficulties. Several examples, however, will allow us to bring together some of the facets of his view. The first example is drawn from the logical domain and concerns the logical presentation of "All *A*."[18] For that presentation to occur in an original way it is not sufficient to survey in fact all *A*, even were it the case that all the particulars in question

[16] *Ibid.*, p. 41. The translation is by Dorion Cairns. See the similar statement by Husserl in "Philosophie als strenge Wissenschaft," *Logos*, I (1910/11), p. 341: "Nur darf man sich *nirgends* der radikalen Vorurteilslosigkeit begeben und etwa von vornherein solche 'Sachen' mit empirischen 'Tatsachen' identifizieren, also sich gegenüber den Ideen blind stehen. ... Es bedarf nicht der Forderung, mit eigenen Augen zu sehen, vielmehr: das Gesehene nicht unter dem Zwange der Vorurteile wegzudeuten."
[17] Cf. Henri Bergson, *Matter and Memory* (New York, 1959), translated by Nancy Margaret Paul and W. Scott Palmer, p. xii; and Aron Gurwitsch, *The Field of Consciousness*, p. 166. See below, note 65.
[18] *Logische Untersuchungen*, II, 1, p. 173. (English translation, I, pp. 391 f.) In addition see Dorion Cairns, "An Approach to Phenomenology," *Essays in Memory of Edmund Husserl* (Cambridge, 1940), edited by Marvin Farber, p. 12; and Aron Gurwitsch, "Phenomenology of Thematics and of the Pure Ego," *Studies in Phenomenology and Psychology*, pp. 246 ff.

were finite in number. Instead a further and founded act of consciousness at the end of the survey must be made explicit along with "All *A*." In other words, only with the original presentation of the logical form as well as the individual *A*'s can one judge that this individual is an instance of "All *A*," and then the fact itself that this is an *A*, that it is such as it is but not otherwise.

As the example suggests, the individuals presented in the survey do not appear simply as actual but mere and bare data. Instead they are also presented and may be explicitly grasped as possible exemplifications or varieties, so to speak, of something permanent and invariant, namely "All *A*." In other words the presented actual *A*'s of the survey need not have any special primacy in the presentation of "All *A*." This last point can be illustrated with a different example – the essence, Material Thing at Large. This is exemplified equally by golden mountains and winged horses, by trees and stones. Regarded as to content, the essence is exemplified by products of the imagination *no less than* by the facts of actual perception and apperception. Clearly to apprehend the essence as exemplified by possible varieties, be they actual or imaginary, in no way eliminates the status of those varieties as actual or imaginary.

Taking these examples together we can state Husserl's view of essence still more precisely: in the process of regarding individuals as possible exemplifications of essences certain features and structures are themselves presented, "given," as unaltered throughout, but exhibited in, that process. All members of the series of *A*'s surveyed, actual and imaginary, are "congruent" in a certain respect, exhibit an invariant form and content of a generic and specific kind regardless of all other differences. Moreover the manifold of possible exemplifications need not be exhaustively surveyed; though the process may be broken off after a given number of steps, it can of course be carried out *ad libitum* – as Husserl expresses it in later writings. Indeed, precisely consciousness of the *ad libitum* continuation makes possible the reference of the essence not only to all those varieties that have been, might have been or will be considered, but also to more *ad libitum*. In short, the essence is seen and grasped, perchance objectivated, as an identity in contradistinction but nonetheless with reference to possible varieties within a given domain of greater or lesser universality. In view of the reference to more varieties *ad libitum*, the extension of the essence in this sense is not exhausted by the possible actual and imaginary varieties. And just as individuals as possible exemplifications of essence may be judged about in original ways, so too essence qua essence may be seen and grasped, objectivated and judged about equally originally regardless of its being non-individual and of whether or not it has possible exemplifications.[19]

It may be said accordingly that if the contents of and relations among essences hold *a priori* for matters of fact, this is because actual things and events must be considered purely *as possible* varieties which happen to be "realized."[20] To regard the actually real as purely possible is, of course, not the same as regarding it as imaginary. Rather the actual is but one possibility among others. There is, as a consequence, a complexity of "specification" which may be formulated as the *a priori* limits of the essentially possible (which may or may not be actualized), the essentially impossible (which cannot be actualized), and the essentially necessary (which must be actualized) in any possible realm of being whatever.[21]

Our examples have also suggested another, though not incompatible, meaning of essence. We noted in the presentation of "All *A*" that one can judge this individual as a variety of "All *A*," and then the fact itself that this is an *A such* as it is and not otherwise. To take another example from the perceptual rather than the logical domain: seeing the pen on the desk. It is of its essence to write well, though it is not of its essence to occupy the place it does on the desk.[22] Here we deal neither with any other pen, but with just this pen; nor do we operate with and grasp the essence of the pen in the foregoing sense as equally exemplified or exemplifiable by other possible (actual or imaginary) pens. Instead we confront the essence of this pen, perceiving and grasping not only *that* it is but also *what* it is, its peculiar nature, its being *such as*

19 See Roman Ingarden, "Essentiale Fragen. Ein Beitrag zu dem Wesensproblem," *Jahrbuch für Philosophie und phänomenologische Forschung*, VII (1925), p. 182.

20 See *ibid.*, p. 182, note 1; and below, § 9.

21 See Husserl, *Cartesian Meditations* (The Hague, 1960), translated by Dorion Cairns, pp. 71 f.

22 See Jean Hering, "Bemerkungen über das Wesen, die Wesenheit und die Idee," *Jahrbuch für Philosophie und phänomenologische Forschung*, IV (1921), pp. 497 f.

it is. Here the complexity of "specification" is distinct from the previous sense of essence. In Hering's words, "each object has one and only one essence which makes up the fullness of the kind peculiar to the constituting of it," and, conversely, "each essence is, with regard to its sense, the essence of something and, more particularly, the essence of this and not something else."[23] As regards its vehicle, essence is individual;[24] moreover it is always relative to its vehicle, while essence in the previous examples remained essence regardless of whether or not there are possible varieties, actual or imaginary.[25] Finally, it must be noted that we can speak as much of the essence of a real individual (e.g., the pen) as we can also speak of the essence of an *ideal* individual (e.g., a verbal expression, a melody, Agesander's Laocoön).[26]

§ 5. A Tentative Schema of Interpretation of Husserl's View of Essence

To say the very least, in the foregoing sections we have employed the term "essence" in a highly ambiguous way. In addition to *"Wesen,"* "essence," Husserl also employed the terms *"Eidos"* and *"Idee"* ("idea"). In the passage cited in § 3 from the *Ideen*, "essence" not only signifies "pure essence" as the Whatness of a real individual in its own being peculiar to it (as in the example of the pen), but it also signifies the highest category as well as its particularizations down to full concretion (as in the example of *"All A"*). The terminological and, to some extent, analytical

---

[23] *Ibid.*, p. 497. This and other translations from Hering are mine.
[24] *Ibid.*, § 2. See also Spiegelberg, "Über das Wesen der Idee," *loc. cit.*, p. 219. Spiegelberg refers to it as the "immediate essence" of the object. He goes on to make the following qualification: "Zunächst ist das Wesen wie schon geschildert im Gegensatz zur Idee ebenso individuell wie sein Träger; nur bei unindividuellen Gegenständen verliert es gleichfalls die Individualität. Das Wesen ist ferner etwas auf den Wesensträger Relatives, was wiederum für die Idee keinen Sinn hat. Die Idee bleibt Idee, ob es Exemplare zu ihr gibt oder nicht. Das äußert sich am deutlichsten darin, daß auch die Idee ein Wesen hat, während von einem Wesen des Wesens zu reden keinen oder einen ganz anderen Sinn hat. Dies Wesen der Idee besteht etwa im Haben bestimmter Elemente oder Bestimmtheiten im So-sein, d.h. im ideellen Entsprechen höheren oder niederen Ideen gegenüber usw., wie das in dieser Arbeit des näheren entwickelt wurde."
[25] *Ibid.*
[26] See Hering's examples, *op. cit.*, pp. 498 f.; Ingarden, *op. cit.*, pp. 168 f. The ideality of the essence must be sharply distinguished from that of the ideal individual; see Spiegelberg, *op. cit.*, pp. 96 ff.; also Dorion Cairns, "The Ideality of Verbal Expressions," *Philosophy and Phenomenological Research*, I (1940), pp. 453–462.

ambiguity here was subjected to critical reflection by Jean Hering who ultimately distinguished between "essence" (*Wesen*), "essentiality" (*Wesenheit*) and "idea" (*Idee*).[27] These distinctions served in turn as the point of departure for Ingarden's full scale clarification of "essence" begun in his essay "Essentiale Fragen" (1925) and continued in his *Der Streit um die Existenz der Welt* (1964 f.).[28] Important as these works are for the development of a phenomenology of essence in the light of Husserl's work, it is not possible to rehearse them here in any systematic way. We can, however, take these distinctions into account by making explicit something which has remained largely implicit in our discussion up to this point, namely the fact that we have regarded essences as objective correlates of specific syntheses in consciousness. And although the temporal syntheses and objective correlates are mutually irreducible, be they real or ideal objectivities, nonetheless they do not exclude each other.[29] In these terms what has been said so far allows of distinguishing between at least three different evident intendings and graspings:

1. The meaning and believing in an individual as of a co-intended kind or essence.[30] (For instance, the *A*'s of the survey, or grasping a tree or a stone as a member of a collection of material things.)

2. The meaning and believing in the essence itself as exemplified in, or embodied or fulfilled by individual varieties.[31] (For instance, explicitly grasping "All *A*" exemplified in All *A*.)

3. The meaning and believing in the essence itself for its own sake, as it were, regardless of whether or not it is exemplified in or embodied by anything at all – unrestricted, in other words, to any given or likely co-intended varieties.

There is clearly a difference between grasping an identical

---

[27] Hering, *op. cit.*

[28] Both "Essentiale Fragen" and Hering's essay are critically reviewed by Spiegelberg, "Über das Wesen der Ideen," *passim*. It should be noted that the German translation of *Der Streit um die Existenz der Welt* is assumed to be not only that, but also an expression of Ingarden's view as of 1964. The original was published in Polish in 1947.

[29] See Aron Gurwitsch, "On the Intentionality of Consciousness," *Studies in Phenomenology and Psychology*, pp. 137 f.

[30] Cf. Roman Ingarden, *Der Streit um die Existenz der Welt* (Tübingen, 1965), Vol. II, 1, pp. 241 ff.

[31] Cf. *ibid.*, pp. 246 ff.; and Dorion Cairns, "The Ideality of Verbal Expressions," *loc. cit.*, pp. 457 ff.

something as exemplified in two or more individuals on the one hand and those individuals grasped as exemplifying the same generic or formal characteristic on the other hand ("All *A*" or Material Thing at Large). But all that is distinct from grasping something identical as constituting the fullness (Hering) of just this rather than that (this pen rather than that one), and, on the other hand, grasping just this rather than that being such as and how it is. In turn, that is distinct from grasping something identical embodied by this individual on the one hand, and this individual grasped as embodying that identical something (e.g., a real rendering of *the* melody) on the other hand.

In each case we distinguish something observable and repeatedly identifiable which stands out in contradistinction but with reference to individuals that are spatiotemporal. In each case we can ask reasonable questions about them and make intersubjectively verifiable judgments about them; in each case we grasp something identical which is objectively existent, but ideal.[32] In the elaboration of Husserl's view in the foregoing sections we have dealt with three such idealities:

1. In a sense narrower than we have employed it up to now, *essence* signifies what is co-intended to in and through the seeing and grasping of a real or ideal individual as exemplifying and, perchance, actualizing what and how it is, its being thus and so.[33]

2. What we shall call with Hering and Ingarden the *essentiality* of something real or ideal is, in contrast, independent and non-individual, though embodied by something.[34] We shall return to this in the next sections.

3. Finally we distinguish "essence" in the sense of *idea*. Here we must mention not only purely formal universals but also material (generic and specific) universals.

In this tentative schema of clarification of Husserl's and a

---

[32] See Cairns, *op. cit.*, p. 454. There is a clear need for terminological clarification in Husserl's writings which would not only bring the first edition of the *Logische Untersuchungen* in line with the first volume of *Ideen*, but the latter in line with later works such as *Erfahrung und Urteil*.

[33] See Hering, *op. cit.*, § 1 and pp. 496, 502 ff.; Spiegelberg, *op. cit.*, § 42, especially pp. 218 ff.

[34] This distinction was first introduced by Hering, *op. cit.*, §§ 2 ff.; it was endorsed by Ingarden, "Essentiale Fragen," pp. 181 f. Later on we shall note Spiegelberg's disagreement with this distinction. Hering himself was not always clear as to what he meant, though at times "essentiality" seems similar to Husserl's use of the term "*Spezie*" in the Second Investigation of the *Logischen Untersuchungen*.

Husserlian view of essence we shall reserve the term *"Eidos"* for all such ideally existing objects and speak accordingly of the *eidetic* seeings and graspings of essences, essentialities and ideas.[35]

In each case essence, essentiality and idea must be examined as to their structures, relationships with each other precisely and purely as they are presented in the seeings and graspings of them. Before turning to the outline of the program of this examination it is worthwhile recalling the occasion for these distinctions in the first place.

At least one aspect of the occasion for Husserl's formulation of his view of essence suggests that a basic problem is that of the nature of the relationship between seeing *Eide* and seeing things. It is no accident that one of the few recent books on Husserl in this regard speaks of his "exemplarism."[36] And indeed it turns out that a basic relation is that of exemplified to exemplifying:

> If one is busied with matters that have the sense of not being temporally individuated, still the individual world is at least inactually co-intended and itself given – though incompletely, as having more to it than presents itself – and, by their sense, these non-individual objects have their varied types of objective "ideal" being, essentially in the relation to the individual world of individuals, e.g., as essences *exemplified* by actual or possible world-individuals, as facts ultimately "about" world-individuals, as cultural affairs ultimately "embodied" in individual things or processes in the world. Thus, in a broad sense, they too are all intended, and perchance originally given, as world objects.[37]

As the passage by Cairns indicates, in addition to exemplification we can also speak of embodiment in certain other cases, and perhaps even of "ideal correspondence" (Spiegelberg). In still other cases we can speak perhaps of "realization" and "concretization" or "constituting in fullness" (Hering and Ingarden).

---

[35] It is necessary to note here that in the first volume of *Ideen*, p. 6, Husserl introduces the term *Eidos* to distinguish "idea" from the Kantian use of the term. Our use of the term "Idea" in the text is more consistent with Husserl's use of the term in *Logische Untersuchung* III (second edition). In any case, our use of the term is not the same as *Husserl's use* of the Kantian term, nor is it the same as Kant's use of the term – either as it agrees or disagrees with Husserl's use. For Husserl's use of the Kantian term, in contradistinction to his use of "Eidos" (our Idea, Essentiality, Essence), see J. Derrida, Introduction to Husserl, *L 'Origine de la Géométrie* (Paris, Presses Universitaires de France, 1962), pp. 147 ff., 156, note 2. The integration of this notion of Idea in the present study is not possible, although it is fundamental to it.

[36] See André de Muralt, *L'Idée de la Phénoménologie. L'Exemplarisme Husserlien* (Paris, 1958).

[37] Cairns, "An approach to Phenomenology," pp. 14 f.

However this may be, it is clear that these relationships are quite distinct from those of subsumption and allied relationships.[38] We can indicate this with a brief example.

Suppose that I am deceived by what I perceive, or uncertain of what it is that I see on the desk in front of me – I cannot decide whether it is a pen or a black Italian cigar. As a rule in recognizing and identifying something I subsume it under a concept expressing the kind of thing it is. Yet only in virtue of grasping a thing X in its idea can I then proceed to subsume it under a concept, or resolve the conflict as to whether it is this or that, a pen or a cigar, or acquire certainty about what it is. Once this occurs, X, as it were, cannot continue to unfold itself in perception along any lines whatever; a limit has been reached where it is seen and grasped as this rather than that. To be sure, further change and alteration of what I perceive is now possible. But that is now possible only on a definite, patterned or predelineated basis – it is now no longer a question of what it is, perhaps, but only of how it is. The point is that to subsume something under a concept I must have already grasped it as to its essence or idea; only then is subsumption possible.[39]

§ 6. Idea and Essentiality

So far as content or "specification" is concerned, the idea "All A" stands out as something identical over against but always with reference to the *formed* real (or ideal) things (affairs). When regarded as to material content, corresponding to the idea, to use Ingarden's language, is its "concretization" or essentiality – in our logical example, the affairs formed.[40] What is important to note is that only in virtue of intending to the idea exemplified in possible actual or imaginary varieties is it possible to proceed to grasp and objectivate the essentiality peculiar to its material content. Equivalently stated, it is possible to grasp and objectivate the idea exemplified by co-intended varieties without of necessity grasping and objectivating the essentiality, the formed

---

[38] See Wilhelm Schapp, *Beiträge zur Phänomenologie der Wahrnehmung* (Göttingen, 1910), pp. 137 ff.

[39] See *ibid.*, p. 140.

[40] See Ingarden, "Essentiale Fragen," pp. 182 f.; Hering, *op. cit.*, p. 529.

things themselves.[41] However, the converse is not the case: no essentiality can be explicitly grasped without an implicit grasping of the idea exemplified by co-intended varieties. For example, I cannot grasp and objectivate the A's surveyed without implicitly grasping the idea "All A." In this connection we can also note that grasping and objectivating an essence is not of necessity grasping, even implicitly, an essentiality, though there can be no grasping and objectivating of an essence (e.g., of this A) without implicitly grasping the idea e.g., ("Material Thing at Large"). In other words, there seems to me to be a sharp distinction between, e.g., the being-pen of the pen (the essence of the pen), the penness of the pen (the what or idea of the pen), and the pen as a member of surveyed items – a member of a collection of items on my desk (the essentiality).

This already indicates that the relationship between idea and essentiality is distinct from that between essentiality and essence. In the former case we said that the idea is "concretized" by the essentiality; the "All A" is "concretized" by the formed state of affairs, "A and A and A. ..." In the latter case we may say that the essentiality is "realized" or "actualized" or perhaps better, embodied, by the essence or essential nature of the thing in question. Earlier we referred in this connection to the "relativity," the necessary "solidarity" of essence with its vehicle; with Fritz Kaufmann we may say that essence fulfills the *"principium identitatis indiscernibilium* not only in virtue of its accidental circumstances, but also in virtue of a principle which is constitutive of its inner form, its intrinsic nature."[42] To be sure, this does not imply that the appearance of each individual being is the outgrowth of an essence. In our by now rather modified example of the surveyed items, the formed and surveyed character of the A's, founded on perceiving the A's, does not of necessity grow out of the individual essences of the A's, out of what they are or

---

[41] See Ingarden, *op. cit.*, p. 182, and Hering, *op. cit.*, § 7. Both Ingarden and Hering are concerned to show cases of material universals to which there is no corresponding essentiality. In turn this is used as evidence that essentiality should not be confused with material universals. In Ingarden's words, "Es gibt Ideen von konstitutiven Gegenstandsnaturen, denen keine Wesenheit entspricht (bei Hering 'unechte Morphe,' 'Morphenkonglomerat,' Beispiel: ἱππότης). Die Auffassung also, daß eine Wesenheit nichts anderes als die Idee einer konstitutiven Gegenstandsnatur ist, ist undurchführbar."

[42] Fritz Kaufmann, "The Phenomenological Approach to History," *Philosophy and Phenomenological Research*, II (1941), p. 163.

how they are (whatever and however they may be, real or ideal individuals). It would make no more sense to say of the pen, for example, that a constituent of its essence is to be surveyed or collected than it would to say that it is of the essence of a given concatenated set of sounds to embody this or that verbal expression. On the other hand, the items in the survey are not presented as mere, isolated items in a mere temporal sequence – this pen *and* this pen ... is a formed state of affairs with definable and sensical or senseful characteristics. And the formed state of affairs is clearly not the form or formal universal.

Yet this does not by any means signify that such characters, such essentialities, are *merely* accidental:

> Characters which do not properly belong to a thing's individual essence may be, nevertheless, of a more than accidental status if they are founded upon this very essence. In this way even the accidental ⟨scl. the survey or collection⟩ may rise above the level of mere chance: the part which it plays in the life of an individual may be determined by the inner form ⟨scl. the essence in our sense⟩ of this being which proves selective of the nature and of the extent of these happenings.[43]

In the case of essentiality we may say that there is a combining of ideality with mutability which is quite distinct from the case of ideas and their exemplification by individuals, or from essences and their "constituting fullness." So far as essentialities are either "concretized" or perchance embodied, they behave, as it were, like essences inseparably presented with their vehicles. But that "inseparability" has the character of contingency, of "historical vicissitudes," rather than that of necessity. As a consequence we cannot say of essentialities that they are individual in any strict sense. Indeed, they are neither individual nor universal – but "singular."[44]

---

[43] *Ibid.*

[44] Whether or not everything Husserl calls "eidetic singularity" can be included here is an open question. For this see Cairns, "The Ideality of Verbal Expressions," p. 459. Likewise it remains to be seen if the "historical vicissitudes" peculiar to eidetic singularities such as verbal expressions are always also characteristic of essentialities. See also Hering, *op. cit.*, p. 520. The account I give here is tentative and preliminary, and differs from Spiegelberg, "Über das Wesen der Idee," p. 229: "So erscheint es als eine diametrale Umkehrung des wahren Sachverhaltes, wenn Hering die Morphe (eine Außenbestimmtheit) für das Fundierende, für den letzten Grund des Rotmoments im Gegenstande ausgibt. Nicht das Rotmoment ist auf das Rotsein des Gegenstands begründet, sondern umgekehrt das Rotsein auf das Rotmoment und sein Verhältnis zur Idee Rot ... Dieser Einwand gilt in gleicher Stärke bezüglich der 'Röte an sich,' der sogenannten *Wesenheit.* Freilich ist es mir nicht geglückt, endgültige

§ 7. Eidetic Generalization and Formalization

We can further unfold the difference between idea, essence and essentiality by referring to Husserl's distinction between generalization and formalization (*Ideen*, I, § 13). The method of free, *ad libitum* variation or "ideation" which we mentioned in the case of idea, i.e., the form "All *A*," can be applied *mutatis mutandis* to essence and essentiality. On the basis of directly seeing, grasping and objectivating them we can proceed not only to state but also to legitimate the *a priori* laws of essence, essentialities and ideas. In this connection the distinction we have in mind was first formulated by Husserl as regards his doctrine of the "forms of meaning" in the *Logische Untersuchungen* (Fourth Investigation, § 10). Here, starting with a proposition such as "The tree is green" we can formalize it to yield the propositional form, "this *S* is *p*." If we substitute material terms for *S* and *p* we can construct an infinite number of propositions such as "This gold is green," "This blue raven is green," etc. It can easily be seen that when "categories of meaning" are not respected mere sequences of words occur:

> We are at once made aware, through *a priori* insight into law, that such intended combinations are ruled out by the very nature of the constituents of the pure patterns in question, that such constituents can only enter into definitely constituted meaning-patterns.[45]

The very freedom of substituting any material terms whatever brings the *limits* to the fore, the "categories" under which the material terms must fall. In other words, there is a sharp distinction between eidetic formalization on the one hand, and eidetic

Klarheit darüber zu gewinnen, was mit dieser Wesenheit eigentlich gemeint wird. Ich kann hier nichts anderes zu Gesicht bekommen als allenfalls die Idee des Rotseins. Die Wesenheit Röte an und für sich soll aber nach Hering nicht mit der Idee Röte identisch sein. Auch soll die Wesenheit Röte etwas schlechthin selbständig darstellen. Röte bleibt aber auch als Idee immer Rotsein *von* etwas, ist immer auf einen Träger bezogen. *Röte für* sich wäre also entweder die Idee Rot oder das Rotmoment." My objection to his in the text is that the alternative here does not allow for such phenomena, it seems to me, as the formed affairs in contradistinction to the form of those affairs, nor for eidetic singularities such as verbal expressions, nor for the historical processes and epochés (e.g., Romanticism) described by Kaufmann in his aforementioned essay. Nonetheless Spiegelberg's point seems well taken as regards Hering's example. Further analysis is required to settle this issue. It cannot be done here.

[45] *Logische Untersuchungen*, II, 1, p. 320. The translation is Findlay's, p. 512.

generalization on the other hand whereby we grasp the "catego-ries," the ideal genera and species exemplified by the material contents that fill the forms with graspable single meanings.[46]

This brings us back to our consideration of essentiality, since essentiality first of all emerges, is grasped in confronting the limit-ing condition, namely that the material terms must fall under definite "categories of meaning" or, more broadly stated, under "regional categories." Essentialities are presented accordingly in acts of consciousness distinct from those in which ideas, for in-stance, are presented. "Thing at Large," or "Empty Something" are presented originaliter in eidetic *formalization*; "the tree is green" is presented originaliter in eidetic *generalization*. That is to say, *either* I see and grasp the logical forms exemplified by possible actual affairs ("The grass is green"), *or* I see and grasp the ideal genera or species exemplified by the material contents filling the forms in question (the green grass). The seeing and grasp-ing of essentialities is founded on the grasping and objectivating of eidetic generalization rather than formalization. To take another example: the idea "Material Thing at Large" is exempli-fied equally by golden mountains and winged horses, by trees and stones. The items mentioned exemplify the ideal generic characteristic, but only the trees and stones are grasped as to their essentiality – the town's hanging tree or the rock of ages.

Stated universally, whereas it is the case that no "regional ontology" allows us to draw any conclusion as to the actual exis-tence pertaining to that "region," nonetheless if there exist ob-jects pertaining to that region they must of necessity conform to the conditions of their essential possibility. Thus if there exist individuals, they must then of necessity be of such and such an essence, embodying such and such an essentiality, exemplifying such and such an idea. Shortly we shall elaborate further these ontological considerations. For the moment we must turn to the relations among the various eidetic seeings and graspings formulated in § 5.

---

[46] *Ibid.*, pp. 320 f. English translation, pp. 512 f. In this connection, see Gurwitsch, *The Field of Consciousness*, p. 196. This is the core of Husserl's answer to Kant's and Kantian criticism that the seeing of essences is not grounded by the facts of experience; see above, pp. 4 ff. To be sure, this criticism ultimately only holds if the relation be-tween essences and the facts of experience is one of analogy; in the previous section I have tried to suggest that this is not the case.

§ 8. The Founding-Founded Structure of Eidetic Seeings

As Natorp rightly pointed out, and as we have emphasized several times, an important aspect of the occasion on which Husserl formulated his view of essence concerned the relation of seeing *Eide* and seeing things. It is here that the problem of Platonic dualism arises and Natorp had charged Husserl with not going far enough to overcome it. However, it follows from Husserl's view that seeing and grasping *Eide* are always of necessity founded upon the purely possible seeing and meaning real individuals as similar or dissimilar to each other, as alike or unlike in some respect or other. Founded in turn on this noetic-noematic stratum is the grasping and even objectivating of that "respect" itself. At a still higher level, founded in turn, is the judgment, for instance, that this is a green tree, or an *A*, etc. The significance of this is that rather than a Platonic dualism of "essence and historical existence" we have a view where "all intention springs from individual awareness" and where essence, essentiality and idea "have the center of their constitution in the very facts which brought them to light":

and the different adumbrations of a general essence, down to eidetic singularities, figure as variations of the very variety that was originally shown through individual experience. This experience, for its part, must be recognized in its concrete historical meaning as given and revised in the horizon and from the perspective of the actual moment.[47]

For this reason and in virtue of the "exemplarism" of Husserl the relation between seeing and grasping *Eide* and seeing and grasping things is not one of analogy at all, let alone one of subsumption or even of similarity of some kind or another. Rather the *novelty* of Husserl's view, namely that eidetic and perceptual seeings are generically alike but specifically different, expresses a *sui generis* concretion which is expressed with precision in these words of Dorion Cairns:

But it would not be correct to say that *all* judgments based on the observation of essences exemplified by reflectively given matters are phenomenological. Indeed, it would not even be correct to say, conversely,

---

[47] Kaufmann, *op. cit.*, p. 161. See also Aron Gurwitsch, "On a Perceptual Root of Abstraction," *Studies in Phenomenology and Psychology*, pp. 385 ff.

that *all* strictly phenomenological judgments are based on observation of essences. The observation of one's individual consciousness provides a basis not only for grasping its general nature but also for performing phenomenological judgments of existence, most notably, the judgment that one's individual consciousness itself is not only purely possible but exists as an actual instance of consciousness in general. And this turns out to be anything but trivial, since it is the basis for every other phenomenological judgment of existence.[48]

In the concluding sections of this essay we shall elaborate in ontological terms the *sui generis* concretion of the consciousness of *Eide* and accordingly the radical shape it gives to Husserl's "Platonism."

§ 9. The Internal Occasion for the Formulation of Husserl's View of Essence

Earlier we noted (§ 1) Natorp's statement that no being is presented to thinking which is not itself posited in thinking.[49] Positing, the positionality of consciousness, is a dimension of consciousness which we have not yet made explicit but with which we must deal if we are to account both for judgment based on observation of essence and judgments of existence. By making this explicit we not only arrive at what we may call the "internal occasion" for Husserl's formulation of essence, but at the elements which constitute the novelty of his view (§ 11) and hence the final, radical shape of his "Platonism" (§ 12).

In addition to the eidetic intuitional moments of the intendings peculiar to consciousness we must also distinguish a "positional" moment; that is to say, not only are things and affairs meant and intended to, intuited as to essence, essentiality and/or idea, but they are also believed in as existing really or ideally. Stated universally, objectivities of all sorts are presented in and through systematically concatenated mental processes, and through those processes they not only disclose their properties, qualities, relations, but also themselves as existent in specific modes – though existence is to be understood as a (syn) "thetic" or "belief" character rather than as a property of objectivities. As a consequence, we distinguish between what is meant and intended to

[48] Cairns, "An Approach to Phenomenology," pp. 13 f.
[49] Natorp, *Die logischen Grundlagen der exakten Wissenschaften*, p. 48.

on the one hand and, on the other hand, that objectivity as it is intended to. For example, I am presently seeing the desk on which I write and, while seeing it, may pay attention to certain features of the desk – its size, shape, color and so forth. But all the while seeing it I am (implicitly) believing in it as existing. By objectivating the noematic sense of the seeing of the desk, its rectangularity, color, shape are made thematic. But by objectivating the character of believing, the mode of existence is made thematic. The seen and meant desk is believed in as existing, as belonging into a spatiotemporal context – the objectivity as it is intended to. This distinction in objectivating points to one in different dimensions of consciousness, such that if one dimension varies, the other varies – if the desk is presented as absent, then it may be believed indubitably, or as non-existent, and so forth.

Using shorthand terms, this distinction between presentationality and positionality of consciousness allows for the development of an ontology in which essence, essentiality and idea and their relationships can be analyzed both as regards their respective presentational and positional modes, both as to the ways in which they are presented or "given" and the ways in which they are believed in. Shortening and simplifying his account, we can refer here to four basic ontological concepts adduced by Roman Ingarden as expressing the fundamental modes of positionality:

1. absolute supratemporal existence,
2. extratemporal, ideal existence,
3. temporal existence, and
4. purely intentive existence.[50]

It is to be borne in mind that the fundamental phenomenological situation to be clarified and explained by the account of essence, essentiality and idea is the correlation of contingent change and necessity. Reformulated in terms of our tentative schema of interpretation, this signifies that on the basis of seeing, grasping and objectivating the essence, essentiality and idea as well as the individual exemplifying, embodying or fulfilling them, the factuality or contingency itself is seen, grasped and objectivated. (To take Hering's example, on the basis of seeing and grasping the

---

[50] See Roman Ingarden, "Les Modes d'existence et le problème 'idéalisme-réalisme'," *Proceedings of the 10th International Congress of Philosophy* (Amsterdam, 1949), pp. 349 f. Cf. Ingarden, *Der Streit um die Existenz der Welt*, I, §§ 14 f.

essentiality Red, it is possible to judge that this is an instance of Red, then that this colored thing is red in color.) When regarded as clarification of this basic situation, the four concepts of modes of existence advanced by Ingarden are immediately seen not only to include (with radical revision) the Husserlian explanation given, but also to surpass it.[51] This gives rise to an occasion *internal* to phenomenology for formulating a view of essence which challenges a basic tenet of Husserlian phenomenology, namely that the *problem* of intentionality is the basic problem, that universally consciousness is both consciousness in and of the world.

To understand the challenge of this occasion in the most direct way we may focus our attention on the fourth mode of existence distinguished, namely purely intentive existence.

Within the general framework of Ingarden's *Das Literarische Kunstwerk* (1930), this mode would seem to hold only for the experience of a work of art which is partly at the mercy of certain significational acts of consciousness. The gist of Ingarden's view, which we shall shortly state in more detail (§ 11), is that what has been said about the constituting of idea in our sense would not hold for works of art,[52] that there is no consciousness *of* idea as regards a work of art. Accordingly, Husserl's account of the universal nature of intentionality at large would have to be *restrictively* revised. However, in *Der Streit um die Existenz der Welt* Ingarden *universalizes* this special case and holds that what is true of the intentionality of works of art is true of all intentionality.[53] Idea and, indeed, all cases of ideal existence, such as essence and essentiality, would then be radically transcendent to consciousness in a manner distinct and apart from pure intentive objectivities, from the noematic correlates of consciousness. Here we need not rehearse the line of thought which leads Ingarden to this conclusion because it is precisely at this juncture that the epithet, if not the charge, of "Platonism" rears its head. And the validity of the charge depends on how we answer the question of

---

[51] Cf. Ingarden, *Der Streit um die Existenz der Welt*, II, 2, pp. 394 ff.; also A.-T. Tymieniecka, "Le Dessein de la philosophie de Roman Ingarden," *Revue de Métaphysique et de Morale*, 1955, pp. 42, 48.

[52] Cf. A.-T. Tymieniecka, *Phenomenology and Science in Contemporary European Thought* (New York, 1962), pp. 26 f. For possible solutions to the problem from a purely Husserlian standpoint, see Cairns, "The Ideality of Verbal Expressions," pp. 455 ff., and Kaufmann, *op. cit.*, pp. 163 f.

[53] See Ingarden, *op. cit.*, II, 1, §§ 46 ff., especially pp. 216 ff.

whether or not Ingarden's assertion signifies anything more than that idea and other cases of ideal existence are irreducible to the modes of consciousness *of* them.[54] Even heuristically granting an affirmative answer to this question, it is still insufficient to hold that therefore some method other than phenomenological reflection is required to elucidate the nature of such ideal existences. This amounts to a sort of "inverse" empiricism where one maintains the existence of universals while denying their reference to the context of consciousness in which they appear, perhaps even denying "consciousness of" them. In terms of Ingarden's universalization of the special case of intentionality found in the experience of the work of art, if anything more is signified than the irreducibility of real and ideal existences to consciousness of them, the serious danger arises of (implicitly) holding that, for instance, the perceptual noema "desk" is not only numerically distinct from the "real desk,"[55] but the unique relativity of essence to its vehicle is vitiated, the essentiality perchance unembodied, the idea unexemplified. In general, can one conclude from the fact that idea, for instance, stands out as self-identical in contradistinction but always with reference to possible actual and imaginary *ad libitum* exemplifications that, as regards its belief character, it is somehow autonomous and non- or "meta-" intentive? This would signify, among other things, that the difference between seeing ideas and seeing individuals such as real perceptual things is a generic *rather than* specific difference. Were this true, then Husserl's view as revised by Ingarden would indeed be Platonism and, more particular, Platonism of the first stage distinguished by Natorp. Yet to say that the perceptual noema "desk" and the idea "Material Thing at Large" are not the same both as regards presentationality and positionality no more asserts that idea is

[54] Cf. *Ibid.*, II, 2, pp. 375 ff.; and *Das Literarische Kunstwerk* (Tübingen, 1960²), p. 121. Fritz Kaufman has put this whole matter in the following way, *op. cit.*, p. 160: Essence "First ... is considered as an object taken separately, i.e., without regard to the context of consciousness within which it appears. The phenomenological emphasis upon the irreducibility of objective meaning, its irreducibility to the stream of conscious acts, does not exclude an understanding of this meaning as somebody's meaning. The object thus is 'reduced' to an objective pole of my experience – or rather, to an objective pole common to the consciousness of an indefinite number of selves, to their 'transcendental intersubjectivity' which is constituted, however, within myself as transcendental ego."

[55] In this connection, see the expert critique of Mikel Dufrenne, *Phénoménologie de l'expérience esthétique* (Paris, 1953), I, pp. 269 f.

not a noematic object than does denying the existence of the desk in any way assert that the desk is rather an object of the imagination.[56]

Finally, in the light of Ingarden's universalization of the intentionality of a work of art it also may be asked whether or not the distinction between presentationality and positionality cuts across all four modes of existence mentioned, or whether or not the fourth mode of existence, purely intentive existence, is not really a mode of existence at all but rather a (limiting?) case of *mere* (pure?) presentationality.[57] These are perhaps the most important questions raised by Ingarden's critical reflections on Husserl since, if true, they would suggest that a *phenomenology* of essence, essentiality and idea is impossible in much the same way that Alfred Schutz found himself forced to conclude that phenomenology is incapable of "establishing an ontology on the basis of the processes of subjective life."[58] It is precisely here that the novelty of the view advanced by Husserl becomes an issue: ultimately whether or not a (transcendental) constitutional inquiry is also an ontological analysis of *Eide*. We can now make that novelty thematic by assessing the consequences of Ingarden's view vis-à-vis Husserl's.

§ 10. The Significance of the Novelty of Husserl's View of Essence

According to Ingarden, ideas, like real individual objects, lie outside our sphere of influence.[59] But to assert this may very well be to maintain that an imputed real relation of consciousness, as a process in the world, to its objects does not hold in some cases – perchance only in the case of intentive objects can we speak of objects within our sphere of influence. In the case of the intentionality of a work of art, it is not difficult to see what Ingarden is driving at: the efficacy of the creative imagination in

[56] See above, § 4. See also the distinction drawn by Husserl between "existential predications" and "predications of reality," *Erfahrung und Urteil*, § 74.

[57] For the difficulties of this view, see the present writer's "William James and Franz Brentano," *Journal of the History of Philosophy*, VII (April, 1969), pp. 184 ff.

[58] Alfred Schutz, "The Problem of Transcendental Intersubjectivity in Husserl," *Collected Papers*, III, pp. 83 f.

[59] See Ingarden, *Der Streit um die Existenz der Welt*, II, 1, p. 253; *Das Literarische Kunstwerk*, pp. 121, 362; Tymieniecka, "Le Dessein de la philosophie de Roman Ingarden," p. 42.

the shaping of the art work. But to consider all intentionality in these terms is to leave one open to the danger of implicitly asserting that there is an objective analogue between intending to something and that something purely as intended to, *and* that real relation, for instance: consciousness and that whereof it is consciousness as real things in time. Ingarden seems to say that if one denies the latter relation in a given case, namely in the case of the first three modes of existence, then one *ipso facto* denies the other relation, namely of intending to something and that something purely as intended to.[60]

To put the whole matter in terms of our initial sketch of Husserl's view, to deny that differences important for perception are unimportant or absent for apprehending ideas is *ipso facto* a denial that there is apprehension of ideas. As Dorion Cairns has put the matter, *in the world* consciousness and its objects are not only related *as*, for instance, perceiving and perceived purely as intended to, but *also* as having objective relationships in time. The two relationships must not be regarded as analogous, and since consciousness only discovers itself in and of the world so far as it is consciousness of the world, the latter is not fundamental but also *sui generis.*[61] (This, of course, in no way implies that consciousness is concretely apart from the world.) Intending to anything, whether it be real or ideal, has no mundane analogue. Obviously the absence of *this* analogue must not be confused with the absence of the analogue between seeing *Eide* on the one hand, and seeing real individual things on the other hand (§ 8). Only by referring essence, essentiality and idea back to the constitutings of them can one avoid even implicitly asserting either analogue. (Likewise the concretion of eidetic and perceptual seeing is also *sui generis* – § 8 *in fine.*)

As already indicated, if one asserts the second analogue then one would be forced to hold that there is no *specific* difference between seeing an essence, for example, and perceiving an individual thing. And in that case differences important for perception would then be also important for seeing and grasping

---

[60] Cf. Ingarden, *Der Streit um die Existenz der Welt*, II, 1, pp. 253, 256 f.
[61] Cairns, "An Approach to Phenomenology," pp. 17 f. Contrast with Ingarden, *op. cit.*, II, 2, pp. 323 ff., especially p. 370.

essences (or essentialities, ideas).[62] Or, if one asserts the first analogue then one is forced to deny altogether seen and grasped *Eide* – ultimately the consciousness of them. As a consequence, to clarify and explain what in truth everyone sees and operates with it is necessary that a constitutional inquiry always be fundamental to an ontological one.[63]

It is this, I believe, which is the philosophical significance of the novelty of Husserl's view of essence: it allows both for judgments based on the eidetic seeing and grasping of Eide and judgments of existence based on the seeing and grasping of real individuals.

§ 11. The "Controversy Over 'Realism' and 'Idealism'"

So far as the internal occasion of the formulation of Husserl's and a Husserlian view of *Eide* is concerned, when pushed to the extreme the question about Platonism turns on the legitimacy of the assertion of the two analogues of consciousness in the world rather than on what Ingarden calls the "controversy over realism and idealism."[64] For there to be such a controversy at all it is necessary to assert the truth of the mundane analogue of intentionality. It is a further novelty of Husserl's view that this analogue need not be asserted to account for seeing and grasping ideal objectivities; a supervenient act of inference, based on the continuity of thought, need not be introduced, for instance, to hold that essence, essentiality and idea are necessary parts of the experienced world – as is the case with the *Kinesis* of Ideas in neo-Kantianism. Equivalently stated, a constitutional inquiry viti-

---

[62] This has serious consequences which are strikingly illustrated in the philosophical significance of certain pathological studies; see Aron Gurwitsch, "Gelb-Goldstein's Concept of 'Concrete' and 'Categorial' Attitude," *loc. cit.*, pp. 378 ff.

[63] Ingarden has suggested that the order of procedure is first, to become aware of what is being investigated as to form, material content and mode of being. The resulting ontology, however, is not the last word; it is to be followed by a metaphysical and epistemological inquiry which provides an ultimate control of the whole analysis, wherein Husserl's constitutional analysis is retained. See Husserl, *Briefe an Roman Ingarden*, edited with commentary by Roman Ingarden (Den Haag, 1968), p. 166; also *Das Literarische Kunstwerk*, pp. x, xii. In shorthand terms, an eidetic ontological analysis is then fundamental to and, according to Ingarden, precedes a constitutional analysis. But just this overlooks the fact mentioned earlier, pp. 82 f., that not all judgments which are phenomenological are based on the observations of essences.

[64] See Roman Ingarden, "Bemerkungen zum Problem 'Idealismus-Realismus'," *Jahrbuch für Philosophie und phänomenologische Forschung*, Festschrift (1929), pp. 168 f., 175 f., 190.

ates the controversy since not all phenomenological judgments are based on seeing and grasping *Eide*, nor are all based on seeing real individuals. And so far as the "struggle for the existence of the world" is dependent on that controversy, on the assertion of the mundane analogue of intentionality, it becomes a pseudo phenomenological problem, the *Proton Pseudos* of both empiricism and (neo-Kantian) idealism. To be sure, even if it is granted that the "transcendentally 'reduced' standpoint" required by a constitutional inquiry is a correct one, it is still legitimate to ask, as Ingarden has shown, whether or not that "standpoint" provides the basis for answering all questions about the existence of the real world, especially ontological and metaphysical ones, ultimately of whether or not that "standpoint" includes, or is at least fundamental to, other "standpoints" as well.[65]

Only in this light can one avoid accepting as philosophical and genuine what is not derived from "evidence," only in this way can one examine the whole range of "evidence": where this is still lacking one's judgments cannot claim any final validity and must, at best, be regarded as possible intermediate stages on the way to final validity.[66] The way to final validity takes the shape not of a controversy about realism and idealism, but instead of a radically altered "Platonism." It remains now, in conclusion, to state the nature of that "Platonism."

§ 12. The Radical Shape of Husserl's "Platonism"

The "Platonism" with which Husserl and Husserlian phenomenology is charged can be expressed in these words of Aron Gurwitsch:

Throughout history, *episteme* was opposed to *doxa*; for *doxa* was conceived as related to the world of common experience, *episteme* to the realm of "being as it really is in itself," a realm with regard to which the world

---

[65] In this connection, Aron Gurwitsch observes that, for example, "In the very possibility of adopting both the naturalistic and the phenomenological point of view, there appears the ambiguous nature of consciousness," *The Field of Consciousness*, p. 166. It is when that "ambiguity" of consciousness is interpreted away, when consciousness is regarded as only in the world, or only of the world rather than both *in* and *of* the world, that the controversy over realism and idealism arises. I have examined this aspect of consciousness in "The Constancy Hypothesis in the Social Sciences," in *Lifeworld and Consciousness*, edited by Lester Embree (Evanston, 1971).

[66] See Husserl, *Cartesian Meditations*, § 5.

90

$28.00 N

#223048

of common experience has been relegated to a position of inferiority in some sense or other.[67]

This is precisely the "Platonism" which Husserl's view attempts to overcome by rehabilitating, as it were, the truth that "everyone sees 'ideas,' 'essences,' and sees them, so to speak, continuously" without interpreting them away. In his 1913 draft of a new preface to the second edition of the *Logische Untersuchungen*, and in this connection, Husserl criticizes those who make the charge of "Platonism" with not taking the trouble to see what he means by ideal objects, by his account of "ideal essentialities." Husserl goes on to point out that his so-called Platonism does not consist in some sort of metaphysical or epistemological substructures, hypostatizings or theories. It consists instead "in the simple reference to a sort of original givenness which, however, is falsely interpreted away on principle."[68] The "givenness" or presentation mentioned is judged about as much in daily life as it is in science. To the extent to which everyone sees "ideal essentialities" everyone is a naive "Platonist." To be sure, there are profound philosophical problems involved, but they are always rooted in the world of common experience. In virtue of this, as Gurwitsch points out,

... the world of common experience is rehabilitated by phenomenology as *the reality* from which all conceptions and constructions of other domains of existence start and to which these domains essentially refer. Accordingly, the *doxa* is reinstated in its rightful place. ... This means that *episteme* in the traditional sense, e.g., specific scientific *episteme*, also falls under the concept of *doxa*, differences of level and scope notwithstanding. ... *episteme* in the specific phenomenological sense is not *episteme* as opposed to *doxa*. Rather it is the *episteme* of the very *doxa*, of all possible *doxa*.[69]

Phenomenology as the *episteme* of all possible *doxa*, the phenomenology of essence, is the radical shape of "Platonism" in Husserl's thought. So far as that is true, Husserl's phenomenology of essence also overcomes the charge of "Platonism" by directly engaging "Platonism" itself through the attempt to clarify and

[67] Aron Gurwitsch, "The last Work of Edmund Husserl," *Studies in Phenomenology and Psychology*, p. 447.
[68] *Loc. cit.*, p. 318. The translation is mine.
[69] Gurwitsch, *op. cit.*, p. 447.

explain the problem of the correlation of contingent change and necessity with an account of the *sui generis* correlation of real and ideal. But engaging "Platonism" itself is the common ground shared by critics and adherents of phenomenology alike, both the external and internal occasion for phenomenological philosophy, "something like a Battle of Gods and Giants going on between them over their quarrel about reality."[70]

Only in virtue of the fact that seeing and grasping *Eide* and seeing individual things are generically alike but specifically different, the novelty of Husserl's view, can *Episteme* be of all possible *Doxa*, can there be phenomenological "Platonism." Clearly this is a program for clarification and understanding of the world in which we live no matter how exalted the battle of Gods and Giants.

---

[70] Plato, *Sophist*, 246A. The translation is by F. M. Cornford, *Plato's Theory of Knowledge* (London, 1951), p. 230.

BERNARD BOELEN
De Paul University

MARTIN HEIDEGGER AS A PHENOMENOLOGIST

Introduction

Edmund Husserl once exclaimed: "Phenomenology, that is Heidegger and me."[1] Yet, this exuberant spirit of co-operation came to a sudden end as soon as Husserl discovered that Heidegger, instead of bracketing Being, had bracketed Husserl. Although from the very beginning Heidegger had accepted the leitmotiv of Husserl's phenomenology *"Zu den Sachen selbst"* (To the things themselves), he took the liberty of interpreting and developing phenomenology in his own way, which resulted in a total rejection of the transcendental subjectivism of Husserl.

Ironically, both Husserl and Heidegger can trace their original inspirations to the same master: Franz Brentano. But, whereas Husserl was gradually led to his phenomenology under the influence of Brentano's conceptions of intentionality, descriptive psychology and ideal intuition (*"ideale Anschauung"*), Heidegger's eyes were opened to the question of Being by Brentano's dissertation *On the Manifold Sense of Being according to Aristotle* which was given to him by Dr. Conrad Gröber.

Now, Heidegger's familiarity with Husserl's phenomenology on the one hand taught him that the traditional naturalistic and rationalistic approaches to the question of Being (*Seinsfrage*) had been too narrow, and that this question must be dealt with phenomenologically. "With the question of the meaning of Being," says Heidegger in *Being and Time*, "Our investigation comes up

---

[1] Herbert Spiegelberg, *The Phenomenological Movement*, Vol. I, (The Hague, 1960), p. 352.

against the fundamental question of philosophy. This is one that must be treated *phenomenologically*."[2] On the other hand, his familiarity with the question of *Being* taught him that the phenomenology of Husserl's transcendental subjectivism was too narrow to deal with the all-inclusiveness of this primordial phenomenon. From the very beginning Heidegger found himself in perfect agreement with the leitmotiv of the Phenomenological Movement as expressed in Husserl's phrase: "Back to the things themselves." Yet, Heidegger has *never* considered himself a member of the Phenomenological Movement in Husserl's sense.

This brings us to the basic issue of this essay on Martin Heidegger as a phenomenologist. The question is as important as it is difficult. Very little has been written on the question "to what extent is Heidegger a genuine phenomenologist?" The ambiguity of this question should not escape us. This question can mean "to what extent does Heidegger still belong to the early Phenomenological Movement?" Thus phrased the question is asked within the perspective of transcendental phenomenology. The authenticity of Heidegger as a phenomenologist is decided upon on the basis of his fitting into the framework of pre-war phenomenology. But the question "to what extent is Heidegger a genuine phenomenologist?" can also mean "to what extent is genuine phenomenology Heideggerian?" In other words, to what extent has phenomenology itself matured and explicated its own ontological roots by extending the problematic of Husserl's intentionality of "pure consciousness" in the direction of Heidegger's intentionality of "Being-in-the-world"? Has Heidegger's existential ontology developed, enlarged and grounded the notions of radicalism, intentionality and consciousness in Husserl's transcendental subjectivism, or has it rather abandoned these notions altogether in favor of a non-phenomenological or even anti-phenomenological ontology?

It goes without saying that this question cannot be answered merely by examining to what extent Heidegger's phenomenology still conforms to the general pattern of the old Phenomenological Movement. We have to examine this question on the intrinsic merit of Heidegger's own original answer to the phenomenological

---

[2] Martin Heidegger, trans., *Being and Time*, (New York, 1962), pp. 49–50. Italics Heidegger's.

problematic. We have to investigate if and to what extent Heidegger's own possible answer entails both a possible continuity with and a further development and radicalization of the early transcendental phenomenology. It is in this sense that we interpret the question "to what extent is Heidegger a genuine phenomenologist?" In order to answer the question or even to understand its full import we first have to sketch the broad lines of Heidegger's phenomenology within the context of his own problematic.

The Genesis of Heidegger's Phenomenology

In his Preface to Richardson's book *Heidegger: Through Phenomenology to Thought* Heidegger himself has given us a recent and rare account of the genesis of his own phenomenology.[3] Here Heidegger tells us how in 1907 at the age of eighteen he received his first philosophical impetus from Brentano's dissertation *On the Manifold Sense of Being according to Aristotle* (1862). On the title page of this book Brentano quotes Aristotle's phrase: τὸ ὂν λέγεται πολλαχῶς, which Heidegger translates as follows: "A being becomes manifest (sc. with regard to its Being) in many ways."[4] "Latent in this phrase," says Heidegger, "is the *question* that determined the way of my thought: what is the pervasive, simple, unified determination of Being that permeates all of its multiple meanings? This question raised another: what, then, does Being mean?"[5] It is here that Heidegger was first aroused by the primordial question of Being which determined the way of his thought, and made him the thinker of Being.

"Meanwhile a decade went by," says Heidegger, "and a great deal of swerving and straying through the history of Western philosophy was needed for the above questions to reach even an initial clarity. To gain this clarity three insights were decisive . . ."[6]

First, Heidegger learned from Husserl the meaning and im-

---

[3] William Richardson, *Heidegger: Through Phenomenology to Thought*, (The Hague, 1963), pp. IIX—XXIII.
[4] *Ibid.* p. X. "*Das Seiende wird (nämlich hinsichtlich seines Seins) in vielfacher Weise offenkundig.*"
[5] *Ibid.*, p. X.
[6] *Ibid.*

portance of the phenomenological method. "Dialogues with Husserl," he states, "provided the immediate experience of the phenomenological method that prepared the concept of phenomenology explained in the Introduction to *Being and Time*."[7] We will revert to this shortly. Heidegger adds here that he interpreted the word phenomenology according to the meaning that its component parts had in Greek thinking, namely: λόγος as "to make manifest," and φαίνεσθαι as "to show oneself."[8]

His *second* decisive insight Heidegger received from his study of Aristotle. Especially Book IX of the *Metaphysics* and Book VI of the *Nicomachean Ethics* gave him the insight into ἀ-λήθεια, the truth, as a process of unconcealment, of revealment, or as the process by which beings show themselves or present themselves.

This insight into the truth as a process of unconcealment or as the process by which beings present themselves led to a *third* decisive insight, namely the recognition of "presence" (*Anwesenheit*) as the fundamental trait of οὐσία, the Being of beings. This discovery of Being as "Presence" (*Anwesenheit*) or as "Present" (*Gegenwart*) "developed into the question about Being in terms of its time-character."[9] Since the traditional concept of time proved to be inadequate, Heidegger in his *Being and Time* revealed authentic Temporality as the horizon of the self-manifestation of Being.

In short, Heidegger's concern for the question of Being found in the phenomenological method the appropriate way to allow Being to show itself, to present or reveal itself. He discovered this process of "self-revelation" to be the "truth" of Being which does not "present" itself unless the horizon of authentic Temporality has opened up. Now, the interconnectedness of these decisive insights clarified, in turn, the fundamental meaning and structure of phenomenology. To quote Heidegger again: "Subsequent to this tentative clarification of ἀλήθεια and οὐσία the meaning and scope of the principle of phenomenology, 'to the things themselves,' became clear."[10]

The fundamental "thing-itself" for Heidegger is *Being* and not the "intentional consciousness" or "transcendental ego" of

---

[7] *Ibid.*
[8] *Ibid.*
[9] *Ibid.*, p. XII.
[10] *Ibid.*

Husserl. For the question of Being has always been in some form or another the primordial question (*Grundfrage*) and the guiding question (*Leitfrage*) of genuine philosophy. "If, indeed," says Heidegger, "phenomenology, as the process of letting things manifest themselves, should characterize the standard method of philosophy, ... then Being had to remain the first and last thing-itself of thought."[11]

From the very start, therefore, Heidegger's phenomenology took on a very different character from Husserl's. This basic difference can be most clearly shown by comparing two parallel statements in the respective writings of Husserl and Heidegger. According to Edmund Husserl "The wonder of all wonders is the pure ego and pure subjectivity."[12] Deliberately, no doubt, Heidegger echoes Husserl's statement in a modified version. In the postscript to *What is Metaphysics?* he writes: "Man alone of all beings ... experiences the wonder of all wonders: *that* beings *are* (*dass Seiendes ist*)."[13] Heidegger concludes his brief but important sketch of the genesis of his phenomenology, which he wrote in retrospect during the month of April, 1962, with the following words: "The Being-question, unfolded in *Being and Time*, parted company with this [i.e., Husserl's] philosophical position, and that on the basis of what to this day I still consider a more faithful adherence to the principle of phenomenology."[14]

Heidegger's Conception of Phenomenology

This brief sketch of the genesis of Heidegger's conception of phenomenology will prove to be a helpful guideline in our attempt to understand the meaning and scope of phenomenology in the early Heidegger of *Being and Time*, and of the controversial attitude towards phenomenology in the late Heidegger, the Heidegger of *die Kehre* (the reversal).

Heidegger begins his *Being and Time* by indicating the necessity of rekindling the question of Being. "This question," he says, "has today been forgotten."[15] It is said that Being is the most

---

[11] *Ibid.*, p. XIV.
[12] Edmund Husserl, *Ideen* III, *Husserliana* V, (The Hague, 1952), p. 75.
[13] Martin Heidegger, *Was ist Metaphysik?*, (Frankfurt a. M., 1949), p. 42.
[14] Richardson, *Heidegger*, p. XIV.
[15] Heidegger, *Being and Time*, p. 21.

universal, undefinable, self-evident concept which needs not to
be questioned. Heidegger retorts that the universality of Being
as all-encompassing universality transcends the universality of a
class or *genus*. It is this mysterious universality which makes
Being undefinable in terms of proximate genus and specific difference. Being is the darkest rather than the clearest of all concepts. To be sure, Being is self-evident in that it "shows itself"
in man who is a being that is essentially always in a "pre-concep-
tual understanding of Being" (*vorbegriffliches Seinsverständnis*).
On the other hand, however, its true meaning is proximally and
for the most part not given and veiled in darkness. This precisely
proves 1) "that it is necessary in principle to raise this question
[of Being] again,"[16] and 2) that "there is need for phenomenology."[17]

Now, phenomenologically, Being (*Sein*) does not manifest itself
as a thing, a substance, a particular being (*Seiendes*), a tool, a
concept or an idea. We have no choice in the matter. When we
go to "the things themselves," we find that only *man* is the place,
the *locus* of the self-manifestation of the question of Being.
Heidegger calls man as the *locus* of the self-manifestation of Being
Dasein (*Da-Sein:* Being-there). Therefore, "if we are to formulate," says Heidegger, "our question [of Being] explicitly and
transparently, we must first give a proper explication of an entity
(*Dasein*) with regard to its Being."[18]

Dasein is essentially an open relation to Being. "*Understanding
of Being is itself a definite characteristic of Dasein's Being.*"[19] In
order to understand the meaning of Being we have to phenomenologically rekindle the question of Being. And in order to rekindle the question of Being we have to phenomenologically describe *Dasein* as Being-there, as Being-in-the-world, as ex-sistence
in the etymological sense of "standing out," of being an open
relation to Being or to totality of all that is.

Now, Heidegger's *Being and Time* is precisely this phenomenological analysis of *Dasein*, of Being-in-the-world, which aims

16 *Ibid.*, p. 23.
17 *Ibid.*, p. 60.
18 *Ibid.*, p. 27.
19 *Ibid.*, p. 32. Italics Heidegger's. The understanding of Being constitutes the
phenomenological distinction between *Dasein*, the essence of man on the one hand, and
Vorhandenheit, the mere presence-at-hand of things, and *Zuhandenheit*, the readiness-
to-hand of gear on the other.

at discovering the fundamental meaning of Being. The existential analysis of *Dasein* in *Being and Time* is not an analysis of man as a human subject, it is not a philosophical psychology or anthropology. The existential analysis of *Da-Sein* in *Being and Time* is rather a fundamental ontology of the differentiated self-manifestation of Being-in-the-world (*logos*). Yet, it is precisely in the light of the phenomenological description of *Da-Sein* that man discloses his essential structure as *Being*-in-the-world. "Every philosophical doctrine of the being of man," says Heidegger, "is *ipso facto* a doctrine of the being of reality. Every doctrine of Being is *ipso facto* a doctrine of the being of man."[20] Those who understand *Being and Time* exclusively in terms of an existential analysis of human existence fail to grasp the true meaning and scope of this modern masterwork. At the very end of this book Heidegger explicitly states: "our way of exhibiting the constitution of Dasein's Being remains only *one way* which we may take. Our *aim* is to work out the question of Being in general (*die Ausarbeitung der Seinsfrage überhaupt*)."[21]

We are now prepared to understand Heidegger's "preliminary conception" (*Vorbegriff*) of phenomenology as he presents it in *Being and Time*. By the phrase "preliminary conception" Heidegger does not mean to suggest "tentative" or "uncertain," but merely that this conception has not yet been explicated and grounded in the existential analysis of *Dasein* which still has to take place. Since for Heidegger the phenomena of phenomenology are the phenomena that are to be "the theme of ontology," that show themselves in the light of the primordial phenomenon of Being,[22] and since the question of Being is still in the stage of a preliminary question that has to be worked out (*Vorfrage*), the conception of phenomenology can only be preliminary (*Vorbegriff*).

For Heidegger the appropriate method for a philosophical investigation which seeks to explicate the meaning of Being is the phenomenological method. Phenomenology expresses the *how* of the investigation rather than the *what* of its subject-matter. And even the *how* of phenomenology cannot be decided upon prior to

---

[20] Martin Heidegger, *Was heisst Denken?*, (Tübingen, 1954), p. 73.
[21] Heidegger, *Being and Time*, p. 487.
[22] Cf. *Ibid.*, p. 60.

its rootedness in the "things themselves" without prejudicing its outcome. In other words, phenomenology cannot be a formalized method, or a mere application of "technical devices." For its maxim is "To the things themselves." This means, positively, that our philosophical investigations have to be guided by the self-manifestations of the phenomena themselves, and, negatively, that we have to free ourselves from "free-floating constructions," "accidental findings" and "pseudo-questions which parade themselves as 'problems,' often for generations at a time."[23]

Here we encounter the reduction from the naturalistic and cultural prejudices toward the life-world (*Lebenswelt*), a reduction which is also found in Husserl. But for Heidegger's radical phenomenology "the first and last thing-itself of thought" is primordial Being which manifests itself in the way of *Da-Sein* or Being-in-the-world. Thus the "eidetic" reduction is unacceptable since Being does not have the nature of a genus. And especially the transcendental reduction of Husserl has to be rejected since Being itself is the primordial phenomenon. As Edie puts it: "The importance of Heidegger's contribution to philosophy and especially to phenomenology lies in his notion of experience-of-the-world (*in-der-Welt-sein*). It is no longer merely consciousness which is intentional (as for Husserl) but the *Dasein*, human reality, as a unitary whole, as a 'field.'"[24] Or as Thévenaz writes: "In Heidegger interrogation pushes still deeper, even below transcendental consciousness, down to the 'foundation of the foundation,'" (*Grund des Grundes* – in *Vom Wesen des Grundes*, 1949, p. 49).[25]

In this sense Heidegger is even a more radical phenomenologist than Husserl. By enlarging and deepening the notion of intentionality from a mere consciousness of essences into the direction of *Dasein* as man's concrete thinking, living, loving and concernful Being-in-the-world, Heidegger's rejection of Husserl's transcendental subjectivism has increased his faithfulness to Husserl's phenomenological maxim: "To the things themselves." Husserl himself has called this principle of "self-evidence" "the principle of all principles." It is this principle which Heidegger has in mind

23 *Ibid.*, p. 50.
24 James Edie, "Introduction," in *What is Phenomenology?*, ed. James Edie, (Chicago, 1962), p. 26.
25 Pierre Thévenaz, *What is Phenomenology?*, ed. James Edie, (Chicago, 1962), p. 26.

when he states that his parting company with transcendental subjectivism constitutes a more faithful adherence to the principle of phenomenology.[26]

We agree with Ludwig Landgrebe, a student of both Husserl and Heidegger, that with the shift from pure phenomenology to existential phenomenology, Husserl's transcendental subjectivism and the Phenomenological Movement in Husserl's sense have come to an end. But also that existential phenomenology is an authentic phenomenology which rightfully develops Husserl's pure phenomenology within the principle of all principles by by-passing subjectivism in its extreme form, and by revealing the primordial phenomenon of Being in its existential intentionality of Being-in-the-world which cannot possibly be equated with *object*.[27]

Being cannot be equated with object. For Being, or the differentiated self-manifestation of all that is, never reveals itself as an *ob-ject* (*Gegenstand*), as something "standing over against" man as a human *subject*, or as something to be "faced" by man as a mere "onlooker." Man as the participant in the event of Being is utterly involved with the whole of his "ex-sistence" in the primordial openness of its self-manifestation. Being is never something that can be controlled or calculated or observed by man from the privileged standpoint of an uninvolved outsider. There is no vantage point "outside" the all-encompassing totality of all that is. Consequently, for Heidegger any philosophy which lets Being appear as an *object* to the outside standpoint of a *subject* is "subjectivism" or *Standpunkts-philosophie* (standpoint-philosophy).

According to Heidegger even the transcendental subjectivism of Husserl fails to enter into the dimension of the *Being* of *Dasein*, fails to formulate an acceptable transcendental phenomenology and to raise the question of the primordial phenomenon of Being.[28] Both Descartes and Husserl leave the question of the Being of consciousness unasked.[29] Transcendental subjectivism, therefore has still too much of a "standpoint" albeit in the form of a "*Rich-*

[26] Cf. Richardson, *Heidegger*, p. XIV.
[27] Cf. Ludwig Landgrebe, *Phänomenologie und Metaphysik*, (Hamburg, 1949), pp. 83–100.
[28] Cf. Heidegger, *Being and Time*, pp. 71–73.
[29] Cf. *Ibid.*, p. 251.

tung," a "direction," or "movement." Heidegger tacitly implies Husserl when he states that phenomenology not only cannot subscribe to a "standpoint" (a view which he shares with Husserl), but also that phenomenology cannot represent any special "direction" or "movement" (*Richtung*) either.[30] This, of course, explains Heidegger's immediate dissociation from the "Phenomenological Movement." What is essential in phenomenology, says Heidegger. "does not lie in its *actuality* as a philosophical 'movement' ("*Richtung*"). Higher than actuality stands possibility."[31] This possibility, for Heidegger, is the self-revelation of the phenomena in the all-encompassing light of the primordial phenomenon of Being rather than in the perspective of the "special direction" of the transcendental Ego.

Since the question of Being involves not only the object in question, but also the questioner and even the question itself, it transcends the dichotomy between subject and object, and is "ontocentric" rather than "anthropocentric." Strictly speaking, the primordial manifestation of Being is not of our own making, but it escapes our control, it is inspirational, posits itself and makes us. "*Es gibt Sein*" says Heidegger. And Being gives itself authentically only in the act in which it is fully received, namely in the authentic *Ent-schlossenheit* which means both the *openness* and the *resolve* of our ex-sistence in its entirety.

Now, the fact that primordial Being and *Da-Sein* as Being-in-the-world transcend the traditional subject-object dichotomy entails two implications of the greatest importance. In the first place, for Heidegger, in contrast with Husserl, our original contact with the world is not a knowing one in the narrow, intellectualistic sense of the term, or in the Husserlian sense of pure consciousness, but rather a *presence-in-Being*. This makes phenomenology for Husserl predominantly *epistemological*, and for Heidegger predominantly *ontological*. To quote Pierre Thévenaz again: "The essential originality of Heidegger's transcendentalism in relation to that of his master Husserl is its attempted resolution of the problem of the foundations without recourse to consciousness, not even transcendental consciousness, which was no doubt still too 'idealistic,' too 'subjectivistic' in his eyes. He bases

---

[30] Cf. *Ibid.*, pp. 50 and 63.
[31] *Ibid.*, p. 63.

himself on a more clearly ontological structure beneath the level of consciousness, the *Dasein*, from which alone one is able to understand the possibility and the meaning of a consciousness or of a transcendental Ego."[32] James Edie puts it succinctly when he states that "with Heidegger any tendency to consider transcendental subjectivity as a disembodied 'thinker' is definitely overcome; man as presence-to-the-world is the only possible point of departure for phenomenological analysis."[33]

The second important implication of *Dasein*'s transcendence of the subject-object dichotomy is the fact that the phenomenon of Being remains inaccessible to those forms of thinking that take place within this dichotomy. The objectifying, calculative and abstractive form of thinking of the positive sciences can neither raise nor silence the primordial question of Being, it remains completely incompetent to deal with the "self-questioning" questions of fundamental phenomena.

This is why Heidegger warns us against taking the expression "phenomenology" in the ordinary (*vulgär*) sense of its component parts. Superficially the term "phenomenology" is formed like "biology" or "sociology," meaning respectively "the science of life" and "the science of society." Taken in this sense, phenomenology would be "the science of phenomena" (*Wissenschaft von den Phänomenen*) in the ordinary, objectifying sense of the positive sciences.[34] We also take the word "phenomenon" in its ordinary, not strictly phenomenological sense when we understand it in its Kantian sense of "empirical intuition."[35] In order to explicate the strictly philosophical meaning of the term "phenomenology" Heidegger appeals to the original meaning of its two components φαινόμενον" and "λόγος" in the Greek philosophical language.

The Greek word φαινόμενον is itself derived from the Greek verb φαίνεσθαι which means: "to show itself," "to come to light." Heidegger shows how the word "comes from the stem φα-, like φῶς, the light, that which is bright – in other words, that wherein

[32] Thévenaz, in *What is Phenomenology?*, p. 57.
[33] James Edie, "Transcendental Phenomenology and Existentialism," in *Phenomenology*, ed. Joseph Kockelmans, (New York, 1967), p. 250.
[34] Cf. Heidegger, *Being and Time*, p. 50.
[35] Cf. *Ibid.*, p. 54.

something can become manifest, visible in itself."[36] Elsewhere
Heidegger relates the meaning of the term "phenomenon" as
"that which comes to *light*" to the conception of the *lumen naturale*, the theory of "natural light" in medieval philosophy.[37] In
short, the term "phenomenon" signifies "that which shows itself"
(*das Sichzeigende*), or "that which manifests itself" (*das Offenbare*).
"Accordingly," says Heidegger, "the φαινόμενα or 'phenomena'
are the totality of what lies in the light of day or can be brought
to the light – what the Greeks sometimes identified simply with
τὰ ὄντα (entities)."[38]

In other words, "phenomenon" is that which shows itself in
the way in which it *is*, and this must clearly be distinguished from
"mere appearance" (*Erscheinung*). Phenomena are not simply
appearances, but rather *that which* appears, or *that which* shows
itself, the being that lights up *in its being*. It goes without saying
that this Heideggerian conception of "phenomena" is a far cry
from Husserl's "pure phenomena" which he first described in his
Idea of Phenomenology, and later in his *Ideas*, as general essences
of empirical data obtained by the eidetic reduction, and further
purified by the bracketing activity of the transcendental reduction.

The second constitutive element of the term "phenomenology"
is the Greek word λόγος. Although this word gets "translated" as
"reason," "judgment," "concept," "definition," "ground" or
"relationship," its basic signification, according to Heidegger, is
"*discourse*."[39] But then we have to make sure that we understand
"discourse" (*Rede*) in its root meaning of δηλοῦν – to make manifest that which the discourse is about. Aristotle, Heidegger reminds us, has explained this function of discourse more precisely
as ἀπο φαίνεσθαι.[40] The λόγος as discourse "'lets something be
seen' (φαίνεσθαι); ἀπο ... that is, it lets us see something *from*
the very thing which the discourse is about."[41]

Now, "the expression 'phenomenology,'" says Heidegger, "may
be formulated in Greek as λέγειν τὰ φαινόμενα, where λέγειν means

[36] *Ibid.*, p. 51.
[37] Cf. *Ibid.*, pp. 171 and 214.
[38] *Ibid.*, p. 51.
[39] Cf. *Ibid.*, p. 55.
[40] Cf. *Ibid.*, p. 56.
[41] *Ibid.*, p. 56.

ἀποφαίνεσθαι. Thus 'phenomenology' means ἀποφαίνεσθαι τὰ φαινόμενα – to let that which shows itself be seen from itself in the very way in which it shows itself from itself."[42]

This, again, expresses the phenomenological maxim: To the things themselves. This maxim, however, should not be mistaken for some sort of naïve intuitionism. The original and intuitive grasping of the phenomena of phenomenology "is directly opposed to the *naiveté* of a haphazard, 'immediate,' and unreflective 'beholding' ["*Schauen*"]."[43]

Since Being is the first and last thing-itself of philosophical reflection, the phenomena of phenomenology are the primordial phenomenon of Being, "its meaning, its modifications and its derivates," in other words, phenomena that manifest themselves in the light of the articulated self-manifestation of Being (*logos*).[44] But since Being is usually concealed although it constitutes the ultimate meaning and ground of all beings, a distinctive "phenomenon" is "something that proximally and for the most part does *not* show itself at all: it is something that lies *hidden*, in contrast to that which proximally and for the most part does show itself; but at the same time it is something that belongs to what thus shows itself, and it belongs to it so essentially as to constitute its meaning and its ground."[45]

Precisely because the phenomena of phenomenology are proximally and for the most part hidden or concealed, is phenomenology required as the unconcealment of the primordial phenomenon of Being, i.e., as the truth of Being as ἀ-λήθεια. In other words, "only as phenomenology is ontology possible."[46] By the same token, however, phenomenology as the process by which beings manifest themselves is truly "radical" only in the light of the primordial truth of Being as the lighting-process by which beings are revealed (ἀλήθεια). For phenomenological truth is rooted in the primordial disclosedness of the phenomenon of *Being*.[47] In other words, only as ontology is phenomenology possible. For

---

[42] *Ibid.*, p. 58. "*Das was sich zeigt, so wie es sich von ihm selbst her zeigt, von ihm selbst her sehen lassen.*"
[43] Heidegger, *Being and Time*, p. 61.
[44] Cf. *Ibid.*, pp. 60 and 187.
[45] *Ibid.*, p. 59.
[46] *Ibid.*, p. 60.
[47] Cf. *Ibid.*, p. 62.

Heidegger, therefore, "ontology and phenomenology are not two distinct philosophical disciplines among others."[48]

Among these other disciplines Heidegger might well have mentioned "dialectics" or *logos* (*Rede*). For, as we have seen, λόγος for Heidegger means first and foremost "discourse," or making manifest what the discourse is about.[49] The meaning of λόγος is not fundamentally the truth as it is revealed in the statement of a judgment, nor the binding together of a subject and a predicate in the copula of logical thinking, but rather the "articulated" way in which Being manifests itself in the world.[50] For "Being-in-the-world" is the fundamental and unitary but structured phenomenon of the self-manifestation of Being. In other words, the way in which Being manifests itself is from the very start an existential "dia-logue." The philosophical way (method) of thinking as the dialectical self-manifestation of Being is at the same time dialectics (dialectical), phenomenology (self-manifestation) and ontology (of Being).

Ontology, phenomenology and dialectics, therefore, are equiprimordial dimensions of the philosophical method. They are not three distinct disciplines or methods, but rather co-original aspects of the fundamental way of thinking. It goes without saying, that especially from the early "Phenomenological Movement" genuine dialectics was conspicuously absent. For the unrelated intentional structures were not rooted in the differentiated self-manifestation of the all-encompassing phenomenon of Being. The little dialectics that remained was only a particular "technical device," namely "the method of free variations" through which we raise our "individual intuition" to the "essential intuition" of the *Wesensschau*. In Heidegger's phenomenology "Being-in-the-world" embraces and supports the otherwise unrelated intentional structures distinguished by early phenomenology. "Even the phenomenological 'intuition of essences' ["*Wessensschau*"]," says Heidegger, "is grounded in existential understanding. We can decide about this kind of seeing only if we have obtained explicit conceptions of Being and of the structure of Being, such as phenomena in the phenomenological sense can become."[51]

[48] *Ibid.*, p. 62.
[49] Cf. *Ibid.*, pp. 55–56.
[50] Cf. *Ibid.*, p. 50 and pp. 201–210.
[51] *Ibid.*, p. 187.

It is in the late Heidegger that this insight reaches its full depth in the light of the λόγος as the dialectics of φύσις. The λόγος sets all beings apart in their essential limits by gathering them in their original togetherness in the primordial luminosity of Being. It is no longer the essential intuition of the *Wessensschau* that reveals the essence of phenomena, but the primordial luminosity of Being as the lighting-process by which beings come-to-a-presence-in-the-World. (In the late Heidegger primordial Being has become clearly identified as *the World*).

Unlike the early phenomenology, Heidegger's phenomenology is not merely descriptive. Phenomenological description is the progressive, dialectical unfolding of the structure of Being, the *logos* of the differentiated phenomenon of Being-in-the-world. And as such phenomenological description is essentially explicative, interpretative or hermeneutic, and not a mere intuition of essences. According to Heidegger "the meaning of phenomenological description as a method lies in *interpretation*. The λόγος of the phenomenology of Dasein has the character of a ἑρμηνεύειν."[52] For Heidegger phenomenology is so radically hermeneutic that as Richardson rightly states, "'hermeneutics' (the process of letting-be-manifest) and φαινόμενα (that which manifests itself), plus λέγειν (to let-be-manifest), rejoined each other to such an extent that 'hermeneutics' and 'phenomeno-logy' became for Heidegger but one. If 'hermeneutics' retains a nuance of its own, this is the connotation of language."[53]

From all that has been said it follows that Heidegger does not regard phenomenology as a separate discipline, or as the only, independent or absolute method in philosophical thinking. Husserl, as we know, states in the Preface to the English edition of his *Ideas* that transcendental phenomenology is "the one science that stands absolutely on its own ground." For Heidegger this is impossible, for phenomenology, ontology and dialectics are equi-primordial. Heidegger can define phenomenology only in function of its co-original dimensions of philosophical thinking. This is why Heidegger concludes his discussion of phenomenology in *Being and Time* not by giving a definition of *phenomenology*, but by attempting to integrate phenomenology in his definition of

[52] *Ibid.*, pp. 61–62.
[53] Richardson, *Heidegger*, p. 631.

philosophy. "Philosophy," he says, "is universal phenomenological ontology, and takes its departure from the hermeneutic of
Dasein, which, as an analytic of *existence*, has made fast the
guiding-line for all philosophical inquiry at the point where it
arises and to which it *returns.*"[54]

Through Phenomenology to Thought

We are now prepared to answer our initial question "to what
extent is Heidegger a genuine phenomenologist?" Insofar as the
early Heidegger is concerned, we have already implicitly answered the question. There is no better way to make this answer
explicit than by quoting Heidegger's comment on the original
title of Richardson's book which was to be: *From Phenomenology
to Thought.* In his Preface to Richardson's book Heidegger writes:
"Now if in the title of your book, *From Phenomenology to Thought*,
you understand 'Phenomenology' in the sense just described as
the philosophical position of Husserl, then the title is to the point,
insofar as the Being-question as posed by me is something completely different from that position."[55]

In other words, if we formulate our question as follows: "to
what extent does Heidegger still belong to the old Phenomenological Movement in the sense of Husserl?" then the answer is that
Heidegger's substitution of existential phenomenology for pure
phenomenology means a radical departure from transcendental
subjectivism. Heidegger has from the very beginning dissociated
himself from the Phenomenological Movement in this sense.

But Spiegelberg is right when he says that Heidegger has never
rejected the Phenomenological Movement in its entirety.[56] For,
as we have seen, Heidegger believes that by substituting *Dasein*
for the transcendental Ego he parts company with Husserl on
the basis of being *more faithful* to the *principle* of phenomenology:
"To the things themselves." This is what the present essay has
attempted to show. If this is true, then we have the answer to
the other formulation of our initial question: "to what extent is
genuine phenomenology Heideggerian?" Phenomenology itself

[54] Heidegger, *Being and Time*, p. 62.
[55] Richardson, *Heidegger*, p. XIV.
[56] Cf. Spiegelberg, *Phenomenological Movement*, p. 279.

has matured and explicated its own ontological roots by extending the problematic of Husserl's intentionality of "pure consciousness" in the direction of Heidegger's intentionality of "Being-in-the-world." This view is shared by most contemporary phenomenologists, such as Landgrebe, Fink, Pöggeler, Gadamer, Biemel, Marcel, Merleau-Ponty, Dufrenne, Ricoeur, Delfgaauw, van der Leeuw, Luypen, Dondeyne, De Waelhens, Wild, Schrag, Kockelmans, and Edie among others.

It is significant that Heidegger, acknowledging his indebtedness to Husserl in the early part of *Being and Time*, mentions only Husserl's *Logical Investigations* without any reference to Husserl's later works. The reason is evident. The *Logical Investigations* announces the *principle* of phenomenology: To the things themselves, whereas in the later works, especially in the *Ideas*, the conception of "transcendental subjectivism" is developed and made into the focal point of pure phenomenology. "The following investigations," writes Heidegger, "would not have been possible if the ground had not been prepared by Edmund Husserl, with whose *Logische Untersuchungen* phenomenology first emerged."[57] On another rare occasion where Heidegger acknowledges his indebtedness to Husserl, namely in his Preface to Husserl's lectures on *Inner Time-Consciousness* (edited by Heidegger) the same characteristic omission occurs.

But Heidegger indicates another possible interpretation of the original title of Richardson's book which was to be: *From Phenomenology to Thought*. "If, however," he says, "we understand 'Phenomenology' as the [process of] allowing the most proper concern of thought to show itself, then the title should read: 'Through Phenomenology to the Thinking of Being.'"[58] In other words, if the primordial phenomenon of Being is allowed to be the first and last thing-itself of thought, then it is through phenomenology as the initial and lasting way of access to Being that we arrive at authentic philosophizing. Now, Richardson who rightly believes that "Heidegger's perspective from the beginning to the end remains phenomenological," took Heidegger's suggestion as a valuable one, and changed the original title *From Phe-*

[57] Heidegger, *Being and Time*, p. 62.
[58] Richardson, *Heidegger*, p. XVI.

nomenology to Thought into *Through Phenomenology to Thought*.[59]

It goes without saying that in Husserl's opinion Heidegger, by substituting human existence (*Dasein*) for the pure Ego, had relapsed into "anthropologism" or "psychologism."[60] Husserl's claim, however, that a phenomenology built on human existence (*menschliches Dasein*) entails some form of psychologism, indicates Husserl's fundamental misunderstanding of Heidegger's position. For *Dasein*, as we have seen, is not man as a human subject, or as a *merely* human reality, the reality of the *homo animalis* as Heidegger calls it in his *Letter on Humanism*. The humanity of the *homo animalis* is based on the metaphysical definition "rational animal," which limits itself to the ontic level of beings, but leaves man's essential relation to Being unthought. "The essence of man," says Heidegger, "consists precisely in this, that he is more than merely man, insofar as his humanity is presented in terms of *rational animal*."[61]

The humanity of the *homo humanus*, on the other hand, thinks *Being*, and transcends the ontic level by revealing man's ontological relationship to the authenticating "e-vent" (*Ereignis*) of primordial Being.[62] Heidegger's phenomenological analysis of *Da-Sein* is not an analysis of the human subject, but of *"Being-there."* This analysis is not merely ontic or existenti*el*, but ontological or existenti*al*. If Heidegger's phenomenology had limited itself to merely ontic descriptions, "if this were all we could find in Heidegger," says James Edie, "we could easily dismiss him, for others have done better. But he is searching for something more fundamental; Heidegger begins where Dostoevsky, Nietzsche, Kierkegaard, Malraux and Camus end."[63]

It has often been remarked that the early Heidegger still belongs somewhat to the Phenomenological Movement on the basis of his alleged "subjectivism," but that the late Heidegger has abandoned phenomenology altogether. Herbert Spiegelberg, for instance, says that "Heidegger undertakes to shift the center of gravity of phenomenology by making human being, rather than

---

[59] *Ibid.*, footnote.
[60] Cf. Edmund Husserl, *Ideen* III, in *Husserliana* V, (The Hague, 1952), p. 140.
[61] Martin Heidegger, "Über den Humanismus," in *Platons Lehre von der Wahrheit*, (Bern, 1954), p. 89.
[62] *Ibid.*, pp. 89–98.
[63] Edie, "Introduction," in *What is Phenomenology?*, p. 25.

consciousness, its hinge. ... The phenomenology of *Sein und Zeit* is still subjectivistic to the extent that it makes man its point of departure. But this is certainly no longer a transcendental subjectivity in Husserl's sense."[64] And here we would like to add "it is certainly no longer a subjectivity in *any* sense of the term!" *Da-Sein* as the *locus* of the self-manifestation of Being transcends as we have seen, any subject-object dichotomy, and is onto-centric rather than anthropo-centric.

It is false, therefore, to accept the early Heidegger as a genuine phenomenologist on the grounds that in his *Being and Time* he still emphasizes the human subject rather than the primordial phenomenon of Being as he does after *die Kehre* (the reversal).[65] From the very start *Being and Time* is *not* a phenomenology of the human subject, but of Da-*Sein*, of *Being*-there, of *Being*-in-the-world as the lighting-process by which beings manifest themselves. And *die Kehre* of the late Heidegger does not mean a reversal in the sense of a departure from his earlier standpoint, but rather its intrinsic intensification and consistent deepening. Heidegger himself is very emphatic about this issue in his Preface to Richardson's book. "One need only observe," he says, "the simple fact that in *Being and Time* the problem is set up outside the sphere of subjectivism – that the entire anthropological problematic is kept at a distance, that the normative issue is emphatically and solely the experience of There-being with a constant eye to the Being-question – for it to become strikingly clear that the 'Being' into which *Being and Time* inquired cannot long remain something that the human subject posits. It is rather Being, stamped as Presence by its time-character, that makes the approach to There-being. As a result, even in the initial steps of the Being-question in *Being and Time* thought is called upon to undergo a change whose movement cor-responds with the reversal."[66]

In short, Heidegger's philosophy is onto-centric rather than anthropo-centric throughout! Those who fail to see this not only

[64] Spiegelberg, *Phenomenological Movement*, p. 303; cf. pp. 301 and 313–16.

[65] The intentionality of Being-in-the-world can be approached from either side of this polarity. In our book *Existential Thinking* we have made an attempt to start from the Being-pole. Bernard J. Boelen, *Existential Thinking*, (Duquesne University Press, Pittsburgh, 1968).

[66] Richardson, *Heidegger*, p. XVIII.

misinterpret the early Heidegger, but also believe that the late
Heidegger has abandoned phenomenology altogether. Yet, the
late Heidegger, as we have shown, is a phenomenologist for exactly the same reasons as the early Heidegger. And even more so,
if his pronounced emphasis on primordial Being, "the first and
last thing-itself of thought," makes him even more faithful to
the principle of phenomenology: "To the things themselves."

Consequently, the fact that Heidegger after 1929 has dropped
all references to phenomenology from both his lectures and his
publications, and that he has even abandoned all phenomenological terminology, cannot be construed as an argument for the
allegation that the late Heidegger has dissociated himself completely from all phenomenology, and not only from Husserl's
version of it. On the contrary, Heidegger's abandonment of all
phenomenological terminology is intrinsically necessitated by his
greater faithfulness to the principle of phenomenology, "to the
things themselves." Heidegger grounds phenomenology in "the
first and last thing-itself of thought," primordial Being, and thereby arrives at a more fundamental insight into the Being of phenomenology.

Already the early Heidegger used the phenomenological terminology very sparingly. From the very beginning he substituted
existential phenomenology for pure phenomenology, and, therefore, he had to dissociate himself not only from the thought of
the early Phenomenological Movement but also from its characteristic ways of expressing itself. Similarly, Heidegger has indicated from the very beginning that he did not reach his goal by
using the language of rationalistic metaphysics either. His fundamental ontology kept groping for adequate and original expression to dissociate itself from both the thought and language
of traditional ontology. This is why Heidegger has often expressed
his growing aversion to all stereotyped labels and traditional clas-
sifications. The fixated and stereotyped use of traditional terminology in both phenomenology and ontology vitiates the fundamental approach of Heidegger's thinking, and leaves their
fundamental truth unthought. These "orthodox" terms are still
too dependent on traditional meanings, and are anything but free
from their "standpoint-philosophical" presuppositions.

In the works of the late Heidegger we find not only that Heidegger has abandoned all phenomenological and ontological terminology, but even that the very terms "phenomenology" and "ontology" have disappeared altogether. This is not, as is often alleged, a tacit admission on the part of Heidegger that his early attempts to build a fundamental ontology and phenomenology have failed. On the contrary, Heidegger does not dissociate himself from phenomenology and ontology, but he dissociates himself from their mutual dissociation. In the very depth of his fundamental thinking the late Heidegger has more than ever become aware of the fact that *der Denkweg*, the way or method of thinking Being is a unitary phenomenon. Phenomenology, ontology and dialectics *are* the differentiated self-manifestation of Being. It becomes, therefore, not only meaningless but even positively misleading to name or define philosophy or *Der Denkweg* exclusively by one of its components. This is why the late Heidegger has created more originative, and phenomenologically more correct terms such as: "thinking" as *Gedank* (thanksgiving); dwelling in the "house of Being"; *der Denkweg* (thinking as method); Being as "grace"; man as the "shepherd of Being," etc. Of course for the classifying mind such a terminology is at best "merely poetic," and at worst "sheerly mystical."

And, finally, the fact that the late Heidegger is often going to the "texts," especially the texts of the Greek thinkers cannot be construed as an argument for the allegation that Heidegger is no longer going "to the things themselves," and has ceased to be a phenomenologist. This allegation overlooks the phenomenological historicity of Being. Heidegger approaches these texts not from the viewpoint of linguistics, but rather from the viewpoint of the truth of Being. Being, for Heidegger, is the e-vent (*Geschehen*) of emerging within the primordial dimension of temporality. Being is *geschichtlich*, historical. Heidegger *is* going to "the first and last thing-itself" (phenomenon) of thought in the Greek texts, namely to Being in its original historical manifestation.

Man is the guardian of Being. And Being is the historical lighting-process by which beings reveal themselves in their fundamental truth. As the guardian of Being man lets the phenomena truly "be." He lets them truly come-to-presence-in-the-world wherever and whenever they show themselves from themselves. Only as the guardian of Being can man be the true guardian of phenomena. And only as the guardian of phenomena can man be truly faithful to the principle of phenomenology. It is through the genuine phenomenologist that fundamental thought comes into existence.

PART II

SYSTEMATIC PERSPECTIVES

Alden Fisher
St. Louis University

MARRIAGE, PARENTHOOD, AND LIFE IN COMMUNITY: A PHENOMENOLOGICAL VIEW

Et s'il est vrai qu'il y a un lien entre l'amour et la mort qui fait que l'amour est aussi angoisse, s'il est vrai que ce lien se laisse déceler jusque dans certains actes de l'union amoureuse, cela ne nous permet pas de dire qu'en se livrant absolument l'un à l'autre, les amants sont portés par une force qui n'apparaîtrait jamais dans la réalité de leurs relations et qui serait la même que celle réglant les combinaisons des cellules. En vérité, on peut trouver à ce lien de l'amour et de la mort un sens qui y est immédiatement vécu. L'amour est le total abandon d'un être à un autre être, le rejet de la dernière dimension de solitude. Cette fin ne peut être atteinte que si chacun s'identifie absolument à ce qu'il est pour-autrui; c'est pourquoi le corps – et le corps tout entier – prend à l'amour une part essentielle. Mais si aimer, au sens humain et charnel du mot, consiste à abandonner le pour-soi au pour-autrui, en les confondant, il y a dans tout désir d'amour un désir de mort.

Mais ceci nous amène à une dernière question, qui vraiment, n'est qu'une question. En quoi l'angoisse pathologique, que l'on soigne, se distingue-t-elle de l'angoisse métaphysique qui est, ainsi que la philosophie contemporaine nous le montre, inscrite au coeur de la condition humaine? Et comment, pour reprendre notre exemple, le désir de mort inclus dans l'amour peut-il ne pas se transformer en mort effective? Il nous semble, touchant ce dernier cas, que le problème se résout en découvrant d'abord que ce désir de mort peut trouver dans la tragédie amoureuse une réalisation, inscrite dans le corps même, qui est susceptible de l'épuiser, si ce désir et cette réalization sont compris; ensuite, que l'apparition dans l'amour, par la disparition des sujets solitaires, d'un intersujet, le couple, doit avoir pour corrélat un rejet de cet intersujet vers le monde, où il devra, comme tout sujet, conquérir la plénitude de lui-même. La mort effective du couple est toujours le signe d'un échec dans l'affrontement nécessaire du monde par ce couple, est toujours un refus de cet intersujet de commencer sa carrière de sujet et, donc, un phénomène pathologique : le vrai amour est mort et résurrection, disparition du pour-soi et naissance du pour-nous. Que ce pour-nous n'achève pas de se faire dans l'épreuve du monde, c'est la preuve qu'il n'existe pas vraiment.

Reste le problème de l'angoisse pathologique. Ce que nous avons dit ne peut qu'en préparer la discussion, en montrant peut-être que l'angoisse pathologique est l'angoisse qui se retourne contre elle-même et se fuit, en une ruse suprême, en se faisant angoisse devant la nécessité. La névrose commence lorsque l'angoisse, de chemin vers la liberté, de découverte de la liberté qu'elle est, se dissimule à elle-même pour feindre de conduire vers la nécessité d'un déterminisme inexorable. La névrose est refus de la liberté qui se masque comme refuse en acceptant l'angoisse mais en la détournant de son sens.[1]

Alphonse de Waelhens, 1958.

The point of view within which the following ideas will be sketched is primarily that of existential phenomenology (with emphasis, perhaps, on the latter term). Let me simply assert, at

---

[1] Free and somewhat interpreted translation by me: "And if it is true that there is a bond between love and death which brings it about that love is also anguish; and if it is true that this connection can be discerned even in certain acts of amorous union; this still does not allow us to say that, in delivering themselves up absolutely to each other, the lovers are carried by a force which would never appear in the reality of their relation and which would be the same as that which governs the combinations of cells. In truth, one can find, in this bond between love and death, a meaning which is immediately experienced (or lived; not necessarily explicitly conscious). Love is the total abandon of one being to another being, the rejection of the lost dimension of solitude. This end can only be attained if each one identifies himself absolutely with what he is for-the-other; this is why the body – and the whole body completely – assumes an essential part in love. But if to love, in the human and carnal sense of the word, consists in abandoning the "for-self" to the "for-the-other" by merging them, then there is in all desire of love a desire of death (in every love-wish, a death-wish).

But this leads us to a final question which, truly, is only a question. In virtue of what is pathological anguish, which is treated, distinguished from metaphysical anguish which is, as contemporary philosophy has shown us, inscribed in the heart of the human condition? And how, to take up our example again, is it possible for the desire of death, which is included in love, not to transform itself into effective death?

It seems to us, touching on this last case, that the problem can be resolved, first, by discovering that this desire for death can find a realization in the amorous tragedy, a realization inscribed in the body itself and which is capable of exhausting it (the desire) if this desire and this realization are *understood;* next (by discovering) that the appearance in love, by the disappearance of the solitary subjects, of an inter-subject, the couple, ought to have as a correlate, a turning of this inter-subject toward the world where it must, as every subject, conquer the plenitude of itself. The effective death of the couple is always the sign of a failure in the necessary facing up to the world by the couple, as always a refusal on the part of this intersubject to begin its career as a subject, and is, thus, a pathological phenomenon. True love is death and resurrection, disappearance of the "for-self" and the appearance of the "for-us." That this "for-us" does not complete itself (really make itself fully into a "for-us") in the experience (and in face of the test) of the world, is the proof that it does not truly exist.

The problem of pathological anguish remains. What we have said can only prepare the discussion by showing perhaps that pathological anguish is anguish which turns back against itself and flees, by a supreme ruse (or deception), by making itself anguish in the face of necessity. Neurosis begins when anguish (turns back) from the way toward freedom, from the discovery of the freedom which it is, and dissimulates itself to itself in order to feign to lead toward the necessity of an inexorable determinism.

Neurosis is the refusal of freedom, which masks itself as refusal by accepting anguish but by turning it away from its meaning."

A. De Waelhens, *Existence et Signification,* "Notes sur l'angoisse dans la philosophie contemporaine," (Louvain, Nauwelaerts, 1958), pp. 187–189.

the beginning, that such a philosophical position is not a simple relativism, a simple subjectivism, nor is it simply descriptive. But it is much less concerned with system building and deductive argument than with an attentive reflection upon the experientially given aimed at the elucidation, the articulation, of the meaningful structures which emerge from this kind of controlled looking. Such a position (when rigorously handled) merges with, even becomes identical with, the best elements in contemporary phenomenology, existentialism, and even aspects of American pragmatism and some current developments in linguistic analysis. Perhaps what these converging trends in philosophy have in common can be summed up by their concern for the concrete and their efforts to render explicit and intelligible the whole of human experience. The philosophical ideal, then, is not that of Aristotelian demonstration through causes, but rather of making manifest and intelligible the given in all its complexity. It is not demonstration as much as monstration.

My effort in these remarks, then, will be directed toward bringing this sort of philosophical reflection to bear, to some extent at least, upon one of the central but complex issues involved in marriage, parenthood, and life in society, that is, upon the question of birth regulation (and, more specifically, contraception). Before proceeding to the central questions, however, I feel impelled to make some preliminary qualifications.

First, I want to underline the fact that mine will be a strictly philosophical reflection, one which prescinds entirely from the theological state of the question. Perhaps this is because I want to be cautious. Philosophers qua philosophers can be and often are mistaken; they cannot be heretical in their arguments. Needless to say, a conclusion drawn can come in conflict with a faith commitment. I would like to think, however, that a more guiding reason is my conviction that the issue in question, as perhaps with few others, requires the philosopher's clarification as a prerequisite for a theological one. On the other hand, although I will not be explicitly presenting here detailed scientific evidence, I would like to insist that the findings of science are, in this case, directly relevant to the philosopher's reflection and that he cannot afford to ignore them. And it is precisely because of new insights into the nature of human sexuality, marriage and parenthood yielded by psychology and psychiatry (to say the least) that we are able to work out a deeper philosophical analysis than was previously possible. Just so, the findings of sociology and demography are directly relevant to the philosopher's more concrete reflection concerning society.

Secondly, I want to call attention to the rather amazing amount of excellent work which has already been done in this area in a very short time. Although obviously much work remains to be done, I am genuinely convinced that in various places and in one way or another, almost everything has been said which needs saying in order to establish the basic groundwork for a clear moral consensus on these issues. I wish to acknowledge at the outset, then, my complete indebtedness to others, the lack of originality of these remarks, and to justify my efforts here solely on the grounds that another and perhaps somewhat different organization of the facts and arguments may serve some useful purpose.

Now, regarding the central issue, I would like to address myself to the question of birth regulation at three different levels, that of the couple in marriage, that of the family, and that of society. I will argue that each of these levels forms a kind of community and that the question at issue impinges directly upon the good of the community at each of these three levels. More concretely, I would like to present a series of philosophical analyses which might be used to justify the following positions. First, that the good of each of the above mentioned interrelated communities may and frequently does demand some form of birth control. Secondly, that the majority of the available means for achieving this good of these communities would seem to be morally neutral when considered abstractly. Excluded as generally acceptable means would be such techniques as abortion or surgical sterilization. (I do not wish to discuss the morality of these procedures in themselves or in all cases, but simply to exclude them as generally acceptable means of birth control.) I would further want to specify that the means which seem to me to be morally neutral in themselves always cease to be such in any concrete instance. Circumstances including intention and goals will dictate whether a particular means is good or bad in a given case. The general conclusion which is instead to result from this line of argumentation is that the most effective means of birth control will under certain circumstances not only be morally permissible but may even be morally obligatory.

Having sketched out the areas which seem to me to demand philosophical reflection, I think you will see the necessity for being somewhat schematic and partial in discussing them; a detailed analysis of each question at each level would be impossible within the limits of a short reflection. In many cases I will be able simply to present a position with little or no supporting argumentation or evidence. I hope, however, to be able to present a sufficiently concrete analysis that the general direction and force of the position can be seen and discussed.

As always with moral or ethical matters, a view of man is presupposed. Along with science, philosophy too evolves, although in a different way. And such is certainly true with regard to our conception of the nature of man. Contemporary philosophy has tended more and more to discuss man as being precisely that kind of existent whose very being is to be both in and present to the world. Briefly, what this means is that the structure or nature of human existence is to be part of the world like other material beings but also to be present to the world and to others in a way impossible for pure things (that is, through knowledge and love). Such a formulation is intended to emphasize several dimensions of human existence. First, man can be-in-the-world only because of his body. But equally, the world can be *present* to man or man to the world only through the body – through perception and affectivity. Likewise human beings can be present to each other only through the medium of the body. Included in this formulation is a new emphasis on man's subjectivity, his interiority, if you will, but also that this interiority is essentially ordered to a beyond, first, to the world of other persons and then to the world of things. This way of viewing man also indicates man's situated character: to exist in a human way is to be situated within a certain perspective both with regard to place and time. Thus, man is essentially also a temporal and historical being. Finally, it becomes more and more clear that existence in the world is coexistence. That is, from the first moment of awareness until my death I find myself co-existing with others, essentially caught up with them in sharing a situation, a history, projects, and ultimately a common destiny.

Moreover, a closer analysis of man's situation indicates that
there are several fundamental modes of being *with* others in the
world – modes which are so much a part of being human that each
is seen to be an existential category, a category of being. Among
these fundamental modes of being-with-others in the world are
work, sexuality, worship, play, and so forth. The way one expresses oneself in one or another of these orders is so intimately
bound up with one's very being that they become expressive of
my existence itself, that is, they show themselves to be so many
ways – both general and individual – for me to be what I must
be: a being-with-others-in-the-world.

For, although man certainly comes into the world with certain
fundamental capacities, man is essentially an existent who
achieves his being only through becoming. And by far the most
significant dimension of human becoming lies in the area of his
relations with others and is, to the extent that man is free, subject
to self-determination. In this sense, it is true to say that with
man, existence precedes achieved essence. Man, as given, is essentially incomplete – and his completion, his perfection as man, is
in and through the various levels of community mentioned above.
Thus, just as one can say that man is a being-in-the-world, one
can equally readily affirm that man is a being-in-and-for-com-
munity. This truth, though phrased in a somewhat novel way, is
as venerable as poetry and philosophy itself.

Now if man is a being in and for community, one can state
fairly easily the general ideals of action which could guide man's
conduct, if he is to achieve his perfection as man. Most briefly
stated, man's human actions are most perfective of himself as
human when they are guided by an intelligence become sensitive
to the ideals of justice and infused with a passionate love which
I shall call natural charity. Thus justice infused with love becomes the highest ideal of morality at whatever level of community man finds himself.

Before turning our attention to the realization of this principle
at the various levels of community, it may be well to pause and
handle one or two of the most standard objections to the view
being developed here. First, nothing in this view goes counter to
the idea that man has a nature, although this nature is seen as
predominantly dynamic and open in character. As someone has

recently said: "human nature is a task, a project of promotion, a work of love." What this means concretely is this: there is a sufficient communality among men to allow one to disengage the central traits of being human. Moreover, one can judge the extent to which this or that action leads to a more complete embodiment of what it is to be human. Thus this view also allows us to hold a version of the natural law, since intelligence guided by a properly ordered love is nothing other than the moral measure of human action. What this view excludes is any reductive or abstractive interpretation of nature and the natural law. From this perspective one cannot, for example, speak of the biological nature of man or the biological end of man. Man's bodiliness is through and through a human bodiliness and man's carnal actions are through and through characterized by their being precisely human actions. As one contemporary philospher has put it, man is not a rational animal. Man is always higher or lower than an animal, but never simply an animal with rationality tacked on.

Let it be asserted then as strongly as possible: what is being presented here is not a simple moral relativism. What we are affirming is the primacy of human intelligence committed to a justice animated by love. Any lesser commitment falls short of the moral obligation (and opportunity) to be human; to realize this ideal wholly is to realize human fulfillment and perfection in as complete a way as it is possible to describe at the level of natural reason. That there are many ways toward this ethical ideal is evident; marriage is only one – however central and important.

What I hope is clear at this point is the following ethical perspective: man is inexorably a being in community. Every human community is more than the sum of its parts yet it must respect the integrity of the part. In other words, in order for a community to be moral, that is, to be a means through which its members can achieve their human vocation, a certain balance between the good of the members and the good of the community must be maintained. And it is here that we find a further specification of the general ethical direction enunciated above. An individual is judged morally faulty insofar as he turns in upon himself and acts only for purely selfish ends, or, on the other hand, is judged

morally good insofar as he turns outward toward the good of
others and 'loses' himself in working for that good. The same is
true of the community at any of the levels which we have mentioned. But no real conflict is present in this apparent paradox.
For it is precisely in turning outward from oneself and working
for the fulfillment of others that one finds the greatest fulfillment
as an individual human being. Nothing more or less is meant by
the two notions already discussed: that man is a being in and for
community and that the general ideal of morality must be justice
infused and animated by love. This *is* the human good.

Let us turn now to examine how these principles are exemplified and realized in the various levels of community already mentioned, beginning with that of the couple in marriage. Again it
will be necessary to be schematic but hopefully not irrelevant to
the central concern of this essay.

As we have seen, man is an embodied subjectivity oriented
toward others and the world. And one of the fundamental modes
of this embodied existence, this being in the world, is sexual. But
to say this is already to refer to co-existence, for sexuality is one
of my fundamental ways of being present to, of being with, others.
That this dimension of human existence can be realized most
naturally and perfectly through the love between a man and a
woman within the framework of marriage with its characteristics
of stability and its ideals of commitment and fidelity, I take here
as a given. If the optimal development of sexuality leads to love
and marriage, it is also the case that sexual intercourse is the
natural and exemplary way of expressing this love and this union.
Without it, marriage would not be true marriage, this particular
kind of community would not be established, and the kind of
mutual becoming which it is of the nature of marriage to promote
would be hindered if not thwarted altogether. For one central
and intrinsic goal of marriage is to allow man to overcome a
lonely and perhaps selfish subjectivity and become this kind
of intersubjectivity, to cease being an isolated 'I' and to become
a truly new subject – a "we". Sexuality in this context is seen to
be both a crucial means to and the most intimate expression (both
real and multi-symbolic – and these are not distinct) of this kind
of community.

But just as an individual subject can turn in upon itself and act only out of self-interest – and thus fail to become truly human – just so the couple in marriage, the new "we," can turn in upon themselves and founder on a kind of selfisness *à deux*, and thus fail in their turn to become an authentic community. And just as sexuality in marriage is seen to be one of the most natural and significant means by which man can overcome his egocentricity and selfishness, leading him hopefully to an authentic co-existence with his partner, just so there is a most natural means by which this new intersubjectivity can turn outward and fulfill itself through a new kind of generosity, the bearing of children, and thereby establish a new community, a new intersubjectivity: the family.

There is an astonishing parallel here. An individual is both drawn toward marriage and in it finds a means for moral perfection. A couple in marriage are drawn toward seeing their mutual love bear fruit in children and are thereby offered new ways - frequently difficult ones indeed, as any parent can testify – for overcoming selfishness and self-centeredness and are thus led to an even more perfect participation in the life of human co-existence. This is so much the case that the individual who cannot or chooses not to marry must find other ways to give and share; similarly the couple who are unable to have children must find other ways of giving of themselves and participating in a broader co-existence.

But the analogy at the level of the individual with regard to the couple, and the couple with regard to the family, sustains itself at the level of the family with regard to society. Families too can turn in upon themselves and refuse that generosity which would invite them to share their good by serving the good of society, by entering fully into this new and even more embracing co-existence. In this regard it becomes a weighty obligation of parents to lead their children to the full acceptance of this generous life at all of its significant levels.

The limit idea of this perspective lies in the sphere of particular societies with regard to the whole of mankind. Societies, too, must not only serve the interest of their own members but also must strive for the good of all mankind. This then is the moral framework which can be traced from the perspective of the kind of personalism being espoused here. And it is within this framework that the morality of birth regulation and more particularly contraception must, I think, be judged.

In moving from the level of essential philosophical elucidation and the formulation of general moral principles to the discussion of more specific moral situations, it may be well to state again the general moral guide lines which have emerged from our analysis up to this point. As we have said, the most authentic guide for morality would seem to be human intelligence committed to justice and animated by love or natural charity. In other words, and in the natural order, the highest moral ideal that is offered to our creative liberty is the achievement of a perfect life of justice infused with a liberating love. A further specification of this principle was seen at the level of the three basic human communities or intersubjectivities which we have discussed: while each member of the community at whatever level should find his perfection and fulfillment in the good of the whole and beyond, the community itself must, in a sense, guarantee, that is, *be for* the fulfilling or perfecting good of the individual member at each level. As we suggested, it is here that a certain balance must be established. For the life of co-existence, the life of participation in community would have little meaning if it were to be destructive rather than perfective of the individual good.

As applied to the specific moral questions being focused upon here, that is birth control and contraception, the major outstanding problem would seem to be the question of the use of contraceptives, that is, physical or chemical devices which positively preclude the procreative dimension of the conjugal act. The issue becomes acute under certain circumstances at each level of community which we have described.

I say that the moral problem centers around the question of the use of contraceptive devices rather than birth control, since there does seem to be considerable consensus with regard to the genuine moral necessity for birth control in the sense of limitation of frequency and number of births for a given couple. Few would doubt any longer that the good of the partners in marriage and frequently the good of the marriage itself demands intelligent birth regulation or control. And no one denies that the principal obligation of parenthood is the continuing concern for the welfare of the child: his growth in the proper atmosphere of love and generosity and his intellectual and spiritual development. And scarcely anyone can doubt that the adequate fulfillment of this responsibility demands an intelligent limitation of the number of children in the family. That this will vary from family to family and in different circumstances goes without saying. Moreover, within particular societies the demands of justice may require a certain real limitation of the number of children born into it. And finally, we are all aware of the fact that the good of mankind itself is rapidly being threatened by over-population. As someone has recently put it, "nature" is rapidly tending toward the destruction of "nature" at this level.

It is here that the ideal of justice animated by love has traditionally met its severest test. For it is true that the intersubjective good of the couple in the marital community finds a natural fulfillment and perfection in a good beyond itself, the community of the family, just as individuals in society find perfection in working for the good of society and societies are perfected by being oriented toward the good of all mankind.

But in fact there should be no genuine conflict here. For, as we have seen, a balance between the good of the participating members and the good of the whole must be maintained. As I indicated above, there seems little question that the good of the marital community, the couple, may be severely jeopardized unless there is prudent birth control. Just so, the good of the children in the family community may be severely jeopardized unless there is prudent limitation of numbers. The same is true at each broader level of community. Let it be said that it is with regard to these matters that the evidence of psychology and psychiatry, of sociology and demography is most important and precious if one truly has the good of others in mind. The findings of these disciplines simply cannot be ignored.

Without detailing the evidence, the knowledge which is now available to us seems amply to demonstrate that, if birth control has now become a moral obligation, whatever may have been the case in the past, it seems equally true that neither continence nor rhythm is an adequate means for achieving this end. Both in their way can be and have been shown to be harmful if not destructive both to the intersubjective good of the couple as well as to the family, that is to the children who need the harmonious atmosphere of a loving and generous family more than anything else, but also adequate training and education.

What then is wrong, that is, immoral, with regard to the use of more effective means, those physical and chemical means which human intelligence has discovered. It is said that they thwart or interfere with a biological process and hence interfere with the nature of the conjugal act. But man is not a biological being; he is a human existent. As we have said, his bodiliness – central as it is to our perspective – is through and through the bodiliness of a human being. To assert that contraception is interference with nature may be to deal in abstractions, not with concrete reality. And, in any case, as Father Johann has recently written, the fact that a person interferes with or disturbs a particular physical process is *by itself* morally irrelevant.

Finally, it is argued that, nevertheless, *the* end of the conjugal act is procreation and the immorality of contraception lies in its interference with this "natural" purpose. But this argument also fails to hold up under careful scrutiny. For we have just seen that other precious human goods are intended by the conjugal act, that is, the most natural means for establishing, maintaining and expressing the intersubjective community of the couple. Since the final moral specification of a human act, both in traditional philosophy and in the present perspective, lies with the human intention involved, and since no one argues any longer that procreation must be intended in each case, it becomes indeed difficult to see the force of the proscription against contraception.

Our own perspective would lead to the view that the meaning of human sexuality and its purpose is complex and manifold. Its moral significance will be found in situating it in its full human context and being guided by the general principles of morality already discussed. If this is done, I would argue, one would find, indeed, a moral obligation to perfect the inter-subjective "we" of marriage in the further perfection of bearing and rearing children, but one would equally well find a moral obligation to regulate birth by the most effective means, prudently and wisely, for the intrinsic good of each of the levels of human community.

Whatever the value of these considerations, I would simply like

to conclude with what may be a statement of human and philosophical faith. It is this: if one really accepts as the authentic
measure of morality the intelligent adherence to a justice animated by natural charity, there is not and cannot be a genuine
moral conflict among the various human goods of marriage,
family, and society.

Erwin W. Straus
Lexington, Kentucky

THE MONADS HAVE WINDOWS

I

Sports together with crafts and arts, with dancing and fighting, are manifestations of the instrumental usage of the human body, directed toward an anticipated accomplishment, such as serving a tennis ball, performing a sonata on the piano, pirouetting in ice-skating, knocking out an opponent, etc.

All of these activities occur on a macroscopic level; an athlete moves his body, his limbs (not muscles) in terrestrial, i.e. in non-Euclidean, space. "Non-Euclidean" refers in this situation not to a kind of Riemanspace but to a space of four unequal dimensions, inward-outward, up and down, forward-backward, right and left, with the gravity-related vertical domineering people in the regions north of the equator just as well as their antipodes.

Practice preceded in all these fields scientific exploration by millennia.

The Greeks of antiquity considered the Olympic games as events of such importance that they chose the first tournament as the Year I of their chronology – the divide separating a prehistorical era from recorded history. Since, according to our own historiography, the first Olympic competition was celebrated in the year 776 B.C., informal athletic contests and shows preceded the scientific investigation of the "machinery of the human body" by more than 2000 years. We can be sure that prior to the Olympics, informal improvised contests foreshadowed organized performance since the days when Cain and Abel were boys.

At Olympia peaceful competition replaced savage combat. The athletes were competing with each other, not fighting against each other. Because athletic performance eliminated direct attacks against an opponent – boxing, wrestling, just as football today, tactfully omitted – the competitors had to be brought into rapport somehow.

The types of mediation and thereby the methods of appraisal vary from contest to contest. A foot race – probably the prototype of athletic competition – might have been decided without judges and stopwatches. For long jumps, however, where athletes perform one after the other, comparative measurements are required ex post facto, and – to give another example – in a gymnastic tournament esthetic evaluation codetermines the verdict. In all these situations there is an amazing contrast between practice and theory.

Whether village boys are competing or trained sprinters enter a race, the participants must share tract and start; they must run together toward a pre-set goal, aware during their own action of the other fellows and of themselves. In the lifeworld this is taken for granted. However, in reflection we may wonder how three or four individual human bodies – each one of them equipped with a particular nervous system and with a particular brain encapsuled in a single skull – could have a territory in common, a spatial area exceeding by far their own size and boundaries. Furthermore, the scientist, bypassing the layman, may add a few more tantalizing questions, e.g. how any one of those brains could ever become aware of other fellows and of itself, and how those brains could turn the attached bodies to a distant place as a common goal to be reached at a future moment?

In a long jumping contest, where the distances covered are measured after each performance, there also is a striking discrepancy between the apparent simplicity of the procedure and the predicament of giving a theoretical account. Let us assume the whole match would have been recorded on a photographic film, then the second jump would be scored several hundred frames apart from the first one, just as in our experience Jump 2 occurs some time after Jump 1. How can any one bring those distant events together for a comparison and nevertheless leave them separate as the actions of Smith, Jones, and Brown?

That the judges who evaluate gymnastic performance must and can see, with their own eyes, the athletes at work is simply taken for granted; they all exist together in one world: nobody in mundane practice would locate the other fellow, still less his own body, in an "external world."

The task before us therefore is:

a. To discover the problems hidden in the naive attitude of mundane life;
b. To acknowledge them without bias;
c. Not to force them in the Procrustean bed of established theories, but to gain an insight respecting human experience and performance.

Some comments concerning the instrumental usage of the human body may be in order.

1) The discovery of new possibilities of comportment has been facilitated sometimes by the invention of a new gymnastic apparatus. Using, e.g., the uneven parallel bars, the athlete can move his body, play as if it were with gravity, in a heretofore untried manner.

2) Basic attitudes, like handling a golf club, taking an archer's position, are not learned through trial and error, nor through conditioning, or reward and punishment. While acquisition of the skills of precise shooting demands a long time of practice, the archer's attitude can be adopted at once; the novice is reproducing in his motor behavior a model visible to him, so that his own position resembles the original almost like a mirror image.

3) There is a characteristic difference between a baby learning to walk, thereby actualizing inherent potentialities and, in contrast, the acquisition of skills, writing, typing, etc. In swimming, for instance, man, defying innate conditions, moves like a quadruped with the arms participating in locomotion which is performed in horizontal position with the legs moving simultaneously (breast stroke).

4) Training and learning based on the possibility of returning to the start poses the problem of repetition of seeing, doing, thinking, *again*.

5) When a boy jumps over a broad ditch fleeing from a bull, or crosses the ditch in the opposite direction on his way to his sweetheart, his action is in the direct service of safety or desire. In

athletic competitions, however, a long jump leads nowhere else; it ends in itself. Success or failure are established indirectly through comparison. Personal ambition is a decisive motive for years of training and the final efforts – that is to say the performance cannot be a response to stimuli. To a boy running from a bull, the goal to be reached is directly visible. To him that very moment of a concrete situation counts. No visible goal is set for the long jump; the athlete could perform at any other place or at any other time.

6) Referees do not participate in a performance. They watch it from a vantage point. The referee's situation resembles that of a scientific observer. Objectivity demands that the presence of the observer does not interfere with the events observed. Yet there could be no observation if the observer and his nervous system had not been affected by the events. No brain has ever known itself. All neurophysiological information has been acquired through direct or indirect exploration of the brains of other creatures – man or animal.

In the region of human action and motion, convictions, coeval with the beginning of modern science, based on the authority of Galileo, Descartes, Locke, Hobbes, Leibniz, prevented or even forbade to ask the proper questions and to develop adequate methods.

Such axioms were: 1) That the scientific method is universal (*mathesis universalis*); it seems therefore fully justified to apply it to man himself, in spite of the fact that science is a human creation. 2) That all human behavior and accomplishments must be explained through the exploration of the "underlying mechanisms" of an "apparatus," receiving stimuli from "an external world" and responding with efferent impulses provoking muscle contractions. "To understand man the doer we must understand his nervous system for upon it his actions depend" (Boring, 1939). "Since the nervous system connects stimulus with response," Boring emphasized, "action always occurs as a response to excitation."

Boring, like so many others, ignored a number of fundamental facts: 1) Men understood their fellowmen everywhere and at all times without any knowledge of the nervous system. (To be sure, not a single one of the participants at the Miami and Chicago conventions (1968), nor of the millions of TV listeners gave a single thought to Rockefeller's or Humphrey's nervous systems.) 2) In the study of the nervous system two brains are involved: that under observation and that of the observer. If "actions always occur as a response to excitation," then the scientist's own action of moving his vocal muscles in speaking, or the muscles of his hand in writing, would be nothing but a group of response to stimuli that – reflected from the brain studied – had acted upon his receptors. The whole process of observation is transferred into the observer's brain. 3) Men have been familiar with their arms and legs, with their eyes and tongues (all on a macroscopic level) but nobody ever had any experience of his brain (he may have had headaches but no brainaches), nor does the brain know itself. Our knowledge of a brain is always that of a brain as part of a human or animal body, i.e., of a brain as material object, not as a complex of stimuli received. (The terminology referring to *the* brain is misleading. There are brains, millions of them. THE brain as such does not exist in concreto.) 4) We cannot manipulate stimuli. We can touch and handle a knife as a visible object, just as we catch a ball, but we cannot catch or touch a stimulus.

To understand man the doer we have to acknowledge, with full and genuine respect for everyday experience – a realm to which we remain bound even though we may transcend it in thought – that in and through sensory awareness the earth is opened to man and animal as a ground of material things between "heaven and earth." This presents us with the problem how causality of stimuli and intentionality of experience can be reconciled. Thereby we finally will reach a position to understand how man the doer can function not in an "external world," but in a world common to all of us, as actors and spectators.

Since athletic performance is but one particular mode of human motor behavior, our interpretation requires first a consideration of man as a motile creature in general.

1) Paraphrasing Hughling Jackson's statement, "The nervous system knows no muscles, it only knows movements," I would prefer to say, "We don't move our muscles, we move our limbs in relation to the environment opened to us in sensory experience." (I am referring here, of course, to muscles as macroscopic units in a morphological sense.) There is a marked topical difference

between the function of particular muscles cooperating in the motion of skeletal parts and the action performed. Example: While the muscles of trunk, pelvis, thigh move the legs in a repetitive sequence, right-left, right-left swinging, though, with a part stop in the hip joint, we proceed on our way continuously, our steps determined by the visible particularities of the road, the anticipated constellation of traffic, and the goal intended.

2) Since we all learned to walk in our early years, it seems not necessary to describe what we are doing; however, to immunize us against certain theories it is essential to say what we are NOT doing: we certainly do not step on optical stimuli! Neither do we walk on optical stimuli projected outward! We set our feet on solid ground, the *subjectum* (*hypokeimenon*), in the original Aristotelian sense of the word, visible in advance and felt in contact.

3) In walking we do not enter "an external world"; we all find ourselves in the world – the world which we share with the others.

4) In contrast to the millions of people able to walk and to talk, to run and to jump, to cook and to eat, there are only a few experts who have any precise knowledge of the muscles involved in such a "simple" performance as catching a ball or signing a name.

5) Even those few who are in the know, cannot voluntarily – certainly not without a long period of artificial training – move one single muscle, e.g., the serratus ant. as such, a protagonist in raising one's arm to the vertical.

There was and still is therefore a sharp contrast between the interpretations given by physics and physiology and the experiences gained in the lifeworld.

Let us imagine a short-distance run at Olympia! A number of young men are forming one group of sprinters; having received a starting signal together, each one starts for himself, although all of them run side by side and simultaneously towards a common goal, marked perhaps by a marble statue. While people in the lifeworld would say that the statue to be reached in the future is visible to all of the runners from a distance, physics tells us that sunlight reflected from the surface of the stone *traveling towards them* had already reached them over this short distance, for all practical purposes in one instant.

The light waves which have the size of microns stimulate the rods and cones of the retina, or other of the retinae; for while we may use the right and left leg in alteration, the right and left eye cooperate under normal conditions in a "cyclopic" function. Yet in spite of the micro-structure of the light waves and receptors, all the participants find themselves in a wide-open landscape closed by the blue vaults of the sky. Lilliputians by astronomic measurements, they are not frightened by the cosmic dimensions of heaven and earth.

The sprinters practically use, although in varying combinations, all their muscles – those of feet, of legs, of pelvis, of trunk, of neck, of eyes, of arms, of diaphragm, of intercostales – all balanced by the vestibularis system. Of course the sportsmen used them, in Olympia as well as in Munich, without any anatomical knowledge of their muscles, let alone the microscopic structure of fibers and fibrils or the biochemistry of actin or myosin. Yet in a race with its constant fast change from right to left leg, a precise coordination of all parts of the motor system, combined with the function of the vestibularis is required. Obviously, a sprinter's brain must function as a globalisator rather than as an analysator.

It is therefore of paramount interest to realize how the interpretation of the function of the precentral motor area has changed in the course of the century, following the discoveries of Fritsch and Hitzig (1870). During a conference on "Brain and Conscious Experience," held in the Vatican Academy in 1964 (edited by John C. Eccles, Springer-Verlag, New York, 1966), C. G. Phillips summarized the situation as follows: "It has gradually become clear that electrical stimulation does not, as some of the pioneers seem to have supposed, evoke natural functioning of the cortical neuronal apparatus within the effective orbit of the stimulating electrodes ... Nothing is known of the locus or nature of the repository of motor skills ..." In the discussion Penfield added: "I think this type of critical, careful scholarly approach that Dr. Phillips is making may begin to tell us what the cortical areas actually do. Stimulation of the cortical area does not tell you the purpose of that area at all: it tells you what corticopetal activation can do and that gives you some reason to assume what the cortex may have been doing ... In man you can remove the leg area (it is comparatively small) completely, using a stimulator to make sure that you have got it all, and still that man will walk and walk quite well." Later on Penfield added: "Vocalization requires the action of the whole mechanism, including diaphragm, lips, mouth, everything, so that it is quite clear that the cortex is utilizing a neuronal mechanism which is in the brain stem lower down."

As a final example let us consider the situation of two tennis players, Jack and Bill, playing together. "Playing together" means in this situation, of course, that they actually are playing against each other; visualizing the same court and net, although "facing" it from opposite points of view.

While the ball hit by Jack and approaching Bill in its flight over the net is seen by both players, the light – or to be more precise – the stimuli reflected in the direction towards Jack are radically different from those reaching Bill; nevertheless, the two players see one and the same thing moving on its way – let us assume from west to east. In a tournament, for instance at Wimbledon, such activities of the players would be watched very carefully by a referee and across the court by a large number of spectators. Turning their heads as in a pantomime, from right to left and from left to right, each one of them – yet all together – will see one and the same performance. They will be aware of the court at rest and of the players in fast action. In spite of their rapidly varying positions and aspects, Bill and Jack will be clearly recognized in their identities. All of those present are convinced that they see and watch the same performance, just as we in a theater are convinced that we like all the others present see the same action on the stage or on the screen. Obviously there must be a polarity in sensory experience, as things visible are seen by everyone in the audience alike. Once again we notice a radical discrepancy between the familiar accomplishments in the life-world reached without any particular effort, compared with the difficult and demanding task of presenting a scientific explanation.

As a rule, a physiologist occupied with experiments to provide deeper understanding of vision takes it for granted that he can see the instruments and the bodies of the other person, especially his eyes and skull, that he knows the structures of instruments used, and that the observed as well as the observer can see under

some arrangements the same object, for instance Snellen's tabulae
– or to use a more scientific expression, to receive equal though
not identical stimuli. Yet luminous agents, whatsoever, are transformed into stimuli only at that very moment when they have
reached and have acted upon receptors. Therefore stimuli are
strictly private and definitely remote from any direct inspection
by others. Jerzy Konorski – one of Pavlov's scientific heirs –
thought that he had found a simple solution for this tantalizing
problem in connecting object and stimuli simply through a hyphen,
referring to object-stimuli. In his book, *Integrative Activity of the
Brain* (University of Chicago Press, 1967), Konorski wrote
(footnote, p. 77): "By the term "stimulus-object" we denote any
event of the external world which acts on the receptors and gives
rise to the unitary perception. The word "stimulus" reflects its
action on the afferent part of the nervous system; the word "object" indicates that the stimulus is not elementary or partial but involves a pattern corresponding to the definite thing or event perceived. To give some examples, by stimulus-objects we shall
denote: visual presentation of a pencil, an apple, a face, a word;
some esthetic presentation of a rough material, or a pencil; gusta-
tory presentation of a piece of apple; auditory presentation of a
whir of a motor, or a human voice, or a spoken word, etc." Following him one could perhaps say that a house across the street reflects
object-stimuli, but when someone crosses the street and enters
the house he then would walk within the realm of stimuli-objects.
Konorski obviously ignored the fundamental facts that the "receptors" – viz, those of a person or an animal used in experiments
– belong to the observer's external world, while the subject's own
perceptions as such are inaccessible to anybody else.

Indeed, those relations of stimuli and objects most familiar in
the practice of life present us with embarrassing problems.

Everyone who has lived somewhere for some time will recognize as one and the same a street, going up and down, he will also
be aware of his own house – outside and inside – all as permanent
structures although the sunlight and thereby the optical stimuli
vary in rapid sequence. Yet in spite of this fantastic speed and
in spite of the drastic changes of illumination from morning to
evening, we all recognize "our town" as the same one, day after
day. The fundamental problem is to understand *not*, how human

experience might be reduced to the function of molecules but that and how human beings as well as animals can and do surpass the realm of physics. A tentative answer may be that also in geometry the apprehension of a triangle, of a circle, of parallel lines, or of numbers, of figures as well as of extension, *transcends* the primary data; for a triangle as such is not recognized by a blackboard or a photographic film. It must be seen by man, silently aware of other possibilities and additional geometrical relations. Two requirements are: a) to grasp the triangle as such in its totality as well as in its essential details and thereby (b) to distinguish it silently from other figures, such as a square, a circle, etc. – reaching far beyond the actually given, – just as the simple remark: "Now they *are* leaving" makes sense only in silent reference to: "They *were* leaving" or "*He will* leave."

The "grammatism" in sensory aphasia is not an accidental symptom.

The fundamental question of sight and insight therefore is: How man can reach so far beyond the limits and confines of his actual corporeal whereabouts.

II

While the program of a modern athletic contest may still be ornated by a vignette of Myron's discus-thrower, the situation has changed markedly during the centuries separating the Olympic games in 776 B.C. from those in Munich in 1972 A.D. At Olympia only men competed in the Pentathlon; since the bikini had not yet been invented, ladies were not admitted as spectators, neither the Aspasias nor the Xantippes. However, in our days the number of contests, of contenders, and of spectators, young and old, male and female, has reached fantastic proportions. Fortunately, a crowd eager to see athletes competing must not wait four years for the next spectacle. In a recently erected stadium in Cincinnati, for instance, 56,000 spectators, seated in ascending circles, may see altogether the same field and watch the same game, although a picture taken somewhere from the highest circle on the south side would differ drastically from one taken down at the first row on the north side.

Discounting for a moment the players, the coaches, the referees, the cheer leaders, the marching bands, the reporters and the photographers, 56,000 spectators would direct 112,000 eyes and with them, according to Sperry, 112,000 cerebral hemispheres to the show. While every one among all those present *views* with his own eyes alone, nevertheless all those present are convinced that they *see* together one and the same contest of football or baseball; just as on a drastically reduced scale a psychologist administering a Rorschach test would be convinced that he and his client see together the same card and picture.

In Lexington, Kentucky, where the coliseum offers 17,000 seats to the fans admiring the Wildcats playing basketball, the stands cover three sides of a huge rectangle with the fourth one left for the doors. Obviously, those seated on the east side have the Basket A to their right and the Basket B to their left while their friends vis-à-vis see the Basket B to their right and the Basket A to their left. Finally, those on the small north side see both baskets in front of them, although separated by some distance. Yet once again all spectators are sure to watch the same performance, although the photic projections change with every run of the players. No doubt, in such a large stadium they see at a given moment only one part of the whole field while they, like the spectators at Wimbledon, must turn their heads from west to east, or from basket A to basket B. Although thereby markedly different groups of optical stimuli follow each other rapidly in time, all the fans are aware of just one huge area, seen in parts and viewed in sequence of time, – nevertheless, recognized as segments existing simultaneously side by side.

There is a strange contrast between the visible experience in the lifeworld shared by millions, generation after generation, and the account of vision and the optical apparatus given by science and philosophy.

Yet the discrepancy is not so surprising. Suppose some one enjoys the "panorama" opened to his view from a high mountain; let him, annoyed by an angry wasp, relax only for a moment the levator muscles – and the whole sight vanishes. This negative effect is not so surprising, for only two small pencils of light, not larger than one or two millimeters in diameter, passed through his pupils, stimulating the rods and cones of his retinae in narrow areas. This "stimulation," then, traveling along the optical pathways will finally reach and activate the cells in the two areas 17 at the optical poles of the brain, placed, it seems, at a right angle to the direction of vision; still worse, covered by the meninges, the dura mater, the skull, and the scalp, these sections of the brain – like all other parts – operate in complete darkness.

In contrast to the strictly local effect of tactile stimuli which makes every one in the coliseum feel the pressure of his seat for himself alone, and in contrast to the separate functions of the two hands – the right one perhaps holding a program and the left one a cup of coca cola – in his sight each one of the spectators looks over the whole floor and the stands of the wide building. Indeed, if the roof would be opened, his view could expand up to the sky. Furthermore, while the illumination must be reviewed from millisecond to millisecond, we all see the floor perfectly at rest.

How can it be understood that a particular "mental apparatus" placed in an intracranial box could ever reach the so-called "external world" and establish there any communication with other brains? How could we account for an athlete's comportment, directed in anticipation of temporo-spatial results of his action – for example, a touchdown – in terms of stimuli and responses, input and output, or afferent and efferent events *within* a nervous system? How can we understand that the rods and cones of the retina need and use magnification through a microscope to inform the cells within the area 17 of – let us say – Professor Hubel's or Professor Wiesel's brains about "single neurons in the cat's striate cortex"?

In his great work on *Physiological Objects* (1867), Helmholtz explained the accomplishments of perception as a result of "unconscious inferences." Helmholtz had accepted Johannes Mueller's doctrine that "sensory sensation is not the conduction of a quality or a state of external bodies to consciousness; it is rather the conduction of a quality or a state of sensory nerves to consciousness brought about by an external cause, and these qualities are different in the different sensory nerves; they are the sensory energies." (*Handbuch der Physiologie des Menschen*, Vol. II, 1837).

Had Johannes Mueller been right, he could not have said what he said; for two reasons: 1) consciousness while somehow receiving sensory qualities does not know their origin; it is completely unaware of the existence of sensory nerves as such; for conscious-

ness is strictly limited to the appearance of sensory qualities; 2)
the sensorium could not speak; even if it were able to innervate
the complex phonetic apparatus, the sound waves produced by
its own body machinery, yet in the "external world," would reach
the sensorium, nevertheless, as the conduction of qualities of a
sensory nerve, its origin completely unknown to the sensorium.
Mueller was convinced that he had found a way out of this dilemma, adding: "but because they (i.e., the sensory nerves) are extended in space, because they can be affected by stimulation ...
impart to the sensorium, when changed by external causes, besides their own state, also qualities and changes in the outer
world ..." In this passage Mueller, replacing "consciousness" by
the "sensorium," accepted the attitude familiar to all of us in the
lifeworld – apparently completely unaware of his methodical jump
that was leading him away from a monadic interpretation of
consciousness and of sensory qualities. Yet if consciousness was
aware exclusively of qualities "imported" by sensory nerves,
such solipsistic consciousness had no access to external bodies,
not even to its own body, except through an enigmatic incarnation.

Helmholtz in the first chapter of his *Physiological Optics* actually took his position in the lifeworld, describing the anatomy
of the eye – an anatomical structure visible under certain conditions to another person, or, following Helmholtz, another brain.
Yet, ignoring his own activities as an observer, Helmholtz then
wondered how a brain jailed in solitary confinement within a
skull could be aware of an external world! He assumed, as mentioned above, that a brain could accomplish such a task by unconscious inference. While Joh. Mueller began his presentation
with a reference to "consciousness," replacing "consciousness"
without much ado by the term "the sensorium," Helmholtz
personified "the brain."

In his book, *The Intelligent Eye* (McGraw-Hill, 1970, p. 30),
R.L. Gregory states: "Helmholtz spoke of perception in terms
of "unconscious inferences." For reasons not altogether clear to the
present writer, this has never been very popular among psychologists. Helmholtz was particularly concerned with the fact that
though sensory activity starts at surfaces of the body, including
the retina, we experience "things out there" ... Helmholtz sup-

posed, though he did not put it quite like this, that the brain continually carries out "unconscious inference" of the form: nearly all retinal activity received is due to external objects. This is retinal activity. Therefore this is due to an external object ... Helmholtz described his "unconscious inferences" in perception in the following words, which I [Gregory] quote at length: "The psychic activities that lead us to infer that there in front of us at a certain place there is a certain object of a certain character, are generally not conscious activities, but unconscious ones. In their result they are equivalent to a conclusion, to the extent that the observed action on our senses enables us to form an idea as to the possible cause of this action; although as a matter of fact, it is invariably simply the nervous stimulations that are perceived, that is, the actions, but never the external objects themselves. But what seems to differentiate them from a conclusion, in the ordinary sense of the word, is that a conclusion is an act of conscious thought. An astronomer, for example, comes to real conclusions of this sort, when he computes the positions of the stars in space, their distances, etc., from the perspective images he has had of them at various times and as they are seen from different parts of the orbit of the earth. His conclusions are based on conscious knowledge of the laws of optics. In the ordinary acts of vision this knowledge of optics is lacking. Still it may be permissible to speak of the psychic acts of ordinary perception as unconscious conclusions, thereby making a distinction of some sort between them and the so-called conscious conclusions. And while it is true that there has been, and probably always will be, a measure of doubt as to the similarity of the psychic activity, in the two cases, there can be no doubt as to the similarity between the results of such unconscious conclusions and those of conscious conclusions."

Gregory wants his book regarded as an extension of that passage from Helmholtz, but he as well as Helmholtz forgot that they actually denied or ignored their own primary presuppositions: namely, that they could see other people, astronomers for instance, and consider together with them objects visible in the "outer world" – objects presented to their own eyes. Had Helmholtz been right, then we must believe that all the basketball-players' individual brains make rapidly changing unconscious in-

ferences about their own bodies, about the floor over which they
are running, about the ball they are driving, about the basket they
are approaching, etc. Each one of those present in the hall must
have been likewise actively producing unconscious inferences –
though each one for himself alone – about the hall, the players,
and neighbors, etc.

We would even have to assume that a dog's brain, while he is
chasing a cat, makes unconscious inferences about an external
world; we – or rather I – could, however, draw such a necessary
conclusion only after placing the dog, i.e., the optical stimuli
received by my brain, through my own inference into an external
world.

With the hypothesis of a brain positing an external world
through "unconscious inference," Helmholtz introduced a kind
of fairy tale terminology into physiology. Maybe he wasn't the
first in line, but, to be sure, he was not the last one; for the pro-
moters of the information theory who claim that the striate area
decodes the signals received from the retina are his disciples.
Gregory in his book *Eye and Brain*, published in 1966, actually
wrote: "Indeed, an object perceived is a hypothesis ... Occasionally, eye and brain reach wrong conclusions, and we suffer
hallucinations or illusions." One may wonder whether Gregory
would approve an application of his dogma in his own case, and
whether he would agree that while he was describing "eye and
brain" of other creatures, his own brain, though unknown to itself
or to himself, indulged in hypotheses never to be tested.

Yet Helmholtz ignored the fundamental fact that in our sensory experience we find ourselves *within* the world, *upon* the earth,
able to see things as objects. When, during intermission of the
ball game one of the fans would enjoy a hamburger, he would
not insert a hypothesis of a piece of food into a body image, de-
tected by inference in an external world, nevertheless known to
him as his own body. Strangely enough, this fellow, according to
science, would have to walk with his own feet on a territory
reached by unconscious inference. No! I – or rather my brain –
does not look through the extremely narrow windows of my
pupils into an external world, having somehow introduced a third
dimension into the two-dimensional images activated on the
retina, No! I find myself within the world – or to be more precise

– upon the earth, aware of my surroundings and of my partners.

We still owe an answer to the question: Can we, how can we understand the situation taken for granted generation after generation by millions in the lifeworld, yet most of the time passed in silence – if not denied – by science and philosophy? A tentative answer might be: Eyes alone are not seeing, brains alone are not seeing, but man and animals do – thanks to their distinct corporeal organization, which enables them, while *awake* to rise against gravity, to stand upright and thereby to acquire each one for himself a central position upon the earth: that of "belonging in opposition."

The physiology and psychology of sensory experience is a study of man and beasts *awake* – even the interpretation of dreams is performed while both the analyst and his patient are awake. When Freud claimed that the interpretation of dreams presented a "royal road" leading to a knowledge of the unconscious activities of the mind," he ignored the fundamental fact that, only when wide awake, people are able to march on that road. Freud also ignored the situation – emphasized centuries ago by Heraclites – that dreams are private experience.

As sleepers, who gave up their op-position within the world, we cannot share individual phantasmagories, even when, e.g., after a long walk in the mountains we are stretched out side by side in a tent. Awake only can we play games together; awake only do we really find ourselves together with others – with our partners – in a common "territory."

The physiology of the *Waking Brain* has been greatly furthered through the studies of Magoun, Moruzzi, and others. Yet we should not forget that such studies silently presuppose: 1) The observer himself must be awake, and thereby fully aware of the actual and the possible conditions of the objects under consideration – be it a mineral, a plant, or the brain of an animal or of a human being. When Bremer, for instance, studied the functions of the *encéphale isolé* of a cat, his experiments required, of course, the perfect functioning of the observer's own brain during his hours of wakefulness; then only was he in a position to note and to describe the behavior of the experimental animal, and to relate the facts observed to other, actual or lost, potentialities. Only when awake was he able – thanks to the functioning of his own eyes and brain – to determine "stimuli" which did produce or did not produce certain reactions of the animal studied, while those very stimuli could never act upon his own "distance-receptors." 2) Studies of the waking or the sleeping brain require, furthermore, an observer able before he ever starts his experiments to distinguish between the general attitudes of sleep and wakefulness of the creatures studied. 3) The term "the brain" is radically misleading, for there actually exist in reality countless individual brains, comparable, to be sure, in structure and function by an observer who with the other creatures shares a common surrounding. 4) Each one of those many brains – the reticular system included – is but one part of the total organism, kept alive and functioning during sleep through breathing, circulation, and homeiostatic functions. Starting to beat in the mother's womb, the heart continues to work without pause from birth to death. It does not rest even while the brain recovers during periods of desynchronized sleep. Refreshed by sleep, with the righting reflexes returning to function, the muscle tone increased, the sleeper is ready to open his eyes, to get up and to "face the world."

When a "neural replication of the external world would be seen across sheets of sensory receptors," as Mountcastle claimed, ("Brain & Conscious Experience," p. 85) when "in neural space and time an isomorphic phantom of the real world would be represented," then Mountcastle – or to be more precise Mountcastle's brain – could never have made such a statement. For his own brain, like that of every other man's, boxed within the skull throughout his life, remains ignorant of Mountcastle's activities during his experiments. Since his observation of others would at best produce isomorphic phantoms within the tissue filling Mountcastle's skull, he could never have discovered the irreality of his own perceptions.

The space of the lifeworld is terrestrial space. It is not isometric. It is not isomorphic. It is not three-dimensional. For with the first cry of the newborn, i.e., with the first act of breathing, the fourth dimension, viz., the relation inner-outer, or belonging in opposition, has been established. It will be kept active day and night, awake and asleep until the last sigh. The skin separates the inner from the outer space, or rather it separates in connecting the inner space of an organism from and with the surroundings.

The exterceptors serve, just like smelling and tasting, the separation and connection of inner and outer space. Breathing and crying, feeding and excreting, will be followed in the normal development of a human baby by the acquisition and growing proficiency of rising, standing, and walking. The space encountered in rising from the ground – terrestrial space – is swayed by gravity: the vertical presenting the one universally domineering dimension. The space of the lifeworld is terrestrial space. Man and beasts are in their existence related throughout to the "mother earth": *gaia*.

Centuries passed before Geo-metry – begun as practical measurement of terrestrial acreage – finally culminated in Euclidean ir-realism, expressed in his famous axioms and summarized 2000 years later in Kant's *Prolegomena* (par. 10): "Geometry takes as basis the pure intuition (*reine Anschauung*) of space." While in Euclidean space a distant point x is separated from the zero point by all the intermediary points of a dimensional axis, in the Lebenswelt a distant point may be visible as a goal to be reached in the future from the present position. "Here," the spot of my aboding at the present moment, is not identical with the intersection of three coordinates uniformly extended from a zero point. The space of the lifeworld is not an abstract immaterial schema. If the sight of the mathematician would not reach beyond the geo-metrical structures, there could be no mathematical insight.

To awaken is often identified in the vernacular with standing and "getting up." Yet the action of rising is intended: it is not automatized like the heartbeat or the peristaltic movements; it is not due to coercive mechanisms like breathing. Awake, I can get up; I must not – in spite of all the stringent reasons. Man and animal stand up through their own power; they are not raised by the air like a cloud of steam or a blimp; they are not carried by forced air currents like a plane. My body provides me with the opportunity of getting up and of holding my stand; yet once accomplished, upright posture still demands my continued efforts. The all-pervading power of gravity never ceases; it remains a counterforce; it requires my constant effort and resistance against the "down pull." Since gravity remains active without cessation, every moment of upright posture is threatened by fall, from this moment "now" to the next "now."

Empowered to counteract gravity, man and animal – certainly the terrestrial animals – are thereby first rendered capable of locomotion. The conquest of gravity provides freedom of motion, "foot-room" and "elbow-room." Walking follows standing. Actually, in walking, standing on one leg while lifting the other one from the ground, we have to overcome gravity for the second time. A galloping horse races through space in leaps; even a caterpillar moves by inching, i.e., by lifting his body in semicircles from a supporting leaf or twig.

The four dimensions of sensory-motor space are not isomorphic: 1) Gravity is domineering terrestrial space, never ending in time, persisting day and night. In getting up and standing everyone establishes for himself a position: *here*, as a starting point wherefrom to reach other points over there in an open space shared by partners, visible to him from his position at the present moment. 2) In the relation inner-outer, the inner zone is strictly secluded, private, while the outer one is common to all of us. 3) The directions forward-backward, having their turning point in the vertical axis, though predetermined by the body schema of the species, vary with the actual position of the individual "facing" the surrounding. The gaze of someone, lying on his back, yielding to gravity, is directed upward, not forward. 4) The antagonism right-left is preponderantly, though perhaps not exclusively, an acquisition of the human race. Yet even in man the active antagonism of coordinated opposition is a prerogative of the arms in contrast to the two eyes with their twelve external muscles cooperating so that the individual has but one view of the whole panorama – notwithstanding the separation of the two parts of the retinae, extended through the chiasm to the striate cortices.

In science the eyes are listed as "receptors." Light reflected from somewhere travels towards them; individual pencils of light stimulate rods and cones of the retinae as "input". The direction of "information-transmission in the visual system" is centripetal, oscillating with the speed of rhodopsin-metabolism. How can it be understood that a particular "mental apparatus" placed in an intracranial box could ever reach the so-called "external world" and establish there any communication with other brains?

Heidegger interpreted Da-Sein as being-in-the-*world*; yet the German word "Da" actually refers to the earth as man's original home. It is the terri-tory on which man takes a position, his stand as a living bodily creature, a *zoon*.

Because man is a son of "Mother Earth," his eyes and ears tally with terrestrial conditions: our hearing with the vibrations of the atmosphere; our seeing with the illumination by sunlight. Yet, since sunlight is pervading the "territory" in all directions, since sunlight before refraction through and reflection from objects is a composite of all the wavelengths, we are blinded in direct illumination, incapable to make any discrimination, exposed as it were to a dense, all-white fog. Direct optical stimulation would provide us no information about the environment. We actually see the differences of our whereabouts only in indirect illumina-tion. Reflected light after all the modifications produced by ab-sorption and refractions permits us to see the landscapes and to differentiate things in their particular colors and contours in permanence and change.

Although reflected light continues to move towards the spec-tator, in looking and watching we see the environment over there, our gaze directed in full opposition to the physical condition of the path of illumination.

That we actually see things in front of us, we ourselves placed at the center of a wide open horizon although only small pencils of light are passing our pupils, that everybody can touch visible objects, turn a page, shake a hand, lift a glass of water towards lips and mouths, although nobody could ever touch optical stimuli, these transformations, I believe, are due to our primary contraposition to the ground, our standing up against gravity when awake. While the sun rises and sets, gravity persists with-out change, dominating the earthly nights as well as the earthly days; gravity never sinks down below the horizon. Stratton and Ivo Kohler actually have demonstrated the dominance of gravity over illumination through their experiments with inverting lenses. When the students and psychologists participating in these ex-periments faithfully continued to wear the inverting lenses for days, they were rewarded with a full correction of sight, seeing things and landscape in a "normal vertical position."

Corresponding results have been established through Held's experiments where apparent deviations from the vertical produced by prism lenses have been corrected when subjects were allowed to walk around, while no corrections were accomplished when the subjects were moved around in wheelchairs.

The fact that awake everyone reaches in his own sight far beyond the boundaries of his body – indeed to the moon, the sun, and the stars – this enigmatic extension has been one, if not *the* decisive motive for dualistic interpretations – positing a soul, a mind, a consciousness, transcending the narrow corporeal boundaries. Accordingly, philosophical and later physiological interpretations postulated a subordination of the motorium to the sensorium, limiting motor activities to locomotion, if not to efferent responses.

Yet my body is not a curiously shaped *res extensa* lost in solitude somewhere in the vastness of Euclidean space; my body as a chthonic formation is located in terrestrial space, counteracting the fundamental invariant – the omnipresent power of gravity.

This power to rise against the force of gravity enables: a) an organism to establish its "here" in contraposition to the world; thereby a living body is transformed into my body; b) provides the indispensable condition for locomotion; c) This situation, namely the position within the world in opposition to it, my existence, challenging gravity makes the intentionality of sensory experience – participation and active receptiveness – possible. d) Facing the encompassing whole to which I belong as a part, I am enabled to meet partners. e) Able to move on terrestrial space, I am in open relation to points over there as potential goals. The intentional relation to visible objects (*Gegen-stände*) presented from a distance is founded in the capacity of conquering gravity. f) The "terra firma" constitutes for our experience as mundane creatures the fundamental, invariant system of coordinates against which also the sun is actually seen as moving.

GUIDO KÜNG

Universität Freiburg (Schweiz)

DAS NOEMA ALS REELLES MOMENT[1]

In einem aus der Zeit um 1918 stammenden Manuskript kommt
Husserl zum Schluss "dass kein Grund ist, das 'Noema' vom
Erlebnis abzurücken und ihm den Charakter eines reellen Momentes zu bestreiten."[2] Dies klingt sehr überraschend, da in der
phänomenologischen Literatur die Unterscheidung von Noesis
und Noema gewöhnlich mit Texten aus den *Ideen* belegt wird, wo
die noematischen Erlebnismomente ausdrücklich als *nichtreelle*
von den reellen noetischen Momenten unterschieden werden.[3]
Man könnte deshalb annehmen, dass Husserl in diesem Manuskript nur ein unverbindliches Gedankenexperiment zu Papier
gebracht habe. Doch scheinen mir die angeführten Argumente
zu beweisen, dass es sich hier wirklich um einen weiteren Fort-
schritt in Husserls Analyse des intentionalen Bewusstseins han-
delt.

Es ist von Wichtigkeit Husserls Lehre vom Noema im Zusammenhang mit der Entwicklung der für die Logik grundlegenden
Probleme der Bedeutung bzw. des Sinnes, zu sehen. Husserl
hatte im Sommersemester 1908 in seiner Vorlesung über "Bedeu-

---

[1] Diese Untersuchungen gehen auf einen von der University of Notre Dame (Indiana) und dem National Endowment for the Humanities (Washington D.C.) unter-
stützten Forschungsaufenthalt am Husserl-Archiv in Löwen während des Jahres
1970/71 zurück. Dem damaligen Direktor des Archivs, Prof. Herman Leo Van Breda,
sowie seinen Mitarbeitern, den Herren Dr. Iso Kern, Dr. Edi Marbach und Dr. Karl
Schuhmann bin ich für die vielseitige mir gewährte Hilfe zu Dank verpflichtet.

[2] Ms. B III 12 Bl. 89. veröffentlicht in *Husserliana* Bd. XI S. 334–335. Die Heraus-
geberin datiert das Manuskript auf 1922 ff.; wie mir aber die Sachverständigen des
Husserl-Archivs übereinstimmend versichert haben, lässt das von Husserl verwendete
Papier eher auf die Zeit um 1916–1921 schliessen; dies stimmt auch mit meinen in-
haltlich begründeten Vermutungen überein, vgl. unten Anmerkung 5.

[3] *Ideen zu einer reinen Phänomenologie und phänomenologischen Philosophie* § 97.

tungslehre" eingesehen, dass die sogenannte ontische Bedeutung (d.h. der Gegenstand so wie er bedeutet ist) als etwas *sui generis* anerkannt werden muss, und dass deshalb die Bedeutung nicht einfach mit einem reellen Moment des bedeutungsverleihenden Aktes oder mit einer Species eines solchen Momentes identifiziert werden kann, wie er früher angenommen hatte.[4] Diese Entdeckung bildete einen entscheidenden Schritt auf dem Wege der Überwindung der noch in der 1. Auflage der *Logischen Untersuchungen* (1900/01) vertretenen rein noetischen Auffassung der Phänomenologie. In den *Ideen* (1913) fand diese Entwicklung mit der offiziellen Einführung des Begriffes des Noema, d.h. des intentionalen Gegenstandes als solchen, einen vorläufigen Abschluss.

Der Text vom Noema als reellem Moment scheint nun aber zu belegen, dass Husserl mit seiner Analyse nicht stehen geblieben ist, sondern schon bald neue Schwierigkeiten entdeckt hat, welche ihn zur Annahme zusätzlicher Unterscheidungen zwangen. Und zwar ist die hier interessierende Schwierigkeit im Zusammenhang mit weiteren Untersuchungen des Zeitbewusstseins aufgetreten.[5] Husserls Gedankengang lässt sich meiner Ansicht nach wie folgt zusammenfassen: Bei einer Folge von Erinnerungen, z.B. an ein vergangenes immanentes Empfindungsdatum, wird dasselbe nun vergangene Datum in jeder Erinnerung notwendig immer wieder anders, nämlich als weiter in die Vergangenheit entrückt, aufgefasst. Das heisst es muss also notwendigerweise ebensoviele verschiedene Noemata wie Erinnerungsakte geben, zwei verschiedene Akte können streng genommen nie genau dasselbe Noema haben. Husserl zog hieraus den Schluss, dass diesen Noemata also keine überzeitliche sondern die gleiche zeitliche Existenzweise zukomme wie den Erinnerungsakten. Genau dies scheint aber der Grund zu sein, weshalb Husserl sich nun nicht mehr scheute, das Noema als ein reelles Moment zu bezeichnen. Er hat nämlich in einem

---

[4] Ich habe erstmals in meinen Aufsätzen "Nowe spojrzenie na rozwój filozoficzny Husserla" (Ein neuer Blick auf die philosophische Entwicklung von Husserl) *Fenomenologia Romana Ingardena* (Warszawa, Studia Filozoficzne 1972) S. 145–156, und "Husserl on pictures and intentional objects" *Review of Metaphysics* Bd. 26 (1973) S. 670–680, auf diesen Wendepunkt hingewiesen.

[5] Roman Ingarden hat wiederholt auf die Wichtigkeit der noch nicht veröffentlichten Bernauer Untersuchungen des Zeitbewusstseins hingewiesen. Tatsächlich scheint z.B. das Manuskript B III 12 Bl. 91–92 (von Husserl mit "Bernau 1918" datiert) mit dem hier behandelten Thema im Zusammenhang zu stehen. Husserl betont dort unter anderem, dass bei einer Synthese der Identitikation genau genommen nicht ein, sondern (den drei Akten entsprechend) *drei* noematische Gegenstände auftreten.

anderen Manuskript ausdrücklich definiert: "Nennen wir alles,
was an einem Erlebnis phänomenologisch-zeitlich gebunden ist,
ein reelles Moment des Erlebnisses."[6]

Natürlich kann es sich hier nicht um einen Rückfall in die
früher vertretene rein noetische Phänomenologie handeln. Das
Noema verbleibt ein durch den Akt Vermeintes: "wir bezeichnen
das Vermeinte als Vermeintes dieses bestimmten Aktes als Noema."[7] Aber es wird nun nicht mehr mit dem überindividuellen
Sinn vermischt, sondern klar als ein weiteres Element *sui generis*
von diesem Sinn unterschieden: "Nannten wir Noema das Vermeinte als dem einzelnen Akte zugehöriges, als anteilhabend an
der Zeitlichkeit, so dürfen wir mit demselben Wort nicht mehr
nennen das über die Zeit hinausgreifende Identische selbst."[8]
Bezüglich der wiederholten Erinnerungen an Vergangenes heisst
es nun: "Der identische gegenständliche Sinn, mit seinen Zeit-
bestimmungen und Qualitäten, ist nur in immer anderen Orientie-
rungen und Zeitperspektiven gegeben, in einem wechselnden
noematischen Wie."[9] Im Wintersemester 1920/21 nennt Husserl
den Sinn ein "Ideelles," und den verschiedenen Satzsinnen ge-
meinsamen Gegenstandspol nennt er zeitweise so gar ein "Ideelles
zweiter Stufe."[10]

Der hier skizzierte Schritt in der Entwicklung Husserls sollte
im Einzelnen noch besser belegt werden. Dadurch wäre es wahrscheinlich auch möglich, ein klareres Bild von dem bei Husserl
festzustellenden Wandel in der Auffassung des idealen Seins zu
erhalten. Die reichhaltigen Husserlschen Analysen sind eines ein-
gehenden Studiums wert, nicht nur aus historischen Gründen,
sondern vor allem weil sie einen wichtigen Beitrag zur analytischen
Philosophie der Gegenwart leisten können.

---

[6] *Husserliana* Bd. XI S. 394 (1922/23).
[7] Ms. B III 12 Bl. 79a (nach 1922).
[8] Ms. B III 12 Bl. 79 (nach 1922).
[9] *Husserliana* Bd. XI S. 332 (1923?).
[10] Ms. B III 12 Bl. 52–53 (1920/21).

Rudolf Boehm
Universität Gent

EINE TRAGÖDIE: WALLENSTEINS UND UNSER ALLER BÖSER GEIST

Descartes zweifelte – selbst an der Wahrheit von Arithmetik und Geometrie: "Equidem non aliam ob causam de iis dubitandum esse ... judicavi, quam quia veniebat in mentem forte aliquem Deum talem mihi naturam indere potuisse, ut etiam illa deciperer, quae manifestissima viderentur. Sed quoties haec praeconcepta de summa Dei potentia opinio mihi occurrit, non possum non fateri, siquidem velit, facile illi esse efficere ut errem, etiam in his quae me puto mentis oculis quam evidentissime intueri": "Allerdings aus keinem anderen Grunde urteilte ich ..., dass daran zu zweifeln sei, als dem, das mir in den Sinn kam, vielleicht habe ein Gott mir eine Natur der Art zu geben vermocht, dass ich mich täusche selbst bezüglich dessen, was das Offenkundigste schiene. Doch so oft mir diese vorgefasste Meinung über Gottes höchste Macht begegnet, kann ich nicht umhin, einzugestehen, es sei ihm ein Leichtes, wenn er nur wolle, zu bewirken, dass ich irre selbst in solchem, was ich mit den Augen des Geistes so evident wie nur möglich einzusehen meine."

Dann wäre die offenkundigste Gewissheit, die höchste Evidenz – am Ende der entschiedenste Grund zur Vermutung einer vollkommenen Täuschung. Wie wäre das denkbar? Als völlig gewiss, ganz offenkundig und vollkommen evident erscheint uns, was sich uns zwingend aufdringt, ganz ohne unser Zutun, völlig unabhängig von unserem eigenen Glauben, Meinen und Wollen, gänzlich unbeeinflusst, ungefärbt von unserer Subjektivität. Darum erstreben wir in Dingen der Erkenntnis die Objektivität des unbeteiligten, interesselosen Zuschauers, dem allein die Dinge in ihrer Objektivität, so wie sie schlechthin an sich selber sind, begegnen können. Sollten wir gerade darin die Opfer der ärgsten Täuschung sein? Es wäre denkbar: wenn nämlich die Dinge "an sich" gerade keineswegs so wären, wie sie sich bei vollkommen objektiver Betrachtung in höchster Evidenz aufdringen, vielmehr in Wirklichkeit tatsächlich mitbestimmt vom menschlichen, wie immer "subjektiven" Verhalten ihnen gegenüber, und erst in dem Sonderfalle unseres interesselosen, bloss betrachtenden Verhaltens gleichsam verfallen zu Objekten, die nur noch durch sich selbst bestimmt sind.

Die Täuschung, der grosse Irrtum wäre dann: blosses Betrachten, Vorstellen, gar Denken bewirke, in Wirklichkeit, ändere an den Dingen nichts, es könne nur – allenfalls um einiges blasser – widerspiegeln, was sein Gegenstand ist. Man gesteht lediglich zu, dass ein solches Verhalten vollkommen objektiver Betrachtung der Dinge schwer zu verwirklichen ist. Doch kein Gedanke daran, dass ein solches die Dinge gänzlich sich selbst und sich selber nur der Bestimmung durch sie sich überlassendes Verhalten eben an diesen Dingen, wie sie an sich selber sind, irgend etwas verändern könnte. Indessen wäre gerade dies der Fall, wenn zu vermuten stünde, dass "die Welt der transzendenten 'res' durchaus auf Bewusstsein, und zwar nicht auf ein logisch erdachtes, sondern aktuelles angewiesen" (Husserl) ist, die Dinge überhaupt, um nicht zu verfallen, angewiesen auf wirksamen menschlichen Beistand, wie ein anderer Mensch, um menschlich existieren zu können, auf mein menschliches Verhalten ihm gegenüber, wie das Leben auf Licht, Luft und Wärme.

Der Irrtum wäre, es vermöchte inmitten der Wirklichkeit, doch in sie nicht verstrickt, bloss unschuldig zusehend, ein Unwirkliches zu sein, genannt Geist, Bewusstsein, Denken: nichts bewirkend, und so aus der wirklichen Welt herausgelöst, allein betrachtend, und so doch wiederum alles – auf geisterhafte Weise – mit dem Blick – umfassend.

In der gleichen Zeit des Dreissigjährigen Krieges, zu der Descartes über jenen trügerischen Gott meditierte, den man seither als das "malin génie" zu apostrophieren pflegt, spielt ein dramatisches Gedicht Schillers: die Tragödie vom Abfall und Untergang Wallensteins. Im Wendepunkt des riesigen Dramas, in der Schlussszene des Ersten Aufzugs des Dritten Teils, wo Wallenstein

sich endlich entschliesst, den Abfall vom Kaiser zu vollziehen,
ruft sein Feldmarschall Illo erleichtert aus: "Nun, gelobt sei Gott!"
Er "eilt hinaus." Wallenstein aber meditiert: "Es ist sein böser
Geist und meiner," der beide, den Kaiser wie ihn selber, betrogen
hat und strafen wird. "Wallenstein" ist in der Tat die Tragödie
des "bösen Geistes" jenes Irrtums, den Schiller zu durchschauen
begann, eine Tragödie, die wir heute zu begreifen beginnen.

"Wallenstein" ist kein Gewissensdrama; zwar werden Recht
oder Unrecht des Abfalls vom Kaiser erörtert, wird mehreres ge-
sagt über seine Erscheinung als Verrat unter dem herkömmlichen
Gesichtspunkt der Kaisertreue und seine mögliche Rechtfertigung
durch die Untreue des Kaisers selber oder durch die für Deutsch-
land durch Wallensteins Wendung eröffneten Friedensaussichten,
doch eine Entscheidung dieser Frage wird weder ausgesprochen
noch auch nur ernstlich gesucht. In *diesem* Sinne ist "Wallenstein"
auch nicht eine Tragödie der Schuld. Schuld ist Wallenstein
zunächst nur – in einem ziemlich aussermoralischen Sinne – an
seinem eigenen Untergang, mithin am Misslingen seines mit dem
Abfall verbundenen Unternehmens, ganz gleichgültig dagegen,
ob dieses nun den Namen Verrat verdient oder nicht; und nur
beiläufig steht seine Mitschuld am Untergange der ihm nächst
Stehenden im Blickfeld. Gleichwohl ist Wallenstein damit schuldig in einem noch tieferen Sinne: schuldig nämlich an einem Verderbnis der Tat als solcher, unabhängig von ihrer Bewertung,
einem Verderbnis des Handelns als solchen, schuldig nämlich an
einem Irrtum, welcher ihn auf den ersten Blick gerade sogar an
allem unschuldig erscheinen lassen könnte.

Allenfalls mag "Wallenstein" ein Schicksalsdrama heissen. Es
ist zuerst das Drama, wie es sich in dem glaubwürdigen Bekenntnis des nahe vor der Entscheidung Stehenden im grossen Monolog
des vierten Auftritts des Ersten Aufzugs von "Wallensteins Tod"
ausspricht:

> Wär's möglich? Könnt' ich nicht mehr, wie ich wollte?
> Nicht mehr zurück, wie mir's beliebt? Ich müsste
> Die Tat *vollbringen*, weil ich sie *gedacht*,
> Nicht die Versuchung von mir wies – das Herz
> Genährt mit diesem Traum, auf ungewisse
> Erfüllung hin die Mittel mir gespart,

> Die Wege bloss mir offen hab' gehalten? –
> Beim grossen Gott des Himmels! Es war nicht
> Mein Ernst, beschlossne Sache war es nie.
> In dem Gedanken bloss gefiel ich mir;
> Die Freiheit reizte mich und das Vermögen.
> War's unrecht, an dem Gaukelbilde mich
> der königlichen Hoffnung zu ergötzen?
> Blieb in der Brust mir nicht der Wille frei,
> Und sah ich nicht den guten Weg zur Seite,
> Der mir die Rückkehr offen stets bewahrte?
> Wohin denn seh' ich plötzlich mich geführt?
> Bahnlos liegt's hinter mir, und eine Mauer
> Aus meinen eignen Werken baut sich auf,
> Die mir die Umkehr türmend hemmt!

Wallenstein ist hier offenbar aufrichtig mit sich selbst. Er gesteht – so kurz zuvor auch vor Illo und Terzky im dritten Auftritt –, er habe "zu frei gescherzt mit dem Gedanken" an den Abfall, "die Tat ... *gedacht*," die "Versuchung" nicht "von sich gewiesen," "das Herz genährt mit diesem Traum"; jedoch:

> In dem Gedanken bloss gefiel ich mir;

> Beim grossen Gott des Himmels! Es war nicht
> Mein Ernst, beschlossne Sache war es nie.

Das ist es selbst in diesem Augenblick noch nicht. Das Spiel mit dem Gedanken aber, bleibt es nicht unschuldig wie ein jedes Spiel, sind denn nicht "die Gedanken frei"? Überdies war das Spiel mit *diesem* Gedanken selber vor allem Wallensteins Sich-gefallen im Gefühl der Freiheit:

> In dem Gedanken bloss gefiel ich mir;
> Die Freiheit reizte mich und das Vermögen.

Was er *könnte*, nämlich am Ende selber sich zum König (von Böhmen) aufwerfen, gibt ihm den Begriff seiner *wirklichen* Unabhängigkeit, die er besitzt, auch ohne dass es dazu der Vollbringung bedürfte. Dass dem so ist, hat der erste Teil des dramatischen Gedichts gezeigt: "Wallensteins Lager."

Nun aber widerfuhr Wallenstein sein – wie es scheint, seltsames – Schicksal: Er schien nur frei zu spielen mit dem Gedanken, der selber ein Gedanke nur der Freiheit, "sein eigenes Spiel zu spielen," war; aber die Wirklichkeit nahm dies Gedankenspiel beim Wort und unterwarf den Spieler einem Zwang, endlich zu tun, was er nur dachte, und zwar dem Zwang, *weil* er es *dachte*, es tun zu müssen. Wie es dazu kommt, legt der zweite Teil des dramatischen Gedichts dar: "Die Piccolomini." Der dritte Teil – "Wallensteins Tod" – beginnt damit, dass er sich fragen muss:

> Wie? Sollt' ich's nun im Ernst erfüllen müssen,
> Weil ich zu frei gescherzt mit dem Gedanken?
> Verflucht, wer mit dem Teufel spielt!

Und gleich darauf, für sich allein, noch deutlicher, nach dem Willen des Dichters mit dem Nachdruck auf den Worten "Vollbringen" und "Denken":

> Wär's möglich? Könnt' ich nicht mehr, wie ich wollte?
> Nicht mehr zurück, wie mir's beliebt? Ich müsste
> Die Tat *vollbringen*, weil ich sie *gedacht*?

Wenn dies sein "Schicksal" ist, dass er zu einer Tat verurteilt ist, bloss weil er mit dem Gedanken an die Tat gespielt hat, dann ist dies Schicksal aber keineswegs ein "blindes," vielmehr im Gegenteil ein allzu aufmerksames, scharfsinniges, kein Schicksal, das "nicht des Menschen achtet," vielmehr ein solches, das ihm noch seine Träume von den Augen abliest – und erfüllt.

Das Dramatische ist also zuerst dies: Es erweist sich, dass der "blosse Gedanke" *nicht* blosses Spiel, gegen die Wirklichkeit "freies" "Vermögen," unschuldig-wirkungslos bleibt noch zu bleiben vermag, wie er auch will, vielmehr selbst in der Wirklichkeit stattfindet, selbst zur zwingenden Ursache unausweichlicher Folgen in der Wirklichkeit wird oder vielmehr von vornherein als wirksame Ursache von zwingender Wirkung wirklich ist. Nicht unschuldig-wirkungslos ist der Gedanke – das will präzisiert sein in seinem zunächst völlig aussermoralischen Sinn: von "Schuld" ist hier zunächst allein die Rede in der Bedeutung, in der man von einem Umstand z.B. sagt, er sei "schuld" am Ablauf irgendeines Geschehens, er sei dafür "verantwortlich" zu machen. "Unschuldig" heisst in diesem Sinne dann gar nichts anderes als wirkungs-, folgenlos. *Das* ist es, was der Gedanke *nicht* ist.

Man könnte ja freilich in Erwägungen über die Frage eintreten,

ob es nicht moralisch unschuldige und moralisch schon als Gedankenspiele verwerfliche Gedankenspiele gibt; als Spiel mit moralisch zulässigen und moralisch unstatthaften Gedanken. Dann
wäre im vorliegenden Falle Wallenstein die Gewissensfrage zu
stellen, ob nicht ein Spiel mit dem blossen Gedanken, wenn es
Spiel mit dem Gedanken an Verrat ist, den Spieler bereits zum
Verräter macht – wenngleich noch nicht in der Tat. Aber nicht
das ist es, worum es hier in erster Linie geht. Es scheint nämlich
ganz und gar, als ob der Gedanke an den Abfall Wallenstein zum
Abfall in der Tat gerade zwinge, *insofern* er im moralischen Sinne
unschuldig, bloss spielerisch, im Bewusstsein eines "unverführten
Willens" gedacht war.

Auf Wallensteins Ausruf: "Verflucht, wer mit dem Teufel
spielt –" antwortet Illo:

> Wenn's nur dein Spiel gewesen, glaube mir,
> Du wirst's in schwerem Ernste büssen müssen.

Und Wallenstein selber begreift, wie er es in dem angeführten
Monolog ausspricht, nachdem er "tiefsinnig stehen" geblieben:

> Strafbar erschein' ich, und ich kann die Schuld,
> Wie ich's versuchen mag! nicht von mir wälzen;
> Denn mich verklagt der Doppelsinnn des Lebens,
> Und – selbst der frommen Quelle reine Tat
> Wird der Verdacht, schlimmdeutend, mir vergiften.
> War ich, wofür ich gelte, der Verräter,
> Ich hätte mir den guten Schein gespart,
> Die Hülle hätt' ich dicht um mich gezogen,
> Dem Unmut Stimme nie geliehn. Der Unschuld,
> Des unverführten Willens mir bewusst,
> Gab ich der Laune Raum, der Leidenschaft –
> Kühn war das Wort, weil es die Tat nicht war.
> Jetzt werden sie, was planlos ist geschehn,
> Weitsehend, planvoll mir zusammenknüpfen,
> Und was der Zorn und was der frohe Mut
> Mich sprechen liess im Überfluss des Herzens,
> Zu künstlichem Gewebe mir vereinen
> Und eine Klage furchtbar draus bereiten,
> Dagegen ich verstummen muss. So hab' ich

Mit eignem Netz verderblich mich umstrickt,
Und nur Gewalttat kann es reissend lösen.

Gerade so, gerade dadurch zeitigt der Gedanke seine Wallenstein
zur Vollbringung der gedachten Tat zwingenden Folgen, dass er
bloss spielerisch gedacht war, nie "im Ernst" an seine Ausführung.
Eben daher nämlich hat Wallenstein nicht daran gedacht, sich
"den guten Schein zu sparen," hat er nicht, wie einer getan hätte,
der wirklich auf Verrat sann, "die Hülle dicht um sich gezogen,"
hat er offen "dem Unmut Stimme geliehen," der "Laune," der
"Leidenschaft" "Raum gegeben" –

Kühn war das Wort, weil es die Tat nicht war –

und das, in der Tat, bestätigt ihm später die Gräfin Terzky, die
ihm die Unentschlossenheit zum Vorwurf macht:

Nur in Entwürfen bist du tapfer, feig
In Taten?

Gerade so entstand ein "Doppelsinn des Lebens" Wallensteins,
der ihn dem Kaiser verdächtig machte, den Kaiser veranlasste,
vorsorglich-vorbehaltlich (vorbehaltlich noch fehlender Beweise
des Verrats) Wallensteins Entlassung vorzusehen, was Wallenstein, dem diese Drohung nicht verborgen bleiben konnte, zu
weiteren Schritten, zunächst bloss zur Sicherung seiner Stellung
gemeint, drängte, die ihrerseits den Verdacht der Kaisertreuen
verschärften, das letzte Vertrauen zerstörten, was endlich Wallenstein in die Zwangslage und zum Äussersten trieb.

Wie dies im einzelnen geschah, wie also es endlich dazu kam,
dass Wallenstein "die Tat *vollbringen*" musste, "weil er sie *gedacht*," ist hier nicht nachzuerzählen. Nur dramatisch ist darzu-
stellen und als Möglichkeit wahrscheinlich zu machen an einem
beispielhaften Fall, dass es einmal so hat geschehen können, hier,
dass einer eine Tat *vollbringen* musste, weil er sie *gedacht*. Der Interpret kann lediglich darauf hinweisen, *was* hier der Dichter am Ende
gezeigt hat und was es bedeutet, eben das Genannte im vorliegenden Falle, dessen Bedeutung fast unermesslich ist: Wenn nämlich
dies *einmal* geschehen kann, dass einer eine Tat *vollbringen* muss,
nur weil er sie *gedacht*, dann ist der Wahn erschüttert, es vermöchte überhaupt inmitten der Wirklichkeit, doch nicht in sie
verstrickt, bloss unschuldig zusehend, ein Unwirkliches zu sein,

genannt Geist, Bewusstsein, Denken: nichts bewirkend, und so aus der wirklichen Welt herausgelöst, allein betrachtend, und so doch wiederum alles – auf geisterhafte Weise, mit dem Blick – umfassend. Gedanken vielmehr wären "Werke" – wie Wallenstein auf seine Frage

> Wär's möglich? Könnt' ich nicht mehr, wie ich wollte?
> Nicht mehr zurück, wie mir's beliebt? Ich müsste
> Die Tat *vollbringen*, weil ich sie *gedacht*?

sich selber antwortet mit den Worten:

> Bahnlos liegt's hinter mir, und eine Mauer
> Aus meinen eignen Werken baut sich auf,
> Die mir die Umkehr türmend hemmt!

Wie aber verhält sich denn zu alledem, wenn es wahr ist, der schon vorangegangene erste Auftritt von "Wallensteins Tod," wo der General nach Betrachtung der Himmelskonjunktur schon ominös beschliesst:

> Saturnus' Reich ist aus, der die geheime
> Geburt der Dinge in dem Erdenschoss
> Und in den Tiefen des Gemüts beherrscht
> Und über allem, was das Licht scheut, waltet.
> Nicht Zeit ist's mehr, zu brüten und zu sinnen,
> Denn Jupiter, der glänzende, regiert
> Und zieht das dunkel zubereitete Werk
> Gewaltig in das Reich des Lichts – Jetzt muss
> Gehandelt werden, schleunig, eh die Glücks-
> Gestalt mir wieder wegflieht überm Haupt,
> Denn stets in Wandlung ist der Himmelsbogen.

Hier scheint er selbst zu ahnen, dass "in den Tiefen des Gemüts" nicht minder als "in dem Erdenschoss" sich "die geheime Geburt der Dinge" vollzieht und eine Macht der Wirklichkeit das, "was das Licht scheut," wie ein Gedanke an Verrat, "gewaltig in das Reich des Lichts zieht." Und überdies – hier scheint er schon zur Tat entschlossen:

> Nicht Zeit ist's mehr, zu brüten und zu sinnen . . .
>   Jetzt muss
> Gehandelt werden, schleunig!

Ist Wallenstein doch unwahrhaftig, wenn er sodann, wiewohl mit sich allein, beteuert:

> Beim grossen Gott des Himmels! Es war nicht
> Mein Ernst, beschlossne Sache war es nie –?

Und wiederum, auch dann noch scheint die Entscheidung nicht ganz gefallen, er selber fällt sie erst im Schlussauftritt des Aktes, und dies nicht ohne zu gestehen, dass ihm denn doch nicht schlechthin (keine) Wahl mehr blieb: Die Gräfin Terzky selbst, die ihn zu dem Entschluss bewegen will, ist überzeugt:

> Gesetzlich ihn zu richten,
> Fehlt's an Beweisen; Willkür meiden sie.
> Man wird den Herzog ruhig lassen ziehn ...
> An einem Morgen ist der Herzog fort.
> Auf seinen Schlössern wird es nun lebendig,
> Dort wird er jagen, baun, Gestüte halten,
> Sich eine Hofstatt gründen ...

Wallenstein aber, vor diese Wahl gestellt, "steht auf, heftig bewegt," und ist nunmehr entschlossen:

> Wenn ich nicht wirke mehr, bin ich vernichtet;
> Nicht Opfer, nicht Gefahren will ich scheun,
> Den letzten Schritt, den äussersten, zu meiden;
> Doch eh' ich sinke in die Nichtigkeit,
> So klein aufhöre, der so gross begonnen ...

Keine Wahl bleibt ihm allein, sofern er "wirken" will und muss, und sich "vernichtet" fühlt, wenn er nicht "wirken" kann. Wie entwirrt sich das?

Wahr ist, dass Wallenstein gezwungen ist, zu handeln, wie er handeln wird, nur wenn er wirken will; es bliebe ihm der Ausweg in die "Nichtigkeit." Wahr bleibt nicht minder sein Bekenntnis – "beschlossne Sache war es nie." Im Angesicht der Himmelskonjunktur war er, gleichwohl, bereits "entschlossen" – doch gerade nicht zur *Tat*, sondern: sich der Notwendigkeit, und ihr allein, zu fügen. Alles klärt sich endlich auf, achten wir auf ein letztes Bekenntnis, welches Wallenstein zu Beginn des Zweiten Aufzuges Max Piccolomini macht, im Unterschiede zu dem des grossen Selbstgesprächs verräterisch beiläufig und ungewollt:

Der Jugend glückliches Gefühl ergreift
Das Rechte leicht, und eine Freude ist's,
Das eigne Urteil prüfend auszuüben,
Wo das Exempel rein zu lösen ist.
Doch wo von zwei gewissen Übeln eins
Ergriffen werden muss, wo sich das Herz
Nicht *ganz* zurückbringt aus dem Streit der Pflichten,
Da ist es Wohltat, keine Wahl zu haben,
Und eine Gunst ist die Notwendigkeit.
– Die ist vorhanden. Blicke nicht zurück.
Es kann dir nichts mehr helfen. Blicke vorwärts!
Urteile nicht! Bereite dich, zu handeln.

Der schicksalhafte Zwang, den Wallenstein zuvor beklagt, er hat ihn selbst *gesucht*. Er wollte "wirken," doch des Entschlusses, und damit der Verantwortung, ja schon des "Urteils," überhoben sein. Er "spielte in der Tat nur mit dem Gedanken an den Abfall, doch in der Rechnung darauf, dass der Gedanke selbst, von einem Gott "gewaltig in das Reich des Lichts gezogen," ihn zwingen würde, ihn zu *"vollbringen"* in der Tat, bloss weil er ihn *"gedacht,"* so dass die Tat die seine – und doch nicht seine wäre. Nicht unaufrichtig war seine Klage, Zwang zu erleiden. Denn mit Leiden, mit Schmerz, wird jeder Zwang erfahren; und Leiden spricht sich in Klagen aus. Doch dieses Leiden, das Gezwungenwerden, eben suchte er, ohne dass freilich bloss daher Zwang und Leiden aufhören könnten, Zwang und Leiden zu sein.

Dies ist Wallensteins "böser Geist," hier tritt über das Schicksalhafte hinaus denn doch seine Schuld ans Licht, eine Schuld auch im "moralischen" Sinne. Aber auch hier betrifft sie nur nebenher und vielleicht den Umstand, dass die Handlung, in deren Notwendigkeit sich versetzt zu sehen er spekulierte, etwa den Namen "Verrat" verdient. Wallensteins Schuld ist vielmehr, dass er Wirken im Leiden, Freiheit im Zwange, Tat in der Notwendigkeit, Ernst im Spiele sucht: und somit schuld ist an der Verderbnis alles Handelns selbst, des Ernstes der Verantwortung der freien Tat.

Die Gräfin Terzky denkt:

Entworfen bloss, ist's ein gemeiner Frevel,
Vollführt, ist's ein unsterblich Unternehmen;

Und wenn es glückt, so ist es auch verziehn,
Denn aller Ausgang ist ein Gottesurteil.

Sie irrt. Wallensteins Tat ist von Grund aus verderbt. Es vermag
nicht einmal das mit ihr verbundene Vorhaben ans Licht zu treten,
so dass ein Urteil über ihre moralische Bedeutung möglich würde. Weil Wallenstein sich selber seine Tat nicht unzweideutig zu
eigen macht, vermag er auch niemand anders, ausser Terzkys
und Illos, an seinem Vorhaben ernstlich teilhaben zu lassen und
somit für sich zu gewinnen. Er steht zuletzt allein. Wie alle Menschen ihn verlassen, weil in Wahrheit er selbst, bloss auf die Sterne rechnend und die "Gunst" einer Notwendigkeit, seine Tat
buchstäblich zur Un-Tat entstellend, zum voraus alle Menschen
verlassen und das Menschliche verraten hat: das zeigt der Ablauf
des dritten Teils des dramatischen Gedichts, "Wallensteins Tod."

Ganz ohne Folgen in der Wirklichkeit bleibt vermutlich kein
einziger Gedanke. Als wahrhaft folgenschwer, so den Zwang zur
Vollbringung eben einer gedachten Handlung nach sich ziehend,
erweisen sich hier aber Gedanken, die keineswegs etwa nur eitle
Träume eines phantastischen Ehrgeizes sind, vielmehr vollkommen gegebenen Realitäten und realen Möglichkeiten entsprechen.
Was sich in Wallensteins Gedankenspielen (scheinbar nur) "wider-
spiegelt," worauf er selber in ihnen "spekuliert," das ist der Lauf,
ein Lauf der Dinge selbst. Sein Rechnen auf die "Gunst" einer
"Notwendigkeit" verrät sich nicht etwa nur in jenem unbedach-
ten Wort zu Max, sondern aufs allerdeutlichste in seinem Sternen-
glauben. Dieser ist der klarste Ausdruck von Wallensteins Sucht,
wirken zu wollen, doch ohne wahrhaft eigenen Entschluss, unter
dem Zwange "objektiver" Notwendigkeit, seiner Spekulation,
durch den Gedanken, mit dem er spielt, sich selbst dem Zwange
zur Vollbringung auszusetzen, die unausweichlich zwingende
Notwendigkeit herbeizuführen. (Freilich erschrickt er selbst, als
dieses Spiel ihm glückt – und wirkt der Zwang nur unter der Be-
dingung, dass jedenfalls er selber doch "wirken" überhaupt will.)
Wallensteins Gedankenspiele sind ernsthafte auf ihre Weise,
insofern er ihnen nachgeht von einem Standpunkt der Beobach-
tung, von der erhöhten Warte des Observatoriums. Astrologie –
das ist ein Zerrbild der Wissenschaft von der Natur in ihrem

grössten Umfang, aber doch ein Bild, ja Vorbild dieser Wissenschaft, verzerrt nur von Spekulationen, wie wir sie am Ende alle, wie Wallenstein, mit der Vorstellung von objektiv und zwingend evident Gegebenem verbinden. Astrologie – das ist nichts andres als der "Geist," der der "Natur" vertraut, von ihr sich leiten lässt, sich ihrem Laufe anpasst und unterwirft und herrschen – sogar sie selbst beherrschen – will, indem er nur ihr eigenes Gesetz vollstreckt. Dies hat Max von Wallenstein erraten ("Die Piccolomini," I, 4); er ist ihm ein geborener Herrscher:

> Mit jeder Kraft dazu
> Ist er's, und mit der Kraft noch obendrein,
> Buchstäblich zu vollstrecken die Natur,
> Dem Herrschtalent den Herrschplatz zu erobern.

Dieses Einssein eines Geistes mit der Natur, deren Orakel er in sich lauscht und die er nur vollstreckt, das ist für Max "das Ungemeine," ja "das Höchste selbst" an Wallenstein:

> Da rufen sie den Geist an in der Not,
> Und grauet ihnen gleich, wenn er sich zeigt.
> Das Ungemeine soll, das Höchste selbst
> Geschehn wie das Alltägliche ...
>   Es braucht
> Der Feldherr jedes Grosse der Natur,
> So gönne man ihm auch, in ihren grossen
> Verhältnissen zu leben. Das Orakel
> In seinem Innern, das lebendige,
> Nicht tote Bücher, alte Ordnungen,
> Nicht modrigte Papiere soll er fragen.

Wallensteins Astrologie, in diesem Licht gesehen, erscheint mit gleichem Pathos, in gleichem Gegensatz zu "toten Büchern," "alten Ordnungen" und "modrigten Papieren," wie die moderne Wissenschaft von der Natur schlechthin.

Illo begreift nicht dieses "lumen naturale," dem sich sein Herr vertraut, wenn er sich von den Sternen leiten lassen will:

> O! du wirst auf die Sternenstunde warten,
> Bis dir die irdische entflieht! Glaub mir,
> In deiner Brust sind deines Schicksals Sterne.

> Vertrauen zu dir selbst, Entschlossenheit
> Ist deine Venus! Der Maleficus,
> Der einz'ge, der dir schadet, ist der *Zweifel.*

"Du redst, wie du's verstehst," antwortet ihm Wallenstein "(Die Piccolomini," II, 6). Sind doch die Sterne, ist doch die Natur ihm selber "das Orakel in seinem Innern, das lebendige." So ruft er endlich aus, als er "entschlossen" ist:

> Geschehe denn, was muss!
> Recht stets behält das Schicksal, denn das Herz
> In uns ist sein gebietrischer Vollzieher.

Sind wir aber denn nicht alle solche Sternengläubige wie Wallenstein? Glauben wir nicht alle, das Rechte dann zu tun, wenn die "Natur" uns selber, klar erkannt, zwingt und vorschreibt, wie wir handeln müssen? Wollen wir nicht alle uns am liebsten jederlei Entschluss entziehen, vielmehr allein von zwingend objektiver Wissenschaft uns leiten lassen, die unser Meinen, Glauben, Wollen ruhen lässt und die Verantwortung uns abnimmt? Ist nicht darum unsere Idee von Wissen, worauf die Menschheit ihre Hoffnung für die Zukunft setzt, noch immer die der Theorie, so dass wir überzeugt sind, auch für die Praxis einer Weltbeherrschung sei die beste Basis die Wissenschaft als reine Theorie in strenger Objektivität? Warum denn? Weil sie ein Handeln möglich macht, das der Natur, wie sie an sich ist, sich unterwirft und anpasst – "mit der Kraft, buchstäblich zu vollstrecken die Natur."

Wie aber, wenn wir alle, wie Wallenstein, so auf die Sterne spekulierend, in Wahrheit die Notwendigkeit, der wir allein uns fügen wollen, erst uns zwingen *liessen*, wenn *wir* erst das "Notwendige" notwendig *machten, weil* wir uns nur zwingen lassen *wollten*? Dieser geheime Wille Wallensteins - muss ich von ihm sagen:

> Es ist sein böser Geist und meiner – ?

Dann wäre Wallensteins Tragödie, wie Schiller sie erriet, die Tragödie unserer Zeit.

Dann wäre Descartes' äusserster Zweifel berechtigter gewesen, als er selber ernsthaft meinte. Übrigens hat diesen Zweifel auch nicht erst Descartes erfunden. Er erhebt sich bereits seit der ersten Darlegung des Ideals rein theoretischen Wissens durch Aristoteles, der bedenkt, dass nach dem Spruch des Dichters Simonides von Keos "wohl ein Gott allein ein solches Vorrecht besitzt, es dem Menschen aber nicht ansteht, nach einem anderen Wissen als dem ihm gemässen zu streben": θεὸς ἂν μόνος τοῦτ' ἔχοι γίρας, ἄνδρα δ'οὐκ ἄξιον τὸ μὴ οὐ ζητεῖν τὴν καθ' αὑτὸν ἐπιστήμην (982 b 30–31). Wenn jenes Wissenwollen (wofür die Philosophie erklärt wird) aber in der Tat den Menschen verdürbe, warum sollte uns ein solches Wissen gleichwohl noch als göttlich gelten?

EDWARD G. BALLARD
Tulane University

"ALMS FOR OBLIVION":
AN ESSAY ON OBJECTIVE TIME AND EXPERIENCED TIME*

If one should hesitate to ask the professional philosopher about time, having despaired of finding a viable definition of anything other than an abstract succession, it might be not unprofitable to inquire of the poet. Suppose, therefore, we were to stop a poet at a street corner somewhere and ask him about time. He might reply with a reference to St. Augustine's profound and evasive remark about it. Or were his memory less medieval, he might reply with the recollection from Shakespeare:

> A Wallet at his back, Time hath my Lord,
> Wherein he puts alms for oblivion.

Or again a poet might suggest that time is like a red carpet which unrolls before us as we move to meet our fate; perhaps adding that we can, if we choose, pause to examine its weave. In any event, the poet would probably answer, if at all, not with a definition but with a reference to something rather like time.

We know from the reflections and speculations of philosophers, if not from our own experience, that time is not an object, nor a class of objects, nor a thing of any sort. Objective time, which is thing-like in that it can be divided and measured in incredibly small or large quantities, is scarcely the time through or in which we live. Nevertheless, experienced and objective times are probably related, but related in a more complex manner than usual

---

* An earlier version of this essay was read, at Professor Herbert Spiegelberg's kind invitation, before the fourth Phenomenological Workshop at Washington University (June, 1969). The present version owes a great deal to criticisms and comments received from Professor Spiegelberg and members of the workshop.

talk of "abstraction" would allow. What sort of being is time like? How many kinds of time are there? How are these kinds related to each other? These questions are not less important because some writers, including some philosophers, are persuaded that objective or clock time is an arbitrary artifice which has robbed action and history of their human character and value.

In this essay I want first to develop the present question about time a little further. Then I shall attempt in a second part to indicate some of the steps leading to a concept of the dependent and derived character of the objective time which is divided and counted; and in the last part I shall suggest something like the time and its structure from which objective time appears at least in part to be derived.

A. The Question about the Experience of Time

If one were asked to describe the passage of time taken, for instance, to eat lunch, the reply might be that it took just forty-seven minutes. If this answer were criticized as being rather too general since it failed altogether to describe the *passage* of that time and referred only to its conventionally measured quantity, then one might attempt to allow for this observation by pointing out that absolutely every existent thing is involved in the passage of time. Thus time is ubiquitous, like being. Everything is in time and modifies its time by its presence; hence, an adequate characterization of the passage of time would have to take cognizance of its infinitely varied contents: an impossible task.

Then, when again asked at least to make an effort to describe the passage of time, one might take refuge in Kant's remark that time itself is not experienced. The request to describe it is, therefore, quite unreasonable since one must in some sense experience a thing in order to have something to describe. What is experienced is just events in succession. There is no time apart from this succession. To suppose that there is a time apart from this succession may be to allow oneself to be tricked by language; the fact that we do make use of a word "time" does not entail that there must be either some empty substantial thing or some impalpable flux to which this word corresponds.

Just the character of this succession called time, however, is in question. There are many kinds of succession. Why is one type of succession called temporal, another dynastic, another dramatic, another mathematical, another spatial? The question is particularly pressing when one contemplates what is often said about time: that it flows "mathematically without regard to circumstance." Such was Newton's description, and such, though somewhat modified, is the belief often held today both by physicists and laymen. But such an empty succession, imagined to occur without regard to circumstance or experience, is most difficult to understand. By what means could one moment of this uncircumstantial flow be distinguished from another?

In any event, time experienced as a passage is phenomenal and will have to be approached through phenomena and their succession. It will not, then, do to identify time at the outset with one of its abstract properties, nor with the full particularity of its contents, nor with some imagined empty and circumstance-less duration.

If one does resolve not to accept such an easy identification of time, then the so-called temporal illusions acquire a particularly puzzling aspect. If one were to drive from New Orleans to Saint Louis and then back again at the same speed and by the same route, the time back would doubtless appear to be much shorter than the time there. But this appearance is usually judged to be illusory, since the clock-time taken up by the two halves of the journey would be approximately equal. Now, this equality is judged by one who is persuaded he already knows what equal time intervals are. He is persuaded a priori that the clock and not the traveler's sense of time is the proper judge. He has tacitly agreed that real time is time viewed through Newtonian analogies, that any other kind of judgment yields only illusion. Still, there are and have been other ways of understanding time. If we are willing to take the traveler's time-sense seriously, that is, if we are really concerned about the experience of time, such favorite ways of judging it as the Newtonian way, must be put aside in favor of the phenomena of time as actually experienced.

Let us attempt to turn directly to the phenomena of time. Unfortunately, the decision not to be guided by sophisticated and quantitative views of time does not indicate in a positive fashion where the phenomena appropriate for study are to be found. The initial step certainly requires choosing events or phenomena in which the essential character of time or the essentially temporal character of experience can be "read off." Then this essence may somehow be rendered explicit. How, though, will a temporal phenomenon be recognized? That is, how can we choose a phenomenon which we are sure a priori will contain all the elements belonging to the kind of succession called temporal? Will the poet or the historian be best able to designate such a phenomenal succession? It is persistently difficult to see at this turn why the successful and generally credited definitions of the physicist should not be accepted as adequate. Surely we do have experience of time pieces. Still, clocks have not always been among us. The fact is that time has a history, and this history may in some way be determinative of time as experienced.

Men have always known that time waits on no man, and now it is frequently taken to be the basic invariant. Thus, the time of physics has always in the modern age seemed to be preeminently real. But only in the modern age. The modern concept has been formed by means of a number of images which have had their day in various historical periods. Time, for instance, has been likened to a woven web, to a spun thread, to a flowing river, to a pathway, to a rotating wheel, to a full or empty container. Analogies such as these have in fact been thought to point to the most trustworthy experience of time. The measuring of time by an object in unaccelerated linear motion or possessing constant angular velocity is merely one among the latest of these analogies. Is there any reason, in the attempt to understand time, why we should not seek guidance from some other than this last analogy? No doubt each of us thinks he can recognize a temporal phenomenon, even if he cannot explicate it further without some such analogy. Hence, I think it desirable to pass in review several of the analogies through which time has in fact been viewed. I begin with one which has contributed something to the objectivist view of time and which likewise manifests some of the weaknesses of this view. Other images will carry this historical formation further. Then this consideration will open the way to a more concrete and perhaps a more basic view of time and its relation to chronometrics.

B. The Analogies of Time

The first analogy belonged to the ancient Greeks and is expressed by Homer in terms drawn from the art of weaving. The full image to which Homer recurs suggests that the effective embodiment of fate is a web or net woven by the Morai at the instance of Fate itself or by command of Zeus and bound upon men.[1] In this web the warp[2] threads are time or length of life. For the Greeks, this time is the duration allowed for living; it is the continuation of the succession of events. Its moments are differentiated by varying experiences. The woof (O. E. *wefan:* "to weave") threads are the fated events experienced, the things ordained. The tapestry, thus woven from day to day and bound upon men according to the design of fate, or of Zeus, is unchangeable. Upon this latter point, it is true, ancient man was not altogether decided. Within undefined limits a freedom was sometimes conceived. A man might live peacefully and in harmony with his fate by his own good choice, or he might make it worse by foolish or arrogant decisions. But how or to just what degree his decisions affected fate was a problem with which he did not attempt to reckon.

Now if this ancient analogy were taken seriously, it might be supposed to render time as duration or succession (quantity of days) accessible by the simple expedient of suppressing the woof threads (time as event). Thus by eliminating or ignoring human events or experiences in all their variety, the warp threads which hold events together in an orderly succession would be laid bare. At least such a separation serves to emphasize certain aspects of the orderliness of temporal succession which conserve some of the factors of the Greek notion of an unchanging and impersonal fate. For instance, time may take from the ancient sense of fate the irreversibility of the order of events. Another fateful aspect of time is the sameness of its pace for all things, the necessity that each of us, indeed of all things in the universe, should reach January first upon just the same instant. It seems to be but a step from the observation of these two properties of temporal

---

[1] E.g. *Iliad* xx, 127; cf. also Plato, *Republic* X, 616.

[2] O.E. *warpen* refers to twisting or spinning a thread. The Greek Καῖρος referred to the thrums to which the warp threads were fastened.

succession, its irreversibility and its constant flow, to the measurement of time. For the irreversibility and the constancy of time hold for all things. These properties appear to be independent of the contents of time and thus to be conceivable separately from "all things." They point to the possibility of dividing temporal succession into intervals which would be equally relevant to any temporal content.

It is also possible to see how the properties of divisibility and measurability became integral elements of objective time by an inspection of other analogies. Another such analogy is the river. If time is a lengthening thread, let it be a thread of flowing water. This image emphasizes the warp character of time and the irrelevancy of the woof (events). For all water is alike as water; thus it becomes easy to think of the events which diversify time as being like additions to the water which change its appearance but do not alter its flow. Cosmic time, then, is like a river which flows irresistibly past the observer on its banks, and carries with it events like driftwood. This flow is irreversible and constant. A water clock is a small representation of this river. It marks the time of an event or a small number of events within a microcosmic part of the universe. Also it is small enough so that its flow may be artificially started and stopped in order to mark the quantity of time of that microcosmic part of the universe. Then the weight or volume of water which flows during an event is identified as the measure of the duration of the event. The quantity of time and the weight of water correspond to each other in a presumably constant manner.

Galileo used the water clock in this way. It was, furthermore, not difficult for him to think of time as moving through other sorts of machines which would divide and measure its flow by means of some handy regularity. According to legend, he sat bored by a sermon in church one day and observed a chandelier swinging to and fro in the changing wind. He idly timed its period by his pulse beat; then the essential fact concerning the pendulum broke upon him: the relation of its period to its length. From the moment of that insight, the invention of the pendulum clock was not far distant. The metaphoric shift is not great which sees time as something which flows like a small river through a water clock, or which moves through one's veins and is marked by the pulse beat, or which flows, as it were, through a clock and is marked by the swing of a pendulum. A more modern analogy might picture time as a magnetic tape with seconds marked on it, running through a tape recorder; the whole universe might be taken as the tape recorder. Thus time became objective, independent of men's experiences, an empty universally measurable quantity, the independent variable of physics.

A modern musician whose mind is possessed by such an analogy might think of this empty flow as a framework to be filled up with the sounds which he likes to hear, very much as some painters think of a white canvas as an emptiness to be filled up with the shapes and colors which interest them. Such time runs on as well without man as with him. It is independent of its content; man, events, history, are merely the contingent filling of its vacancy. Once the warp of time – its quantifiable duration – is separated from the woof (its contents), the two soon come to appear to be intrinsically separate and independent of each other. Time comes to appear to be one and the same empty and characterless duration, receptive of infinitely varying contents. Thus we might speak quite seriously (and literally) of pre-historic time, or of the eons which the nebulae spun out before the hardening of the earth and will spin out after its destruction.

This objective time is, then, in sum, independent of its content; it is an irreversible, constant, divisible, and hence a measurable flow or succession. For our purposes it may be viewed as a sophistication of the warp threads of the fateful web imagined by the Homeric Greeks to determine or to limit human action or it may be the flow of a river which carries events steadily and irrevocably upon its course. But, if it be thought in this manner, the question arises how it may be related again to the events, human and other, which happen in history. Our metaphors have suggested a separation of events, the temporal content, from the time flow which bears them on. We must ask: how radical is this separation? How does it happen that events seem to make all the difference in human time and none in objective time?

In what way are events and the empty duration which they occupy related to each other? Merleau-Ponty points out that the observer of events must admit that he himself is in time; that is, he himself is one of those things borne along by the river of time. He does not stand independently aside on the bank watching the flow. As soon as he admits his own temporal flowing, then he tends to identify himself with his life-time and so to think of events as objects along the bank which he views as he passes them. Now one of those things (or contents) observed along the banks of time are the warp threads of our previous analogy. Also the constant flow of the water in the clepshydra, the flow of blood punctuated by the pulse, the abstract flow in the clock, or the empty succession which the physicist measures, all are objects which the observer has found or has made and has left along the banks of time as his history bore him along. Strangest of such possibilities is the suggestion that convictions about the independence of time or its non-relation to its contents may be events in time which eventually are to be borne away on its flow. Observations like these suggest the artificial nature of objective time and are disturbing to those who hold the objective aspect of nature to be certain, basic, and given. And yet in fact, not only was the separation of the warp from the woof of time a human act, but in the first place the intimation that time bore a significant resemblance to a woven web or to a river was a historical human achievement.

These latter reflections loom like a comic reversal in the drama of time. It is as if the weight of water which passed through a clepshydra were to be measured by the duration of an event rather than vice versa. The same might also be true of the more sophisticated mechanisms for measuring the constant flow of time. So soon as one considers the matter, it appears that the tape which passes through the recorder of the universe must have had the seconds already marked upon it by someone who knew the measure of time. The same point is made by the Newtonian philosophers who attempted to argue for the necessary constancy, the mathematical flow, of time. This regularity simply could not be established, as Newton had hoped, without regard to circumstance. The circumstance selected by Newton was the movement of the stars. But he himself was quite aware that this regularity was itself an event in time and needed to be compared to some other orderly serial event by which its regularity might be measured and judged. Some philosophers today seek in nuclear disintegration the instance of perfect regularity, but one may still

ask by what measure of time this regularity is measured and established. In any case, the measure of constancy would be an
event or a temporal series of events, and such temporal circumstances are just that which are to be measured. Our conclusion
must be that the woof and circumstance of time cannot be altogether and clearly separated from the warp. In short, the warp
is imaginable only as one of the factors in the web of time.

The metaphor of the moving thread or flow, yielding time as
an independent measurable quantity, breaks down if followed
out in this manner. Hence, we must confess that the supposition
of an empty and irreversible but real and constant flow is clearly
a reified analogy, or rather it is a portion of an analogy taken
apart from its total context, as if that portion possessed an independent truth. Thus it becomes a meta-physical assumption.

To many people, some philosophers included, this objective
time appears to be the only real time. Time in any other sense is
"merely subjective," just a fantasy probably bred by linguistic
confusion. It will be interesting and useful, therefore, to suspend
these assumptions and definition of objective time and to attempt
to describe time as experienced prior to the reification of physical
time. I want, finally, to suggest that this objective time is derivative; it is a human product, made for the purpose of guiding
one in a certain way of selecting, ordering, and interpreting events.
Also convictions about the irreversibility, divisibility, constancy
and measurability of time, which guided us to the meta-physical
interpretation of it just outlined, are themselves at least events
in time, whatever else they may also be. If, therefore, we are interested in acquiring a less narrowly circular view of time, we had
best return to that concrete order to events in which we are now
living, whose orderly succession we wish to understand, and begin
again.

C. The Structure of Lived Time and of Objective Time

Another perspective upon objective time is got by returning
to and elaborating upon the human character of the passage of
events. These lived events are represented by the woof threads
in the ancient image. The woof is just that which is laid aside and
forgotten by the objectivist metaphysician and physicist. We,

on the contrary, shall now transfer our interest from the warp of the web of time to its woof.

Time understood as event is subjective; it is simply unconceived and unconceivable apart from man who lives events. It is always man who imagines the woof, the warp, and the weaving of fate or history. Even the highly contrived and sophisticated Newtonian flow, providing the independent variable for physical equations, is a meaning which men conceive and which has its being in their subjectivity. Acquaintance with it and power to use it are acquired only through a very specific discipline offered by some cultures but not by all. Time as eventful flow is obviously nonexistent apart from the beings, men, who live events. To understand time as it is experienced, then, we ought first to attempt to search out that aspect of human life which is most sensitive to, or most expressive of, the passage or the succession which – when factored with the help of an appropriate analogy – will ultimately be known as objective time.

There have been in recent years a number of attempts to characterize time as lived.[3] I shall not now review these views; rather, I shall develop a brief analytic description of time as lived, choosing as my analogy an event which will exhibit certain kinds of recurrent events or intervals. By beginning with recurrent intervals through which all men live, it may be possible to see a way to a better grasp and evaluation of the kind of time which admits of (regular) artificial divisions and measurement.

It is worth noting again the initial need and difficulty involved in choosing an instance of the awareness of time and in selecting the appropriate manner of viewing this instance. The living of time might be viewed primarily from the perspective of the future, of the past, or of the present. For instance, one who emphasizes the present is aware chiefly of the peaceful waiting, the continuous and persistent, or perhaps the boring, character of his temporal movement. One who perspects time mainly from the future senses it as anticipation of novelty, as anxiety, or as revolutionary excitement; such a one would tend to phrase his descriptions accordingly. Similarly, one who lives in the past would sense time

---

[3] Cf. H. Bergson, *Essai sur les données immédiates de la conscience* (Paris, Alcan, 1889); M. Merleau-Ponty, *Phénoménologie de la perception* (Paris, Gallimard, 1945), pt. 3, ch. II.

as a determined order, a tradition which must be conserved, else life itself be lost. Though each of these emphases is experienced and might quite validly be described, each one tends to ignore the other two. I believe it possible, on the contrary, to acquire a sense of the wholeness of time and to discover events in which the unity of its several dimensions becomes evident[4]. But we shall, in the search after such events, also have to be careful that the concrete temporal character be not allowed to disappear either in the abstract unity of a mathematical eternity or in the ineffable unity of a mystical *totum simul*. We are interested in the whole of time as commonly experienced.

Once in possession of an instance of lived time in its complete-ness, one might be able to read the essential character of lived time out of such an instance, were it adequately described. Emphasis here must fall upon the completeness of the time-inter-val, for only if it is complete, can we feel confident that we are not inadvertently contributing to the tradition of vicious ab-stractions.

Here, physical or objective time having been put aside, we are returned to our earlier question: what would be a fair illustration of a complete temporal interval? And how shall we know when an adequate example has been selected? Would a concerto which one hears to the end offer a fair illustration? But in this instance one is relying upon composer and musicians to determine what a complete interval of musical time is. Then the composer's or someone's life? But here one must rely upon the biographer to decide whether this lifetime was complete or not. Then an epoch or period in history? And here one must accept the historian's judgment when, for instance, the epoch properly began and ended. Perhaps we may avoid this dependence upon specialized and perhaps prejudiced or official viewpoints by searching for a characteristic temporal interval which belongs to the common experience of all men. There are many such items of common ex-perience from which to choose. There are the larger rhythms of birth, life, and death, the yearly recurrences of seasonal change, or the diurnal-nocturnal experiences of waking and sleep. These

---

[4] Eugene Minkowski describes cases of the disintegrated sense of time which, by way of contrast, are instructive in this regard; cf. his *Le temps vécu: études phénomé-nologiques et psychopathologiques* (Paris, 1935).

experiences appear to be needlessly complex for the present purposes. Happily, in addition, there are smaller natural intervals
marked off in the course of life, intervals such as the winking of
the eye, breathing, the beating of the pulse. Of these latter three,
I believe there is sufficiently common agreement that the heart-
beat is a quite regular recurrence. It has been thus used in history;
we have recalled that Galileo so used it upon a crucial occasion. I
choose it, therefore, as an instance of a simple, common, and essential temporal interval.

But whose pulse shall be chosen? Surely not that of Edgar
Poe's melodramatic story, "The Telltale Heart," for this heart-
throb was the voice of fear; the persistent presence of guilt, not
the passage of time, was its burden. Conversely, the heart-beat
of the healthy worker is too unobtrusive, too much an unnoticed
part of the background of his eventful activity. But though any
person can attend to his pulse, we desire our phenomenological
observer to attend to nothing else, but to attend to it with sufficient penetration to perceive its structure. Perhaps such an observer will do well to recall the attitude of a heart-disease patient
who, as he delicately feels his pulse, wonders "will there be another?" for he, surely, is aware of the living phases of his heart-beat
and of the recurrence of his pulse as a *sine qua non* of time.

Whether our patient or observer merely feels his pulse or
whether he watches the complex wave form of his cardiac rhythm
upon an oscilloscope, he will remember that each recurrence of
this rhythm is formed by three partial phases. These phases are
initiated when the auricles of the heart fill with blood from the
veins, contract, forcing blood through stop valves into the ventricles. Then, the expanded and filled ventricles contract, forcing
the blood, through other valves, into the arteries. This cardiolo-
gical detail is, however, not actually experienced and therefore
not especially relevant to one who is concerned primarily with the
experience of this rhythm. But it is to the point to observe that
the attentive patient can experience this systolic-diastolic action
as three moments within one rhythmic period: first a slight pause,
then the characteristic "lub-dub," then the same over and over
again.

He is aware upon reflection of a beginning moment, which is
followed by a mid-moment, which then comes to its conclusion

in an end-moment. Then, to his relief, the pattern begins over again.

As actually experienced, I suggest that these three moments are rather simply related. It is clear that they are not three separate elements. Rather the beginning moment is distinctive in that it is sensed as related "forward" to the mid-moment; whereas the end-moment is felt as related "backward" to the mid-moment. These two moments might be described as monadic or uni-directional; although they are directed in opposite ways, one "forward" and one "backward." They might be symbolized thus → and ← respectively. The mid-moment, however, is related in both ways, "backward" toward the beginning of the period, and "forward" to the end (like a pulse of alternating electric current). It might be symbolized thus: ↔. This symbolization suggests that the beginning and ending moments may be regarded as separated elements of the dyadic or di-directional middle moment. This latter, the middle moment, has the abstract character of a "now" or present moment as it was described by Aristotle. It is always between a past and a future. However, a "now," characterized merely as between past and future moments, is remote from a present united organically to its beginning and ending phases. Aristotle was interested in time as the measure of motion; however, we are in pursuit of a time which is more like the measure of a human action phenomenally accessible to us.

The heart-disease patient, our phenomenological observer, would further notice that the three moments of a cardiac life-interval are mutually inclusive or hierarchically ordered in a characteristic way. That is, the middle includes the beginning as leading it forward, and the end includes the middle as, so to speak, having led it forward. Hence the end moment includes the middle which in turn includes the beginning.

At the same time, the man with his finger on his pulse, projects himself on beyond the end of a given pulse-beat, in anticipation or hope, to a new beginning. That is to say, the end, which includes the middle and the beginning and so completes the period, also looks forward as a whole to a following renewal of this complex rhythmic interval or period. Such a period includes the preceding period, which in its turn includes in memory the period immediately preceding it. Ideally any period includes all the preceding and looks forward indefinitely to others. In fact, though, these retentions and anticipations break down into groups which coincide with – or are – recollected or anticipated events. Thus, there is first a hierarchical order within the life interval or period; and, secondly, each period is hierarchically related to the others preceding and following. Our lived time is this kind of ordered passage; we are, organically speaking, in this cardio-temporal becoming.

The continuity of our patient's being is a function of this rhythmic recurrence. It is not difficult to conclude that this rhythm with its peculiar structure is time itself, one's life-time. Or rather "life-time" is a pleonasm; lived time *is* life. This is the kind of time which is the condition of one's being.

It is important to emphasize at this point that the time of which we are now speaking is not an empty flow independent of its contents. Here container and contents are no longer separable. The time in which the weaver lives as he weaves is a time no longer conceivable on the analogy of a warp separate from the woof. If the analogy is to be retained, then the web must be imagined to come into existence as a unity. The living of the weaver's life-time is precisely the continual uniting of warp and woof. Only in retrospect may the warp be considered separately from the woof. Such is the burden of the expression: time is life.

Three observations must now be added to amplify and modify this view. The first is to admit that this characterization of lived time differs from that offered by many philosophers, for instance by Bergson. Bergson's famous descriptions of time as duration *vécue* emphasizes its continuity. This emphasis follows, it seems to me from his perspecting time primarily from the present. My attempt was, however, to reach a grasp of time as a whole. Time observed thus appeared partly discontinuous, its basic unit being an organic periodic interval analyzable into three components. But these periods are not altogether discontinuous; I expressed the continuity of these unit intervals in terms of the hierarchical relation among them, a relation which is observable.

My second remark must hasten to add that the significance of this cardio-time is shared by other kinds of organic rhythms.[5]

[5] An argument, however, for the quite fundamental character of cardiac time might be developed from the sense of close identity between the person and his heart; cf.

We might also have chosen the rhythm of breathing in which to localize the sense of the passage of life-time. Indeed we might choose any such bodily rhythm commonly identified with the continuance of life and presence as the temporal condition of one's continuance in being. For the artist, the weaver for example, the usual temporal rhythm may become the set of habitual movements which constitute the activity of his art and its necessary divisions.

Assuming, now, that the heart-beat does constitute a fairly typical and basic example of inorganic life-interval, also assuming that we have succeeded in reading off from this instance the essential structure – the hierarchically related beginning, middle, and end – of a complete interval of lived time, then it should be possible to find the same structure in other more complex temporal activities. And in fact it is not difficult to discover a similar structure in listening to a concerto, for instance. Or, it can be found in an artist's acceptance of a task, his actual work, and his complete embodiment of the design in materials. Or again this structure is present in a drama which presents an interval of the protagonist's life defined by his decision, his struggle to live out the terms of this decision, and his culminating insight into the real nature or possibly the inappropriateness of his decision. The same structure is likewise present in the largest time-interval, the birth, life, and death of the person. Time conceived in this manner, as precisely the concrete and rhythmically structured flow of human life, is probably best instanced in dramatic action, a complete action, as Aristotle expressed it. Thus, even if the event chosen for analysis – the cardiac patient's feeling for his pulse – was a trifle over-dramatic, it was not altogether inappropriately so. The temporality of other human activities, as well as their dramatic involvements, imitate these organic rhythms. "Time," then, may also be used in a collective sense to name the whole family of organic and lived temporal intervals and series of the same. Some of these kinds of experienced time may include others, as a long breath may include several cardiac intervals. No doubt the expression "lived time," when not otherwise modified, is normally used in this collective sense.

H. Plügge, *Wohlbefinden und Missbefinden* (Tübingen, Max Niemeyer Verlag, 1962), ch. IV.

It will in the third place be useful to observe briefly at least one further characteristic of the relations which unite the parts of an interval of time and which unite the intervals of time among themselves into a flow. I now have in mind intervals of time more complex than such organic intervals as the pulse or breathing.

An important property of these relations is indicated, I will suggest, by the concern which I have already expressed several times, for beginning with an appropriate illustration of temporality, an illustration from which the whole essential nature of time might be read. This anxiety points to a certain freedom for choosing one's guiding analogy. It also suggests an obscure conviction that one already somehow "knows" what time is and need, therefore, only take care to use this knowledge in selecting a fair example for analysis. Now one important point at this juncture is to see that the anxiety and this obscure prior knowledge already constitute a reference respectively to the future and to the past. These two references are sensed now; they are unified in this present which is constituted by the inquiry into the structure of lived time. The event of this present, in other words, like an actor in a drama, defines its own interval of time by its intrinsic references to its relevant past (its beginning) and to the future. Thus, the present inquiry functions like a confirming instance of the structure which has been disengaged.

This structure, furthermore, as thus exemplified, as now referred anxiously to the future and with conviction to the past, clearly contains noetic components. Indeed, it is not too much to say that the references of a lived present to its future and to its past are like meaning references. Lived events are significant events and are so constituted by their meaning references. These references may be the relation of symbol to referent, implication, suggestion, analogy, and the like.

The supposition that time can be used and viewed as a language is nothing new. It has been observed that time is constantly so used; for instance in the business world the interval a person is kept waiting for an appointment with an associate tells quite unmistakably whether the associate will be receptive, indifferent, or hostile.[6] This lapse of time indicates, therefore, the way in

---

[6] Cf. E. T. Hall, *The Silent Languages* (New York, Doubleday, 1959), ch. I.

which their appointment will begin. In general the relations among the elements of an interval of lived time to each other are or are like meaning relations. For example, the beginning of a significant life-interval refers (like a symbol, or perhaps like an implicans) to the middle, which in turn refers to the end. If this view is true, then the ancient observation that only man, the language using animal, lives fully through time becomes tautological. Other animals live only through some form of organic time.

Thus, in conclusion, the relations connecting the time intervals of a drama, of a single human life, or of an historical epoch are meaning relations and acquire their shape and structure in virtue of these relations. This point might be developed in detail for the several kinds of lived human time. We are concerned here, however, mainly with the relation of lived to objective time.

Here I pause to summarize: Lived time is constituted of discrete lived organic intervals having a characteristic triadic structure; the continuity of time results from its hierarchic character – from the inclusion within a present phase of its immediately past and future elements and from the inclusion of other intervals in any given interval by way of memory and anticipation; overlapping series of intervals of this sort form a family of kinds of lived time; each such interval and succession of intervals are structured in the more complex instances by meaning relations.

Of such a nature is time as lived. It is clearly inconceivable as an empty objective flow to which contents may or may not be added. It is not like a container, independent of its contents. On the contrary, lived time is woven of its contents, of events, experienced as passing.

Nevertheless, we do believe that time in some important sense is an empty objective flow to which contents may or may not be added or which is measurable independently of its contents. In what sense is this conviction justified? Now, I suggest that the kind of freedom from contents which objective time enjoys may best be seen by observing the kind of lived time which is most like an empty objective flow. In effect I want to suggest that objective time may be developed out of – or abstracted from – a certain sort of experience. This experience is that in which the natural articulations of an interval of time, its beginnings and endings, fade into insignificance.

Objective time, in other words, can scarcely be supposed to be abstracted from the temporality of just any experience. Rather it is derivable from the experienced time which is already not unlike an empty flow. Such a time is that wherein the beginnings and endings of organic intervals fade away and finally become indiscernible. But even when not discerned, we must suppose that the structural elements of a temporal interval remain as aspects of the infra-structure of lived time, so to speak, only they are not used and so can be ignored. For instance, in ordinary healthful work the rhythm of time comes from one's activity; then the pulse beat or breathing or other organic intervals are not noticed. Still these latter remain and might be elicited by an act of attention.

During periods of complete or almost complete inactivity, when attention is diffuse and expectation is at a minimum, then one may experience something approaching a contentless, event-less flow. Here nothing begins, nothing ends. Time then is experienced as a kind of waiting, a gap between matters of greater moment. This is the time which Shakespeare had in mind when he remarked,

> Thou hast not youth nor age,
> But as it were, an after-dinner sleep,
> Dreaming on both.

The objective character of such an almost contentless somnolence is not yet evident; it is still duration and is experienced as a temporary oblivion. Such a time is a vague "now" or series of nows which one may imagine to be divisible *ad libitum*. For this duration contains no intrinsic divisions. And just because one moment of it cannot be distinguished from another, it can be divided anywhere. Hence, it can be divided so as to become isomorphic with the equal divisions of (say) an Euclidean line. Then the divisions may be counted. Here the living events and rhythm of time having faded away, its sense of passage and uni-directionality disappear also; only the event of the isomorphism counts.

Furthermore, the experience of an impersonal flow, a mere passage, is objectively relevant in another way. Without much exercise of the imagination and without much effort of projection, this time may easily be attributed to unconscious objects. Inanimate objects begin nothing of themselves; they end nothing. Their time may be thought as an endless somnolent waiting; now, equal intervals of this impersonal time-like flow may be selected, and the objective time of physical objects may be defined into being. The important operation which the imagination must perform in projecting the almost meaningless duration of oblivion or somnolence upon the world of non-living objects is to remove from this world the notion of events. This operation is performed by reversing the isomorphism just indicated and ascribing to the temporal extension just and only the properties of the line which measures it. Then, the constancy of the flow of time is translated into the seriality of points of intervals along a line both in respect to the time of the (somnolent) self and the time through which an object endures and moves. We are returned, it seems, to the web from which the woof threads have been removed. Only warp threads remain; they are isomorphic with numbers, and they so may be counted. Thus is reached a view of time which is deprived both of beginnings and endings as well as of the sense of passage. There remains only an isomorphism between a set of numbers and of numbered objects (e.g. days); such an isomorphism is established in the eternal present of abstract relations.

For a man, though, no matter how routinized or absent-minded, time cannot but retain in some sense its discrete and rhythmic structure. It may be that Husserl was assenting to this observation when he described time as a structure of the "now" plus protention and retention. Protention and retention are the spontaneously anticipated and retained elements of a "now."[7] They are "passively generated." Husserl appears to have believed that the passively generated layers of experience (the "hidden achievements") are difficult, perhaps nearly impossible, to reach and analyze. I am suggesting, on the contrary, at least in the instance of time, that its structure is that of any dramatic event or – on the less complex plane – of any felt organic interval. However, when time merely flows and when beginnings and endings are indiscernible, they are nevertheless possible. Time as mere duration

---

[7] Cf. *The Phenomenology of Internal Time Consciousness*, tr. by J. S. Churchhill (Bloomington, Indiana Univ. Press, 1964), §§ 7, 10, and *passim*.

retains as a possibility the structure of time as event and as interval. Time, then, if human, is possible meaning; it is the realm of possible beginnings and endings. Only upon giving up these structural elements do we attain the abstract oblivion which is objective time. Even then, the abstract structure of meaning remains. Objective time is still something, devised by men; it has a beginning in history and may be used for an end. It marks the end of history only when this beginning is forgotten.

ROBERT SOKOLOWSKI

Catholic University of America

TRUTH WITHIN PHENOMENOLOGICAL SPEECH*

> "Since 'Know thyself' is not said to the mind ... as it
> is said, Know the will of that man: for this it is not
> within our reach to perceive at all, either by sense or
> understanding, unless by corporeal signs actually set
> forth; and this in such a way that we rather believe
> than understand. Nor again as it is said to a man, Be-
> hold thy own face; which he can only do in a looking-
> glass. For even our own face itself is out of the reach
> of our own seeing it; because it is not there where our
> look can be directed. But when it is said to the mind,
> Know thyself; then it knows itself by that very act by
> which it understands the word 'thyself'; and this for no
> other reason than that it is present to itself. But if it
> does not understand what is said, then certainly it does
> not do as it is bid to do. And therefore it is bidden to
> do that thing which it does do, when it understands the
> very precept that binds it."
>
> St. Augustine, *De Trinitate* X, #9.**

The problem of truth within phenomenology is the problem of
how we can mean anything after we have carried out Husserl's
transcendental reduction, and how we can verify our meanings.
How can we talk philosophically after we suspend our natural assertion of the world as an assumed, real background of experience?
Can we talk at all after we disengage this underlying belief which
is the condition for all our speech about things in the world? Is
there anything left to say, and if so, how are we to decide whether
what is said is true or not? Within philosophy, within the transcendental reduction, do meaning and truth work the same way

* This essay was written in 1969 and a more extensive version is being published
as a chapter in my book, *Husserlian Meditations*, Northwestern University Press.
** A. Haddan trans. in P. Schaff, ed.: *A Select Library of Nicene and Post-Nicene
Fathers*, vol. III (Grand Rapids, 1956), p. 140.

they do in ordinary, non-philosophical consciousness? To ask about philosophical discourse in Husserl is therefore to ask about the transcendental reduction, which we will interpret as Husserl's way of showing how we can speak philosophically about consciousness, and how we can speak about the world from a philosophical point of view.

1. Three strata of judgment

The linguistic principles we must use are found in Husserl's theory of judgment as expressed in #13–#16 of *Formal and Transcendental Logic*.[1] Husserl there distinguishes three ways in which a judgment can be realized: vaguely, distinctly, and clearly.

(a) A judgment is realized vaguely when it is passively received. It is not executed or carried out explicitly, but simply assimilated "by association." It dawns on us, or we passively read or hear it, and just accept and entertain it without thinking. Even such confusedly entertained judgments must conform to correct syntax, Husserl says. If they are judgments at all they must be formally structured, they cannot be just a heap of words. Their formation is governed by a set of rules, by syntax or morphology (*Formenlehre*). But because such judgments are not explicitly executed, we do not worry about contradicting ourselves when we entertain them. The realm of vaguely realized judgments is the domain of opinion without thought, where we can say one thing and hold its opposite without discomfort. There is no consciousness of contradiction. Vague or confused judgments are formally structured but need not be formally consistent.

(b) A judgment is brought to distinctness when it is explicitly executed. We take responsibility for it instead of merely entertaining it. We are willing to defend it as ours, and must eliminate formal contradictions because to maintain a contradiction would be to hold something as both ours and not ours. Distinctly executed judgments are formally structured, like vague judgments, but in addition they are formally consistent with themselves and with the other judgments the speaker asserts.

(c) In clarity we become concerned with the judgment as pre-

---

[1] *Formale und transzendentale Logik* (Halle, 1929); English translation by Dorion Cairns (The Hague, 1969). Henceforth abbreviated FTL.

tending to express a state of affairs. We are no longer occupied with
the judgment simply as our meaning, but as that which expresses
something beyond itself. The adaptability of the judgment to
things now becomes an issue. Clarity in a judgment is its successful capacity to express what is, its capacity to be the expression
of an intuition. To possess clarity in a judgment, besides being formally consistent and syntactically correct, must be verifiable or
falsifiable.

Here we leave purely formal criteria and examine the matter
or content of the judgment. The meaning-contents that compose
the judgment must be compatible and coherent. They must belong
to the same language game, fitting with one another and with
what is meant. A judgment like, "Tall virtue sleeps furiously,"
fails in this test. It is syntactically correct, formally consistent,
but meaningless and incoherent. Its words do not work together
with one another in respect to their contents.[2] Husserl says the
realities the words express could not be experienced together, in
the totality of a single experience, hence such a judgment could
never be brought to evidence or verification, whether positive
or negative.[3] But judgments like, "The house is red," or "Courage
is good," are meaningful and have their own methods of verification or adequation programmed into them. They achieve not only
distinctness, but also clarity.

Distinctness and clarity reciprocally condition one another. A
judgment cannot be a candidate for clarity unless it is formally
consistent, but neither can one be executed distinctly if it is incoherent. In #89 of *Formal and Transcendental Logic* Husserl
says that incoherent judgments (like our "Tall virtue sleeps furiously") simply fall outside the scope of contradiction and non-
contradiction. The compossibility, the coherence of the content-
parts of a judgment – as opposed to its formal parts – is a condition for the existence of the judgment as a distinct meaning.
The coherence of the content-parts in turn depends on the possi-

---

[2] This is so only if we take the words literally and univocally. In metaphorical
speech, "meaningless" expressions do convey sense, and such distorted, non-literal
discourse is essential in the constitution and growth of language. Husserl does not
examine metaphorical discourse because his chief concern is with scientific language
and consciousness, where univocity is required for the unmistakableness of what is
expressed.

[3] FTL, #89, B; #90.

bility that these contents can be intuited together in a single pre-judgmental experience.

How are vagueness, distinctness and clarity related chronologically? There is certainly a temporal interval between a judgment vaguely assimilated and the same judgment executed distinctly. The two states could not be contemporary; one must precede the other. But there is no temporal interval between a judgment distinctly executed and the same judgment established in clarity. Because distinctness and clarity mutually condition each other, both dimensions come together when we explicitly execute a judgment. The temporal motion is from vagueness on one hand towards distinctness and clarity on the other. Both distinctness and clarity emerge simultaneously out of vagueness, and vagueness can harbor both inconsistency and incoherence. Still, distinctness and clarity are two different dimensions; formal consistency is not the same as material coherence. Our example, "Tall virtue sleeps furiously," is meant to show a dimension (clarity) in which a judgment can be deficient while it is adequate in another (distinctness, formal consistency).

But the example is obviously contrived. No one who knows the language would ever make a judgment like this. Are there any kinds of judgment that can seriously be distinctly executed while still deficient in clarity? There are two: first, judgments using metaphor. "Red is a loud color," or "That is a friendly building," are formally consistent but materially incoherent if the words are taken literally. Of course they are not meant to be taken literally; they are distortions made artfully and on purpose, and are necessary to the life of the language. But their "decidability" and "verification" work in ways different from univocal speech. Before we decide whether the judgment is acceptable, we have to let the metaphor sink in, we have to tolerate the manifest incoherence. We are not misled because we know the words are not used univocally. But the decidability of a judgment using metaphor is not reached by saturating the intention with a familiar perception; rather the metaphor is an attempt to make us perceive differently. It wants to provoke a new perception, to make us aware of differences that have not been institutionalized in univocal, accepted speech. A metaphor, with its surprising incoherence of meaning, makes things appear fresh to our shocked sensibility. Its "verification" consists in making truth, not matching it. Therefore the success or failure of a judgment with metaphor is not expressed by saying that the judgment is "true" or "false," but that it uses a "good" or "bad" formula. We cannot say that "Red is a loud color" is true, while "Red is a soft color" is false; if the propositions were so definitely decidable, they would not contain functioning metaphors. The metaphors would no longer be lively, but would have settled into established meanings. Rather the first judgment is better than the second in most circumstances, but there could be cases where the second metaphor is better to arouse the perception that is appropriate and desired. To carry out their function, judgments with metaphor must achieve distinctness; if they were formally contradictory they might serve to express a paradox, if we wished to retain them at all, but then their metaphorical disclosure would be subordinated to that purpose. Thus a judgment with metaphor subsists on the difference between distinctness and clarity, for it possesses distinctness, being explicitly executed and formally consistent, while it defies clarity.

The second kind consists of pretended philosophical judgments, those we want to reject as being "wrong" philosophically. They may be proto-philosophical maxims or proverbs, or the initial attempts of someone beginning philosophical analysis, or even the fully articulated but unsuccessful judgments of a certified philosopher (for instance Locke's judgments about abstract ideas as interpreted by Berkeley). Judgments like, "Things are just what I see with my eyes," or "Democracy is the best way of life," are formally consistent and can be explicitly executed and even preserved as a permanent belief, but they contain latent incoherence. They fail in clarity. And unlike metaphors, their incoherence is not something we are conscious of when we accept such statements; therefore we are misled by philosophy. Success in achieving distinctness deludes us into believing we have clarity as well, when we do not. This is the kind of category mistake or confusion of language games that Wittgenstein and other philosophers have said is endemic to philosophical discourse whenever it tries to do anything more than discover and unravel such incoherences, that is, whenever it makes a positive truth claim of its own. Without agreeing that all philosophical judgments are incoherent, we can say that those we consider wrong are rejected either because they are incoherent, meaningless, deficient in what Husserl calls clarity, or because they are inconsistent. We will explore this theme more fully when we examine philosophical or phenomenological judgments and the kind of polemics that occur within philosophy.

Thus language goes on holiday in two ways in respect to the clarity of judgments: recreatively, when it responsibly enjoys the games, fancifulness, disclosure and discovery of metaphor, and misleadingly, when it is on vacation but does not know it and keeps all the strain of work without pay, because it labors philosophically with incoherence under the conviction of belief.

The three strata of judgments play an important role in the splendid and tightly organized argument of *Formal and Transcendental Logic*. To each level in judgment there corresponds a particular type of analysis. All judgments, even those in vagueness, call for the *Formenlehre*, the formal syntax which simply lists the possible combinations and formal structures which are available for categorial objects and categorially structured meanings. Judgments that reach distinctness call for a science that describes structures of formal consistency. Husserl calls this science "pure analysis" (*die pure Analytik*)[4] and claims that it can be carried on in two ways: as formal apophansis it examines the consistency of judgments as meanings, and as formal ontology it gives the rules of consistency for objects as given in categorial formulations.[5] Formal apophansis talks about judgments and complex meanings, formal ontology talks about states of affairs (*Sachverhalte*), groups, relations, etc. in their formal complexity and consistency. Throughout #17–#54 Husserl examines the intricate relationships among pure analysis, formal ontology, and formal apophansis, as well as the place of mathematics within these disciplines; as Jules Vuillemin has indicated, the ideas he develops are of considerable originality and great value for logical and mathematical theory.[6] The third level of

---

[4] FTL, #17.
[5] FTL, #25.
[6] *La philosophie de l'algèbre* (Paris, 1962), vol. i, pp. 479–506. The contrast between modern algebra and ancient mathematics which Jacob Klein has discovered was certainly made more visible by Husserl's notion of the intentionality of mind, an intentionality which functions even in formal systems. Klein shows that modern formal

judgment, clarity, demands still another science, which Husserl calls "truth logic" (*Wahrheitslogik*). Here we begin to talk about bringing judgments to evidence, bringing them from empty intention to saturation. We are concerned not only with consistency but also with truth. In order to carry out this logic, however, we must start talking about subjectivity and its intentional actions, because bringing an intention to fulfillment is a performance achieved by consciousness in action; truth is not discovered simply in the consistency and interrelationships of words and propositions. Truth logic is the description of transcendental consciousness in its process of establishing truth. It is studied in Section II of *Formal and Transcendental Logic*.[7]

2. The two fundamental forms of consciousness: empty intentions and saturations

We must situate the three strata of judgment more accurately within the structure of consciousness. In the *Logical Investigations*, under the genus of "objectivating acts," Husserl introduces a distinction which persists as the most fundamental duality throughout its philosophy. He says there are two basic and irreducible forms of consciousness: (1) acts of empty intending, of empty meaning; (2) acts of fulfillment, saturation, or intuition.[8]

systems (since Vieta) are characterized by referring to symbols of conscious operations with things, not to things themselves. Ancient formal systems referred directly to things, but taken as indeterminate or without content. Husserl's phenomenological understanding of formal systems, especially formal ontology and mathematics, is much more akin to the ancients than to the moderns in this regard. For Klein's ideas see: *Greek Mathematical Thought and the Origin of Algebra*, trans. E. Brann (Cambridge, Mass., 1968), esp. #9, and "Phenomenology and the History of Science," in *Philosophical Essays in Memory of Edmund Husserl*, ed. M. Farber (Cambridge, Mass., 1940), pp. 143–63.

[7] Husserl says that the three strata of judgment and the three levels of formal inquiry (morphology, consistency, truth logic) are fully articulated only in FTL; see pp. 11 and 71 of the English translation, 10 and 62–63 of the German. Parts of these investigations are present in some of his earlier works, however; for instance the problem of clear judgment and truth logic is the theme of the sixth *Logical Investigations* especially Section II, and appears also in *Ideas I*, #153. Both differentiate truth logic from consistency. Pure analysis is treated in *Ideas I*, #10–#16, together with the distinction between formal apophansis and formal ontology, which is anticipated in *Prolegomena* #67, where Husserl distinguishes between *Bedeutungskategorien* and *gegenständliche Kategorien*. Formal syntax is studied in *Logical Investigations*, IV, where Husserl discusses pure grammar and syncategorematic terms.

[8] *Logische Untersuchungen* (Halle, 1901), VI #14, p. 524, #15 p. 525. Henceforth abbreviated LU. References will be to the first edition, since the section numbers should suffice to determine the passage in the second edition.

The importance of these two contraries in his thought is similar to the force of the Pythagorean polarity between the determined and the undetermined in Greek thinking, and Husserl's "presence" and "absence" has much in common philosophically with the classical contrariety. All other intentionalities presuppose either one (or a mixture) of these two, but neither of the two can ever be reduced to the other. Each is equally fundamental to consciousness, and the task of describing the relationship and transitions between the two contraries comprises the phenomenological problem of evidence.[9]

(1) Empty intentions are executed in the absence of what they intend. Consciousness can mean something in the absence of its object. It is not bound only to respond to the immediate presence of being, but can take the initiative and intend without actual presence. In the *Investigations* Husserl points out that even such empty intentions require a basis in sense impressions; there must be, to use the terminology of the *Ideas*, a hyletic component even in this case, but the hyletic dimension is only "symbolic."[10] It is the sensory data of words, for example, or of other signs whose sensory impression is entirely different from the impression that the object itself would make on us if it (or its picture) were present.

(2) Acts of fulfillment or saturation actually present their objects. What is meant is actually given; here meanings are verified or brought to adequation, and in the case of judgments, truth or falsity is established. In the *Investigations* Husserl gives two degrees of such saturation. The most intense saturation is reached when the object is actually present itself; the sense impression made on us, which serves as the foundation for the perceptual intention, is the definite impression that only this particular object or type of object can make. Husserl describes how degrees of

---

[9] Empty intending and saturation are immediately involved with evidence because objectivating acts are defined as those that allow the identity and identification of an object to be constituted, and evidence is precisely the bringing of an object "itself," as "the same," to consciousness. Cf. LU VI #14, p. 524: "Demnach können wir die objektivierenden Akte geradezu als diejenigen definieren, deren Erfüllungssynthesis den Charakter der Identifikation, deren Enttäuschungssynthesis also den der Unterscheidung hat; oder auch als diejenigen Akte, welche phänomenologisch als Glieder einer möglichen Synthesis der Identifikation oder Unterscheidung fungieren können ..." See also VI #8.

[10] LU VI #25, pp. 560–62.

fullness in saturation are possible even in the direct, bodily presence of the object. But he then allows another, weaker type of saturation when the object is presented by its copy (a picture, painting, or other representation) or by its image in our imagination.[11] An imaginative phantasy serves as an actual presentation in copy of the thing itself; in imagination and in picturing, the sensory, hyletic impression on us is similar to that made by the thing itself in its actual presence. Thus pictorial presentation is not merely symbolic, not an empty intention, but a weak form of having the thing present itself.

The interplay between presence and absence, between saturation and empty intending, operates in two dimensions: (A) in simple, non-syntactic intentionalities, and (B) in complex, categorial intentions, that is, in cases where we deal with a synthesis of meanings put together syntactically.[12]

(A) Non-syntactic intentions are exemplified by ordinary perceptions; in perceiving any physical object, presence and absence combine. While I mean one side in actual presence, the other sides are absent and meant only symbolically or emptily. When I perceive a melody only the actual, present phase is meant in direct saturation; the rest of the melody is also meant, but meant as absent (as either anticipated or retained). When I perceive another person his bodily presence is accompanied by the contrasting absence of his mind, that is, his mind is given to me as that which can never be given the way the body is. It is meant as absent. Furthermore the same chiaroscuro of presence and absence prevails even when I mean a physical object, melody or person in my imagination.

(B) Such simple intentions are what Husserl calls the domain of "sensibility" (*Sinnlichkeit*) as opposed to "reason" (*Verstand*).[13] In the domain of reason we deal with complex, categorial, syntactically combined meanings and objects. Here we mean and saturate propositions; we can emptily intend, "Peter is taller than John," "Water seeks its own level," "Virtue is its own reward," and we can also bring such empty complex intentions to their saturation and intuition, in keeping with the style of evi-

---

[11] LU VI #17, pp. 539–40; #20, pp. 550–51.
[12] LU VI #46–#47.
[13] See the Introduction to LU VI, p. 478, and the title of VI, Section Two, p. 600.

dence proper to each statement. Since in dealing with such complex intentions (of which judgments are the primary case) we are
dealing with assertions or claims to truth, the saturation of such
meanings serves to decide their truth or falsity. The problem of
truth arises in its fullest form when we come to the phenomenology
of the saturation of complex, categorial meanings. This is why
Husserl says that the *Logical Investigations* culminate in Section
II of the sixth investigation.[14]

Now how do the three strata of vagueness, distinctness and
clarity in judgment criss-cross with the types of intentionality
we have distinguished? Since they are levels of judgment, it is
obvious that they fall under complex, categorial intentions; but
how do they fit within the dichotomy of empty intentions versus
saturations? Do they straddle the dichotomy, or can they fall
within one of the alternatives?

All three levels of judgment can be realized within empty intentionality, without actual saturation. This is easy to see regarding vagueness and distinctness, for both formal syntax and formal
consistency are conditions for holding the judgment simply as a
meaning, and even the "explicit execution" of a distinct judgment means that we are willing to accept it simply as our intention.

The case of clarity is more difficult. Husserl does speak of a
"clarity of actual possession" which can be realized only when
the thing meant is present and the intention is intuitionally
saturated. However he also mentions a "clarity of anticipation,"
in which the judgment simply prefigures, strives towards, antici-
pates the things it means, while not having them present at all.[15]
But the anticipation is important, for now we are concerned with
the judgment not simply as a distinct meaning, but as anticipating
and striving towards the things themselves. The pretention to
truth now becomes a factor, and a wholly new dimension is added
to the judgment even though it is not saturated in any degree at
all. The anticipational clarity of a judgment means that the judgment can be brought to adequation, that it can possibly be saturated. Clarity promises that it makes sense to bring this judgment
to evidence, but it does not of itself mean that the judgment is

---

[14] Introduction to LU VI, p. 478.
[15] FTL #16, C; see also #59.

saturated. That is, a distinct and clear judgment may not yet be
decided as true or false. It may still await verification and decision, still await being brought to intuitional evidence of things
in the "clarity of actual possession." Judgments like, "The
Supreme Court building is fifty feet high," or "Beagles run faster
than terriers," are clear but can still be only empty intentions;
they must be verified, brought to evidence and saturation, to be
decided as true or false. Judgments in anticipational clarity are
"on the verge" of saturation because they are fully qualified to
be saturated by virtue of their coherence; but such anticipation
is not saturation itself.

In this essay we always use the notion of clarity in judgments
in a minimal sense: we refer to the clarity of anticipation only.
Whenever we speak of judgmental clarity, we mean judgments
as empty intentions with no saturation but anticipating their
fulfillment.

Still another distinction must be made within the types of
judgments we can execute. This distinction is a refinement of
Husserl's basic duality between empty intentions and saturations
and introduces the factor of time. We distinguish: (I) Judgments
made simply as meanings, as opinions, *before* we have any saturation or evidence as to their truth. Before seeing Monticello or any
pictures of it, I may be given the statement, "Monticello is red
with white trimming." All I can do is entertain it as an empty
meaning pending evidence. Years ago the statement, "The moon
has a hard surface" had the same status. When there is no evidence yet, not even the assurance of other persons, such statements are more properly questions than assertions. However they
must be distinct and clear if they are to have hope of evidence.
(II) Judgments made *during* saturation or evidence. They are
the actual expressions of evidence: looking at Monticello I describe its color, or standing on the moon someone says it does indeed have a hard surface. (III) Judgments made *after* they have
been saturated. Once their truth has been established we assert
them as true even though we do not enjoy their evidence at the
moment of assertion. They have become our convictions, "habit-
ualities" of our intentional life which Husserl compares to the
habits that become part of our ordinary personal life.[16] Judg-

---

[16] These three states of judgment can be distinguished effectively after Husserl

ments in this category can still be meant emptily; I can merely intend them without a perception or imagination of what they say, but I mean them as true and valid. I cannot remove the fact that in my conscious history they have been established or verified at some time, so even when I mean them emptily I must mean them with conviction.

Thus (I) and (III) can fall under the scope of empty intentions, which we numbered (1) above; only (II) is exclusively restricted to the domain (2) of saturations.

Our tripartite division brings out more fully the problem of truth in Husserl's theory of judgment; the duality between empty intentions and saturations was not refined enough to do this adequately because truth is not simply equivalent to saturation, although it presupposes it. Case (III) is an example of a true intention which is not actually saturated while it is asserted as true. The division is based on the three dimensions of time, the three states being classed as before, during and after evidence. This implies that the problem of truth in Husserl cannot be dissociated from the temporality of consciousness. Judgments cannot be decided as true in a trans-temporal context; they must be referred to the event of evidence, which is achieved by acts located in the time-filled stream of consciousness. Truth logic can be carried out only by referring to the intentional actions of transcendental subjectivity, which are events in the ego's history.

Just to round out the place of distinct and clear judgments within the various forms of intentionality, we may add that such judgments may be realized even within category (I); a judgment may be executed distinctly and clearly, with consistency and coherence, and still be prior to any saturation and undecided as to its truth. But only if it is distinct and clear does it make sense to try to determine its truth by evidence. Only judgments are decidable.

3. Judgments and other intentions in the natural attitude

In any intention executed in the natural attitude, all saturations are accompanied by a horizon of unfilled, empty meanings.

introduces genetic phenomenology into his thought. For instance they fit well with *Cartesianische Meditationen* (The Hague, 1950), #27, #32–#33, #36–37.

Presence is always accompanied by absence. We never reach full closure in any intention in the mundane attitude, because we never eliminate the empty intentions that accompany evidences. We do have evidence, but it is never final. In mundane consciousness there is always a distention between saturation and empty intending, always an interval between what is directly given and what we mean. As long as we remain in the natural, non-phenomenological attitude, we can never entirely eliminate this interval, never close this distention. In the case (A) of simple, non-syntactic intentionalities, any object we perceive always possesses absent dimensions, sides or parts which we do not have directly present but mean only *in absentia*. This is due to the spatiality of physical objects. Any perception of them is surrounded by a horizon of absent parts that are merely intended and not given. Likewise parts of a melody are always meant as absent at the same time we directly perceive its present phase, and the inner experience of other minds or other psyches (such as those of animals) can be meant by us, but can never be given the way their bodies are to our direct perception. The interval between intention is therefore always kept open, a perpetual obstacle to our ever reaching "unsurpassable" evidence. The mind is never totally at rest in perception, but must always move on to further perceptions to saturate what it now means only emptily and symbolically.

This open interval, furthermore, is not a defect of fault of our consciousness, not the result of some sort of epistemological greed, weakness or imperfection, as though we always mean more than we should, or bite off more than we can chew. Our unclosed intentionality is based on the kinds of objects we know in the world. They exist in such a way that they do not present themselves fully at any time. It is not a question of somehow getting around a thing more quickly in order to see all the sides at once, or compressing the melody so that we can hear it without retention and protention; such "ideals" of total simultaneous presence would destroy the very objects we want to experience. There is no other way for such things to be manifest except through the mixture of presence and absence. As Husserl says, even a divine intellect, if it were to perceive a physical object, would see it only one side at a time.[17] Therefore the obstacle or hurdle presented by the

[17] *Ideen I* (The Hague, 1950), #150, p. 371; see also pp. 98 and 101.

interval between empty intention and saturation is an obstacle grounded in the things known to mind, and not the result of some failure or limitation of mind itself. The mind is distended in perceiving because the objects it knows are distended.

The same interval or distention, the same mixture of presence and absence, also arises in the cases (B) of judgments or other complex, categorial intentions made in the natural attitude. Consider how it functions in judgments that are executed (I) before, (II) during, and (III) after saturation.

If we want to bring a judgment from (I) to (II), from total indecision to saturation and evidence, we have to find things out. We must reach new evidence. How we do this depends on the type of judgment we are dealing with: historical, aesthetic, financial, chemical, biological, medical, political or geographical judgments are all verified in different ways. But in any case we have to do something, we must ask, perceive, read documents, excavate, form experiments, measure things, turn things around, read instruments, go places, mix things, and get new information in order to attain saturation. It is never enough just to think about the empty intention, to think about what is said in the undecided judgment. Even if the judgment is distinct and clear, fully understood, there is no guarantee that it is true, nor do we yet have the evidence for its truth available to us. There are obstacles outside us, in the world and its objects, that we must overcome in order to decide our judgments.

Suppose we have reached evidence and saturated our judgment, and are in state (III) where, although we no longer actively saturate it, we maintain the judgment as our permanent conviction, as a truth we have once verified, as a habituality in our conscious life. Even such an "assured" judgment is still conceivably subject to further questioning in view of later evidence. That is, there is always the possibility that something may arise which will return this judgment to state (I), to indecision, or even to negation. In the natural attitude everything is radically provisional, never free of subsequent questioning, possible revision, and even rejection.[18] Even if I assert a judgment as true in full evidence ("Glass is breakable," "Richard Nixon was President of the United States

---

[18] *Ideen I* ,#138; *Cart. Med.* #6-#7.

in February, 1969") it makes sense to say that something could conceivably arise to change my once saturated and verified judgment back into a merely intended one.[19] Of course Husserl does not mean that we trifle with well established evidences and irresponsibly turn certainties into doubts; if a judgment has been established by evidence, we have no choice but to accept it unless other evidences that shake our conviction actually arise. The modalities of judgment are not subject to our wills.[20] But there is always the conceivable possibility that such disturbing new evidences may indeed appear. No mundane evidence excludes the conceivability of counter-evidence, because every categorial intention has conditions and implications that are only emptily intended and not verified or saturated. Subsequent saturations (or negations) of these conditions and implications may force us to reassess the evidence and verification that were once given to the judgment itself. In addition, the evidence of judgment is based on the evidence of simple perceptions, which are never totally saturated and may, in the course of filling up empty dimensions, bring about a correction of earlier presentations.

The interval between saturation and intention, the absence that always accompanies presence, thus constitutes an obstacle to bringing a judgment from (I) to (II), and also constitutes an irremovable threat to keeping a judgment in (III).

4. Phenomenological judgments

Now let us consider phenomenological judgments, the assertions made by the philosopher after he adopts the transcendental viewpoint. How do his judgments compare with those made in the natural attitude? First of all, they can have the same three strata we initially found in mundane judgments: (a) they may be vague if passively received and confusedly formulated; (b) they reach distinctness when explicitly executed, with formal consistency; and (c) they possess clarity if they are materially coherent and meaningful. But the three levels still keep us within

---

[19] FTL, pp. 109-111.
[20] *Ideen I*, #46. In the translation by W. R. B. Gibson (New York, 1931), p. 145, we read: "The world is not doubtful in the sense that there are rational grounds which might be pitted against the tremendous force of unanimous experiences, but in the sense that a doubt is thinkable ..."

empty intending; what is the relationship between empty intending and saturation in the realm of philosophical judgments?

If we approach this problem by examining the three temporal
states of judgment as: (I) before, (II) during, and (III) after saturation, we find that the three states, which are irreducible to and
separated from one another in the natural attitude, lose their
separation in the transcendental focus. When we are doing phenomenology, once we bring a judgment to distinct and clear
existence as a meaning, once we bring it to state (I), we are in
possession of all that we need to decide its truth or falsity. There
is no obstacle left, and no traverse necessary between (I) and (II),
between empty intention and saturation. Once we execute a
phenomenological judgment distinctly and clearly as a mere intention, its truth or falsity should dawn on us immediately; there
is nothing else for us to do, no evidence beyond what we already
have must be reached. Nothing can get in our way to hinder us
from verifying the judgment. This is quite different from mundane
judgments, where considerable effort may be required to overcome the obstacles between (I) and (II).

Husserl's description of the awareness consciousness has of itself explains why this is so. When consciousness experiences itself,
nothing it means and wishes to thematize can remain absent from
it. There are no unavailable corners of consciousness. In mundane
experience there are always and essentially obstacles to evidence
built in to all our intentions. The obstacles, causes of the permanent interval between intention and saturation, reside in the nature of what is experienced, not in any defect of human consciousness. Some absence is a constant accessory to all evidence in
mundane experience, and always keeps the gap between meaning
and saturation open. This is not so in the self-experiencing of
transcendental reflection. The object here has no independent
distance from the consciousness that perceives it. Everything is
immediately available to intentions, every meaning can be saturated at will.[21] We can never be in the position of being "unable
to reach" (through reflective perception or imagination) judging,
memory, inner time, emotions, imagination, and the other "parts"
and actions of consciousness, as we might be blocked in natural

[21] *Ideen I*, #44 and #46.

experience from reaching the presence of certain objects that we need for evidence. There are no obstacles to evidences in reflective transcendental experience.

It is true that in *Ideas I*, #44, Husserl admits temporal profiles within the pure immanence of consciousness.[22] These profiles bring with them a sort of obscurity and absence which has to be overcome within phenomenology itself, because what is already available to consciousness may not yet be available distinctly and clearly. We shall examine this in #5. But the obscurity based on time is essentially different from the absence and unavailability based on space in mundane experience, and does not hinder the statements made in phenomenological description from being *decidable* as soon as they are *understood*.

For example consider the statements Husserl makes in noetic phenomenology (his descriptions of noeses and hyletic data and their relationships, his analysis of simple intentions and categorial acts and their relationships, the definition of evidence, the contrast between privacy and intersubjectivity, analysis of the temporal dimensions of present, protention and retention, etc.). All the judgments he makes in these analyses are such that when we *understand* them, we have all that we need to *decide* if they are true or not. They must be expressed and understood distinctly (explicitly and consistently) and clearly (with coherence), but if they satisfy these two requirements, these two criteria of understanding, no more needs to be done before they can be decided as true or false. We are never in the position of saying: "I clearly and distinctly understand what Husserl means, but now I must attempt to see whether it is true or not." We never stand suspended in the interval between intention and verification. Once we understand his meaning we do not have to go anywhere to find its truth, because what he speaks of is constantly available to us. There is nowhere else to go; consciousness is present to itself.

Furthermore, once a judgment in phenomenology has been saturated, once it reaches state (III) and becomes a permanent, habitual conviction of ours, there is never any danger that what was once asserted in evidence will never be put back into the state of a question. Phenomenological evidences do not run the

---

[22] pp. 103–104.

risk, as all mundane evidences do, of ever being countermanded by subsequent evidence. Phenomenological judgments are all carried out in strict apodicticity and once achieved distinctly and clearly, are permanently valid. There is never any threat that they will fall back into the state of mere intentions; indeed it makes no sense to say they would fall back into (I) because, as we have seen, (I) is itself in immediate contact with (II) and would lead us right back into (III).

Thus states (I), (II) and (III) are squeezed into direct contact with one another when we speak philosophically. The move from one to the other is instantaneous; as soon as (I) is reached distinctly and clearly, the saturation or verification of (II) is immediately available, and established philosophical judgments in state (III) never leave the immediate accessibility of their evidences and saturation in (II), so there is never any fear that they will be subverted.

Philosophical judgments have a curious circularity; once one reaches state (I) its truth is really already decided, so it simultaneously has acquired state (III), it already is a judgment that has been saturated. Likewise when we execute state (II), when we actually bring a phenomenological intention to the intuitional presence of the things it means, we do so with the awareness that we already know it is true; that is, (II) is like (III), and all three states are equivalent to one another.

This self-verification (or self-falsification) of statements made in phenomenology is illustrated by a remark Husserl makes concerning the attempt to psychologize logical laws. He says in the *Prolegomena*, "I would almost say that psychologism lives only through inconsistency, [and] if anyone were to think it through rigorously (*Folgerichtig*) to the end, he would already have abandoned it . . ."[23] The remark is incidental and is not intended to express the nature of phenomenological speech, but its very casualness makes it a good example. Just "thinking through" the position of psychologism makes it self-destructive, for when we do work it out rigorously, we find that we have "already" decided its falsity (*habe ihn schon aufgegeben*). No further evidence is needed.

---

[23] *Prolegomena zur reinen Logik* (Halle, 1900), #25, p. 78.

The separations of states (I), (II) and (III) from one another are temporal separations based on the relationships of before, during and after evidence. Because phenomenological judgments compress these states, they have a kind of intemporality, a sort of eternity. Once they are established they are permanently valid. There is never any question of new facts, information or evidence arising which will throw them into a new state or "move" them from where they are to some other position. Once distinctly established, they are no longer "on the way" or "in motion" to truth in any sense, hence they no longer have the temporality or historicity which is the measure of awareness of the motion towards truth.

The reason they have no motion is that they have no absences. States (I), (II) and (III) are compressed because the interval between (1) empty intentions and (2) saturation is also compressed in phenomenological intendings. The separation between presence and absence (between actuality and potentiality) is removed, because what we intend in phenomenology is only what is actually and totally available to us in consciousness.

Should we say there is no difference at all between (1) empty intention and (2) saturation in phenomenology? Is the evidence for truth given right in the empty intention itself, so that it is just a matter of analyzing the terms of the judgment in order to see its self-evident truth? In a judgment about inner time, for instance, do we simply inspect the terms of the judgment and see that they express an irrefutable, apodictic truth? The difficulty in agreeing to this is that it would make truth in phenomenology merely a function of meanings and intentions, and not of intuitions, of the evidence given by the objects meant. We cannot say that truth comes merely from the inspection of terms; it comes from the saturation of meanings by the presence of what is meant, by the presence, for instance, of temporal consciousness to itself. To use Kant's classification, phenomenological judgments are not analytically true, but are synthetic a priori assertions. Even in phenomenology and the mind's presence to itself, there is a difference between the intending and what is intended, a difference between empty intending and presenting the object in saturation. The basic duality between empty intentions and verification still exists, except that it is a duality with no distance between the poles. There is no obstacle in getting from one to the other because consciousness is always present to itself.

Another reason for asserting the difference between simple intention and saturation in phenomenology is the fact that we sometimes do entertain a simple intention without the presence of what it means. We can emptily mean a description of a certain emotion without actually experiencing or even imagining the emotion at the time. I do not need to be angry, or imagine myself angry, to understand and confirm a phenomenological analysis of that passion; I do not need to be counting or imagine myself counting in order to understand and confirm Husserl's phenomenological explanation of numbering or collecting. I can mean such things emptily, without intuition or saturation; but provided I have understood the meanings distinctly and clearly, I can never really mean phenomenological judgments as undecided, as being in state (I) and not yet capable of being brought to the saturation of (II). To mean them emptily can only be to mean them in state (III), where they have been decided and are known as such, even though the actual presence of what they mean may not be achieved at the moment.

It is even somewhat misleading to say that we *first understand* the meaning of a phenomenological judgment, and can *subsequently verify* it whenever we wish because of the constant presence of consciousness to itself. Rather, the verification or deciding is more in the nature of remembering; upon understanding the judgment distinctly and clearly, we know immediately by a kind of memory that things have indeed always been this way. We do not have to activate the action or part of consciousness we judge about to "see" whether it really is so. We can verify the judgment through remembering, which of course is not saturation, not even saturation through pictures or imagination. When we read a phenomenological analysis of perception, for instance, we need not even imagine perception to decide its truth or falsity; we simply "recognize" that it is true or false. However this verification through memory works only if we are given phenomenological judgments already constituted by someone else. If we were to constitute the judgments originally ourselves, we would require imaginative presentations as the datum upon which to formulate the judgments. But even then the decidability of the

judgments would come simultaneously with their being understood.

5. *Other aspects of phenomenological judgments*

If the interval between intention and saturation is no obstacle,
why is there any difficulty in doing phenomenology? If phenomenological judgments are timeless and permanently true, why
don't we go from one sudden flash of effortless illumination to
another, touching these truths the way the pre-existent Platonic
soul touches eternal, changeless ideas? There may be no difficulty
in getting from meaning to saturation, from understanding to
verification in phenomenology, but there still remains a great
problem in getting to distinct and clear understanding. We still
have the hurdle of bringing our reflective judgments from (a)
vagueness to (b) distinctness and (c) clarity, to consistency and
coherent meaningfulness. We often find this in Husserl: when he
refers to problems still outstanding in phenomenology, he calls
them areas that are still vague and confused, unexplored horizons,
places where contradictions may still be present and where new
vocabulary has to be established.[24] We can intend these areas,
but only vaguely at first, as horizons left over from evidences we
do have. There is room for progression and work in phenomenology
but the progress does not entail verification of meanings we already have; rather the labor of phenomenology (and philosophy
in general) is the constitution of these meanings themselves. As
Husserl often says, the elaboration of univocal meanings (meanings without confusion and vagueness) is the first and most difficult task he faces in his first philosophy.[25] Likewise, for the
student of phenomenology, for someone reading Husserl's statements, the labor exerted is a work of understanding, not of verification as something distinct from understanding.

Thus although we eliminate in phenomenology the time-stretch

---

[24] On the methodological problem of getting from obscurity to clarity, see *Ideen I*,
#66–#70, and also, p. 370.
[25] Cf. *Prolegomena*, #67, p. 245; LU Introduction, #2, p. 7; see the remarks on
terminology at the end of the Introduction to *Ideen I*, pp. 8–9, and those on terminology and equivocation in LU V #13. As an example of what Husserl means, see his
clarification of ambiguities in the terms "sign" and "expression" at the beginning of
LU I.

which exists among states (I), (II) and (III) of judgments in the natural attitude, we do not eliminate temporality from the passage between vagueness on one hand and distinctness and clarity on the other. There still remains this motion, traverse, interval and distention. This is where the obstacles of phenomenological and philosophical self-understanding exist: in the clarification of what is immediately present to us in a confused but certain way. This is where the historicity and temporal stretch of philosophy reside, because clarification of confusion and vagueness is achieved only through time.[26]

If phenomenological judgments are brought to distinctness and clarity, their truth is self-evident to everyone who understands their meaning and who experiences the things they talk about (and every listener must experience what they talk about, because they discuss the very consciousness which constitutes him as an intelligent listener and speaker). The self-evident truth, the "tautology" and necessity of phenomenological statements is obvious to all who understand them; then as Husserl expands his work, as he gradually describes more and more of the structure of consciousness, the progression in his science is carried out entirely in a network of self-evident and necessary judgments.[27] The progression in one of Husserl's meditations is a process of distinguishing and clarifying, of removing vagueness and penetrating unexamined horizons. None of it is merely hypothetical, awaiting the evidence of further information to decide its truth, nor is any simply factual, subject to the counter-evidence of later truths. Phenomenology is apodictic as it proceeds, a rigorous science throughout.

The self-evident truth of phenomenological speech is shown by the way disputes are carried on within it. Since the only progression is from the vague to the distinct and clear, the only way of attacking another position in phenomenology is by accusing it of being either contradictory (violating distinctness) or meaning-

---

[26] Cf. "Vom Ursprung der Geometrie," Appendix III in *Husserliana* VI (The Hague, 1954), p. 379: "Wie verschlossen, wie bloss 'implizite' mitgemeint dieser Sinn ist, ihm gehört zu die evidente Möglichkeit der Explikation, der 'Verdeutlichung' und Klärung. Jede Explikation und jedes von Verdeutlichung in Evidentmachung Übergehen ... ist nichts anderes als historische Enthüllung; in sich selbst wesensmässig ist es ein Historisches und trägt als solches wesensnotwendig den Horizont seiner Historie in sich."

[27] Cf. *Ideen I*, #75 and the Section entitled "Zur Terminologie" in #84.

less (violating clarity). For example Husserl rejects scepticism as well as the theory that evidence is an inner feeling, by claiming that such doctrines are contradictory or lead to contradictions, or that they are confused.[28] His attack on some traditional concepts in logic says the tradition does not distinguish logical structures from the acts that constitute them, and also confuses formal apophansis with formal ontology, thereby remaining in vagueness where neither distinctness nor clarity are reached.[29] In such polemics it is always a question of how we are to express and understand what we experience; it is never a disagreement about the verification of a meaning we all agree upon. The dispute is in the intention, in the meaning itself.

These reflections on philosophical speech help us understand why there can be no such thing as a "summary" of someone's philosophy. In mundane sciences, where the main problem is to verify truth claims, it is possible to abbreviate the meanings and give the collected results of investigations without demanding that everyone go through the process of verification which the original investigator carried out. I can accept as true the results of a sociological survey or a physical experiment without experiencing the survey or the experiment. But there are no "results" separate from the process of expressing philosophy, because the expression is the clarification of philosophical meaning, and the process of philosophy is simply this clarification. Its truth is in its understanding. It is a gradual crystallization of intelligibility, and in order to understand it and appreciate its truth, one must experience the process itself.

In order that phenomenological judgments be brought to distinctness, it is also necessary that they be explicitly articulated;

[28] *Ideen I*, #20–#21.

[29] FTL #11, #25–#26, #47. Countless passages illustrate the fact that Husserl rejects opposing positions because they are contradictory, absurd, confused or meaningless. E.g., *Ideen I*, pp. 44–47, 106, 134 (where he says, "If anyone objects ... we can only answer that he has not grasped the *meaning (Sinn)* of these discussions;" Gibson, p. 168), 136, 189–94, 224; LU pp. 64, 67, 70–72, 79–80, 132–33, 135, 160, 165–66, 179–82, 196, 354, 401–402, 655, 658, 671. The entire *Prolegomena* are based on the claim that psychologism in regard to logic is self-destructive and contradictory. See also the claims of contradiction and obscurity in the critique of Brentano's theory of inner time in #6 of the lectures on time. Husserl is able to judge these various contradictions in philosophy because he undercuts them all by uncovering the basic contradiction that provokes and fosters all of them: the mundane conviction that reality can be meant as independent of consciousness, that it can be thought as a consistent and coherent totality in itself, apart from consciousness.

distinctness, as we have seen, involves both that the intention be explicitly performed and that it be consistent with itself and with the speaker's other judgments. Therefore phenomenological judgments have to be "made our own," we have to express them as ours and take responsibility for them. This is implied in Husserls frequent insistence that phenomenology begins with each person's own subjectivity and with his explicit reflection upon it. A judgment which is not explicitly made our own is accepted associatively, simply entertained, accepted in a sort of "associative dreaming." In contrast a distinct, explicit phenomenological judgment is a "remembering of the forms," since it brings to clear and distinct awareness what is already possessed by us, but forgotten and obscured. Like the Platonic *anamnêsis*, Husserl's process of making phenomenological judgments distinct is carried on in a dialectic with other philosophical positions, which he attacks by reducing them to the dilemmas of contradiction and incoherence. For it is in dialectic that we establish ourselves as speakers in the face of our interlocutor; we identify ourselves, we find our identity, with a given philosophical position and strive to protect ourselves from the one weakness that can break our defenses and split us into disorganized pieces, the weakness of inner contradiction and incoherence. Such weakness can be ours if we have accepted a philosophical position by "associative dreaming" instead of authentic remembering, if we entertain it vaguely instead of distinctly articulating it as our own. Errors in philosophy are due to the precipitation and rashness with which we assume philosophical positions publicly as ours before we have thought them through as our own, before they truly reflect ourselves. We have not had the patience to let them crystallize through time. The effort of phenomenology, as Jacques Derrida has stated, is to defend ourselves from confusion, forgetfulness, and irresponsibility.[30] It does this by making us strive to assume a distinct and clear possession of what is already ours.

[30] In his introduction to the translation of Husserl's *L'origine de la géométrie* (Paris, 1962), p. 38.

6. Judgments in noematic phenomenology

Most of what we have said and the examples we have used so far deal with noetic phenomenology, the description transcendental consciousness gives of its own structures and acts. How do the principles of phenomenological truth function in noematic analysis?

The eidetic descriptions of various regions of reality, the phenomenologies of physical things, life, society, animals, art, sport, and so on, demand that the philosopher make statements which are not factual propositions, but necessary and apodictic judgments that cannot be falsified by subsequent experience of the things described. For instance we have judgments that material objects occupy space, appear as figures against a background and cause changes in one another, that they have inner and outer horizons, that colors exclude one another in a given place, and that we experience other persons only through the mediation of bodily presence.[31] In such noematic analyses Husserl considers the objects described in their appearing, in their presencing to consciousness. Since he has performed the epoché and reduction, things are present to him as phenomena, and he speaks of them as phenomena, in their process of appearing.[32] The eidetic descriptions are the ground rules, the boundary conditions, the factors essential for an object's being present to consciousness at all; eidetic structures are how things must *be* in order to appear. For instance an object that is not extended cannot appear as a material object in the *Lebenswelt*. It violates the "essence" of physical objects, it breaks the ground rules for material appearance. If we try to de-spatialize a physical object it "explodes" as a phenomenon. It cannot be experienced this way.

Noematic analysis uncovers the structures and principles that are operative as anonymous, hidden assumptions in the non-philosophical experience we have of things. Both ordinary ex-

---

[31] Such analyses are carried out extensively in *Ideen II* (The Hague, 1952).

[32] *Ideen I*, #47 and #50; in the latter Husserl says: "It is this which remains over as the 'phenomenological residuum' we were in quest of: remains over, we say, although we have 'suspended' the whole world with all things, living creatures, men, ourselves included. We have literally lost nothing, but have won the whole of absolute being, which, properly understood, conceals in itself all transcendences, 'constituting' them within itself." Gibson trans., pp. 154–55.

perience and scientific experience could not take place without these assumptions, and the expression of ordinary and scientific experience in speech could not come about except upon the anonymous assumption of eidetic structures and principles. But only noematic phenomenology, not ordinary mundane consciousness, expresses these structures and principles themselves and understands the role they play in the appearing of being to consciousness.

But even if it is true that ordinary, mundane consciousness generally does not concern itself with eidetic structures, that it limits itself to an attitude which assumes them, takes them for granted anonymously, and speaks about what can be said after these assumptions are made – would it not be possible for someone in the natural, non-philosophical attitude, in a reflective moment, to bring his eidetic assumptions to light and express them in words? Can't someone in the natural attitude state, for instance, the eidetic structures of physical things, their spatiality, causality, etc.? Do we have to perform the transcendental reduction in order to let essences become public?

Husserl admits that eidetic analysis can be carried out in the mundane attitude.[33] What would be lacking if the transcendental turn is not made, however, is the ability to understand the status of eidetic structures or essences. We would be at a loss to situate essences along with facts and things, because in the natural attitude we do not talk about things *as phenomena*. The transcendental turn makes us focus on them as phenomena; we become conscious of their appearing as appearing, we focus on their phenomenality, their correlation to consciousness, and we realize that there may be differences in the way things appear. We are then able to understand essences or eidetic structures as the anonymous conditions for the appearing of things as individuals and as facts, but conditions which in their turn can also become manifest to consciousness through essential intuition. Thus essences function in the appearing of things, and it is only when we focus on the appearing of things that the status of essence becomes intelligible. The transcendental viewpoint lets us do this.

---

[33] In *Ideen I*, #7–#9, Husserl talks about eidetic sciences that need not be transcendental, and he often mentions an eidetic psychology as possible in a pre-philosophical attitude; cf. *Cart. Med.* #35.

In the mundane attitude we focus on things as existing independently of consciousness. We simply assert them as various types of objects, in various relations, as true or illusory, as modified in certain ways, but in all this we are not conscious of what appearing is, what truth or illusion are, what object means; in short we are not conscious of a phenomenon as phenomenon, and remain ignorant of the various dimensions and status possible among phenomena. Forgetfulness of all this actually defines the natural, mundane attitude, which accepts phenomena but forgets what phenomenality is. The epoché is supposed to shake us out of this forgetfulness by suspending our mundane convictions, and the transcendental reduction opens us to the awareness that the world can be seen in another perspective or focus: it can be wondered at in its phenomenality.

Without the distinctions that the phenomenological attitude towards the world can give us, we are helpless to handle the status of essence and the objects of apodictic, noematic judgments. We fall either into a nominalism which denies the reality of eidos altogether, or into an exaggerated realism which either places essences as things in the world along with ordinary objects or constructs another world for them parallel to the world we experience. Or we fall into a conceptualism which makes essences a part of mind. The reduction makes us see essences in their proper context, as structures enabling the presence of things to consciousness to happen. We are able to appreciate phenomena as correlative to intentional consciousness.[34] The transcendental reduction is needed to bring this about, for the eidetic reduction alone does not change our mundane attitude towards phenomena.[35]

---

[34] The reduction is also necessary to prevent us from using any mundane science, such as physics, psychology, sociology, anthropology, history, and the like as the explanation of what consciousness, meaning and being are. Phenomenology must be carried out as a self-justifying and uncontaminated discipline more basic than these other sciences. See *Ideen I, #32*.

[35] Would mathematics satisfy the criteria for philosophical discourse as we have described them? No, according to Husserl, for the following reasons: (1) mathematics is a deductive science, whereas no inferences are made in phenomenology (*Ideen I, #73*). In a discipline where deductions must be made, certain propositions are not immediately true but need to be related to and mediated by others in order to be decided. This is not the case in philosophical speech. (2) Mathematics as a technique of reckoning does not reflect on the status of the ideal objects it uses, such as numbers, axioms, theorems, rules and operations. Only a reflective, transcendental focus can analyze them, and it can do so only in the wider context of analyzing logic, both formal and transcendental (see FTL #52).

To give a historical analogy, doing eidetic analysis without the transcendental reduction would be like trying to appreciate Aristotle's philosophical analyses of life, politics, ethics, chemistry, or biology without knowing his metaphysics. The former analyses express essences of various things, but only metaphysics studies the status of essence as such, that is, it examines the difference between saying something as an accident and saying something "in itself" of a thing. The metaphysics examines what being is and how it can be spoken in judgment; in doing so it focuses on the various ways being can be realized, and shows how these differences come to expression in speech through definition and predication in its various modes. In order to make such distinctions about being, however, we must step back from our normal unquestioning acceptance of being, our habit of taking it for granted. To question what being is, *ti to on*, does not mean that we doubt being or annihilate it, but that we change our focus towards it; we try to see what we can say about it simply as being. And this is precisely what Husserl's epoché and transcendental reduction are supposed to make us do. We suspend our spontaneous belief in the being of the world in order to thematize this belief and its correlate, the being of things. Only this step moves us into radical science, because it alone questions the fundamental assumption that underlies all other convictions we have; only this step allows us explicitly to raise the question: what is being?[36]

In noematic phenomenology is there an interval between (1) empty intention and (2) saturation? Once we bring a judgment in noematic description to distinctness and anticipational clarity, is there still a further problem of deciding its truth? The answer is the same as in noetic phenomenology. The interval between intention and perception shrinks to insignificance in noematic speech. Once we bring out judgments to clear and distinct formulation, no one familiar with the region of being we describe will need anything more to decide the truth or falsity of what we say. If we say colors exclude one another in a given place, or bodies are extended and cause changes in one another, no one who has experienced colors or bodies will need to do anything more to see the truth of our judgments. The self-evident truth of the judg-

[36] See *Ideas I*, #30–#31.

ments can be "remembered" by anyone familiar with the objects they refer to. And since the interval between intention and saturation dissolves, the temporal distentions among states (I), (II) and (III), before, during and after saturation, also vanish, as they do in noetic phenomenology. The timelessness of philosophical judgments also holds in noematic phenomenology; when eidetic truths about a region of being are stated, we immediately recognize their truth and think "we always knew it was so," because in fact these eidetic truths are anonymous assumptions that we have always accepted and taken for granted in our experience of the world.[37]

Although it is easy to recognize truth in expressed judgments about noemata, it requires effort and insight to elaborate these judgments in the first place, and to do so distinctly and clearly. Progress in this part of phenomenology also consists in moving from vague possession to distinct and clear understanding, always within the context of apodictic speech. In the development of phenomenology we never are in the position of having to say, "I once claimed p, but now the facts show I was wrong." Rather, correction and progress are expressed by saying, "I once held p, but now I see that it was confused and vague, and should be replaced by the clearer and more distinct judgment I now make."

But there is the condition, as in noetic phenomenology, that we must have experienced the kind of being which is described. Someone who has not experienced music or paintings or sport will not understand eidetic analysis of such things, because the analysis simply gives the structures that underlie the presence of such realities to mind. Without this experience the meanings combined in the descriptive, apodictic judgments simply will not make sense, and the judgments will lack clarity; the coherence or meshing of the content of their terms will not be apparent, so the listener will not even be able to understand the judgment, let alone determine its truth.

What we have discovered about phenomenological speech within the transcendental reduction has importance for the prob-

---

[37] The sense of "pastness" and "remembering" involved in recognizing the truth of phenomenological judgments suggests not only Plato's *anamnêsis*, but also the past tense of Aristotle's *to ti ên einai*. I wish to thank Thomas Prufer, Gregory DesJardins, Fred Kersten and J. R. A. Mayer for comments on earlier drafts of this paper.

lem of philosophical speech in general, and helps us understand the peculiarities it has: that it is non-empirical, that is, not simply factual nor hypothetical discourse; that it seems to carry its own verification and necessity within itself; that it seems to tell us things we "already know" or can somehow recall from a forgotten past; and that it claims to be ultimate speech, spoken from a final and universal, underived, and even timeless viewpoint.

Finally a problem can be raised about the value of philosophical speech. If it is self-explanatory and not informative, if it deals primarily with self-referential consistency in meaning, what value does it have, what good does it promise, and how does it avoid triviality? It would be in keeping with Husserl's thought to reply that the good which philosophical speech brings is integrity; not specifically the social integrity of an honest man who means what he says and keeps his word, nor specifically the psychological integrity of a man who is well adjusted with himself and with others, nor specifically the technical integrity of a craftsman or the artistic integrity of a novelist or painter – the integrity philosophy promises is the self-possession of a man who can talk theoretically with consistency about himself, his world, and what he knows in its totality; he refuses to abandon himself to the discord and dis-integrity, the distintegration of separating science and life, politics and values, theory and practice. Whether such total integrity is achievable is itself a problem, but the constant search for it is certainly the meaning Husserl gives to philosophy.

JOHN MAYER
Brock University

THE PHENOMENOLOGY OF SPEAKING

Firstly, I would like to approach my topic in a negative way. I would like to point out that what is not being done in a phenomenology of speaking is the phenomenology of language, even though it is not an irrelevant project and has both philosophical significance and a considerable bibliography showing the endeavor that has already gone into it. Language has been discussed from the point of view of structure, of content, of function, and so on. It has been analyzed by linguists, semanticists, grammarians, etymologists, as well as philosophers with a variety of biases. Our task will leave the nature of language unexplored, save that it is necessary to point out that speaking has language as one of its conditions. What I mean by "condition," however, is somewhere between the conventional meaning of that word and the technical meaning of "intentionality" in the phenomenological tradition. Perhaps the best way to clarify my meaning is to propose an analogy, which may serve to illuminate not only the relation of language to speaking, but also of thought to its object, and to the extent that each of the pairs of terms in the analogy can be grasped intuitively as inter-related one with another, light can be shed on several problems with respect to the relationships.

The proposed analogy is the following:

Thought : its object = Speaking : language.

This analogy is fertile because it helps to penetrate for example, the realist-idealist controversy. Seeing, however, that this is not the central subject of the present paper, I shall diverge for but a minute to stimulate further thought on this issue and to clarify my meaning.

Traditionally, the question has been raised as to whether objects in the world exist as objects independently of their being perceived; and if so, do they resemble the perceptions normal perceivers have of them under normal physical circumstances? The man with the natural attitude, (which may be considered pre-philosophical), would in fact, answer positively. On the other hand, brief reflection indicates that such an answer is not only in principle unverifiable, but also is logically weak. Natural objects are not accessible twice – once independently of perception and the second way through perception – and hence, one cannot compare the object as unperceived with its perceived form. Further, inasmuch as what are thought of as single objects can be perceived in a variety of distinct and dis-similar ways (by different senses, and from different perspectives) one has to ask how it is possible for one object to resemble each of its percepts, and if it doesn't resemble each, which is the more accurate and why? These puzzlesome problems have led some philosophers to the idealist conclusion, namely, the view that there are no objects apart from their percepts, hence percepts do not resemble anything other than perhaps each other. Such a conclusion undermines the natural attitude and brings about a *skepsis* which can be cured only by reconstituting the world into sensibilia and sensors – a philosophic possibility, which, however, is generally resisted in spite of its apparent plausibility – a plausibility which perhaps masks a fundamental implausibility.

Phenomenologists will recognize that the problem as formulated above has many implicit presuppositions, which are in fact responsible for the dilemma. Of course the primary pre-supposition underlying the problem is the I-World dichotomy which gives rise to the question of "bridging," that arises in every dualism. With our analogy we can gain insight into the problem.

Just as language can be abstracted from speaking, but is presupposed to it, and just as prescriptive and/or descriptive grammars can be written, so one can abstract the natural world from its variety of presentational givennesses in perception, memory, imagination, symbolic or natural representation – but just so do we presuppose the natural world to the experiencing of it. Just as expression can be formally and ideally anticipated and/or pre-constrained by conventional and grammatical habits, so experiences in perception can be anticipated or preconstrained by scientific theorization about objects in nature. And yet, just as speaking can transcend language habits and rules, so perception can transcend traditional theories about objects. On the other hand just as language as such does not depend on any particular utterance, though it can be modified by it, so objective nature does not depend on any specific perception, although scientific theories about nature can be modified by particular perceptions.

But enough of digressions – let us get back to speaking. We have said that all we will now claim about language is that it is one of the several intentionalities of every speaking. For speaking not only presupposes language, it is also the expression of a will to communicate, a will-into-being of language.

"Speaking" is a single word in our language, but a careful scrutiny of the phenomenon of speaking reveals it to be a wide variety of acts, each of which has distinctive characteristics. Furthermore speaking is fundamentally intertwined with what are often thought of as other activities, other modes of being, usually expressed in the words "thinking," "reflecting," and even "imagining," which in turn are recognized minimally as implying but more radically as being congruent with being-in-the-world. If, therefore, speaking and thought are interdependent, speaking is not an accidental activity of man, but lies near the center of man's essence.

However, here a first difficulty arises. What has been said so far may seem plausible, even perhaps cliché, but its truth can be questioned by the facts of infancy and muteness. If speaking is a fundamental aspect of being-in-the-world, how is it with infants and with the mute?

Infancy is the simpler matter to deal with. The humanity of the infant is recognized because his speaking exists as project and potentiality. It is interesting to note that we speak to infants; we address them. However, the language in which babies are addressed is special not only because of its simplistic vocabulary – but primarily because of the special inflection and tone we adopt, so characteristic of "baby talk." Making faces is also characteristic of baby talk. What does this reveal? That not only do we accept babies as people, but also we distinguish them as belonging to a different realm – a realm apart from the world of men. It is the fact that we speak to infants which constitutes their entry into the world.

But muteness poses a problem. Until relatively recently the congenitally deaf were constrained to live as people unable to communicate. As Gusdorf puts it: "Deaf-mutes used to be reduced to a kind of idiocy, a vegetable existence, at least until the day when someone discovered the means of reestablishing with them in indirect ways the communication they lack." (p. 94)

This reveals, however, that deaf-mutes, like infants are construed as potential speakers, who cannot speak until they are spoken to. Speaking to deaf-mutes might entail different body-movements from ordinary speech, but it is nonetheless a speaking to them that constitutes the breakthrough to speaking, and therewith the entry into a fuller human reality. The deaf-mute's speaking may differ mechanically from ordinary speaking, but it is intentionally identical with speaking. In fact the action of the vocal chords in the analysis of speaking is relatively insignificant and uninteresting.

This first hurdle, the problem of the infant and of the deaf-mute in fact provide us with a first essential insight. Speaking must be considered from the other side – the side of hearing or comprehension, which presupposes the other as speaker. Indeed it becomes clear that speaking as an activity is impossible without a prior being spoken to. To will a language into being which can express my lived world is to become aware of language as expressing the lived world of others.

Speaking, then, is constituted as the expression of the lived world. However, one must realize that this expression does not follow the constitution of the lived world, but is self-identical with it. Occasionally, however, the expression is suppressed into an interior utterance.

But more of this later. The important point to note is that active speaking presupposes and necessitates "being spoken to." Speaking in its primary sense does not arise independently of this reciprocity.

If this thesis be true, and if it be the case that thinking is a mode of suppressed speaking, the definition of man as the thinking animal can be translated into man the speaking animal (cf. Gusdorf, p. 4), which in turn is grounded by man in the encounter of language; man is the animal who constitutes his world as addressing him. This is perhaps no different than the fundamental Buberian claim that self-awareness is fashioned out of being aware of the other as person, as speaker; thus that the traditional problem of other minds puts the cart before the horse. Other minds, others, are more fundamentally given in experience than our own self. Thus the tendency to solve the problem of other minds by supposing that we construct them from an analogy to ourselves is mistaken. We construct ourselves in terms of our encounter with being spoken to, our encounter with language, which is at first the expression of the other.

A supporting phenomenon is to be found in the relative difficulty of speaking the first word. If I sit in a train and eye a stranger sitting opposite me, it is the first word that one of us says to the other which is found difficult. All the rest follow.

Similarly, in formal meetings the task of introducing a speaker eases his presentation to a group. And for chairing meetings, we tend to choose the most respected, the most eminent member, who can shoulder the responsibility of speaking the first word.

Yet another instance of the difficulty of the first word is the formalized nature of greeting. The greeting breaks the ice. Once greeted it is easy to carry on the encounter in speaking.

All this then reveals the root of speaking as founded in the experience of being addressed, of constituting a phenomenon not as sound or noise, but as language, the carrier of meanings.

Another insight can be generated at this point. In an earlier version of this analysis I had presented various modes of speaking ordered according to a nice logical schema. I started with soliloquy, then went on to dialogue, then to conversation, then to public address. The conceptual order was readily discernible. I started with talking to no one else, then went on to talking with one other, then to speaking, and finally, speaking to many. I am afraid that that schema was in some ontological sense unsatisfactory. Being addressed, and hence, dialogue is the fundamental mode of speaking, and both soliloquy (which is but one tiny step removed from thinking) and conversation are modelled on it.

Writing is clearly a formalized subset of speaking. It is the transformation of speaking into a different spatial and temporal modality. The written word, even though it usually conforms to formal strictures more rigorously than spoken ones, is originally spoken, and then captured into other symbols whose temporal span is of a different order. Nowadays we face the possibility of capturing the spoken word in all its spoken nuances on tape or disk, thereby combining some of the richness of the nuances of speech which is lost in writing with the transtemporality of the written page. However, the possibility of a high culture or civilization depends on the ability of mastering the evanescence of the spoken word. From this it follows that literature, and all that it entails, are grounded in speech. Accordingly we can conclude that not only is speaking (and encountering languages as world- and self-constituting) the foundation of individual humanity, it is at the same time a necessary condition for social, cultural collective self-creation.

Let us now come to some more mundane phenomenological considerations arrived at through the observation of speaking as phenomenon. I shall first consider the noematic aspects of speaking, and then when some variations have been presented proceed to some of the noetic analysis, which in good Husserlian style must accompany each noematic study lest it be thought of as merely an exercise from the natural standpoint, carried to conclusions which are not suitably subjected to the phenomenological epoché. Regrettably in this paper we cannot claim comprehensiveness. Indeed one needs must omit variations which are present and readily at hand after even cursory thought.

Speaking is done by the vocal chords according to physiological evidence, but phenomenologically the speaking body with its postures, gestures, grimaces is the origin of speech. In fact, one would not be aware of vocal chords if one had not studied physiology. The voice can come from various aspects of the body: the stomach, the chest, the mouth, the nose and the head. Time alone prevents us from characterizing the associations with voices originating in these bodily locations. Facial and hand gestures reveal not merely the objective meaning of the spoken word, but primarily the bearing of the speaker.

Firm, sharp hand movements emphasizing the cadence of the sound, the words flowing with rapid eloquence reveal conviction, competence, the desire to persuade, to convince, to overpower on the part of the speaker. On the other hand, a hesitant, slow artic-

ulation accompanied by chin-grasping or mouth-covering movements of the hand reveal uncertainty and deliberateness.

Often, if the words desired need be accurate, but are elusive,
the speaker, in a symbolic search will look around for them rather
than maintaining eye-contact with his interlocutors. The words
in that situation come in staccato groups, with non-grammatical
pauses between successfully found word sequences, or even words.
This kind of speaking reveals concern and the relatively high level
of felt need to communicate successfully.

Speaking that is not free and creative but tied to a previously
written text, be it one's own work or that of another, will tend to
accelerate gradually, become monotonous in pitch and sloppy in
phrase separation unless the reader has acquired a very conscious
mastery of this tendency.

More subtle physiognomic expressions while speaking reveal
excitement, anxiety, insincerity, nervousness or levity. Variations
in intonation, rhythm, volume, rate, pitch, cadence, may express
and communicate sarcasm, uncertainty, anger, desperation, or
the ceremonial or protocol function of the speaking, as in preaching
or public prayer.

Whispering can be of at least two sorts: one conveying intimacy,
as in sharing a secret to which the other alone is privy, another,
one which breaks into the focussed attention of another say at a
lecture or a concert, reveals a need to communicate, to become the
object of the attention of the addressed, to divert his being-to-
ward-something-else.

The choice of vocabulary reveals the cultural horizon of the
speaker as well as his attitude toward the hearer. A highly
polished erudite vocabulary, intermingled with foreign phrases
and proper names is impressive but often deliberately chosen to
impress. On the other hand, very short sentences which contain
frequent ungrammatical sequences reveal the person with limited
intellectual and aesthetic capacity. In contrast, the aesthete and
the punster demonstrate in their speech an awareness not only
of the meaning but also of the sound-pattern of words and their
tonal interrelationships. It is fundamentally this awareness which
is the generator of one kind of poetry.

I would now like to turn to the noematic question once removed, "who can speak to us?" At some obvious and foundational

level only another person can speak to us; furthermore, another who is in our sensory region or vicinity. However, as one matures, conceptualizes, and develops a degree of socialization, variations on the "who speaks" become possible. Through the mediation of another, be it a person (as when I regret that you say), an object (a book, a diary, a radio, or a phonograph), a person who is not spatially or temporally proximal to us can address us. But this is still trivial.

More interesting is the possibility of being spoken to by the non-person. Here we shift from the noematic to the noetic. Crucial to this experience of being addressed by the non-person is the noetic act of personification. Typically, nature is often experienced as speaking to us.

> "One evening in the verdant wood
> Can teach you more of man,
> Of moral evil and of good
> Than all the sages can,"

says Wordsworth. If one looks at the "language of nature" (which is contrary to what we did concerning the language of man), one can further see that nature can be experienced as speaking to us in at least two different ways. One of these is more from the natural standpoint, as when signs are perceived as signs. An example may be the overcast sky portending rain, or the second robin (and, to be honest, even the first) heralding spring. For phenomenologists one need not emphasize the non-objectivity, the constituted nature of such a "speaking."

But surely this is not what Wordsworth had in mind when he wrote the above cited stanza. Rather, it is the perception of natural events as symbols rather than signs that holds more interest for us. Firstly, let me remind you of the traditional distinction between symbol and sign in the positivist fashion and then ponder about a phenomenologically more viable distinction. The sign is usually thought of as objectively associated with its signification, often as one or the other pole of the cause-effect relation – in the case of the cloud-formation-rain situation, the cloud-formation is thought of as a causal antecedent of the rain, but in the case where I take my six year old son Michael's clean hands or knees as a sign of his having had a very recent bath,

the sign is seen as the effect of signification rather than its
cause.

However, in the case of a symbol, there is no cause-effect relation assumed between the symbol and the symbolized. Rather
the symbol is intentionally related to the symbolized, which requires the assumption of purposiveness. An example might help
here. Supposing that someone were to observe a squirrel busily
collecting and storing acorns and nuts. If this person were suddenly
to feel guilt and remorse for not being materially provident, or
if he were to then be inspired to deposit some money in the bank
instead of spending it on a previously planned pleasure trip, he
would have perceived this squirrel and its activities symbolically.
The critic may say that the symbol in the example chosen is
laden with culture embedded meanings; that the person looking
at the squirrel did not originate his meaning but associated his
phenomenon with a previously familiar cultural horizon. But this
is exactly the point. Being spoken to can occur only within the
context of a previously apprehended, cultural context, the language. The exact significance for me of what is now being said
to me is constituted by me within this socio-cultural horizon of
language and its historically partially determined significance.
Thus, like the organism, the language is alive, dynamic, building
its present gestalt of significance upon the past, and yet in each
sentence (except for prevocal utterances) adding something radically new to its historical content. This "radically new" may or
may not enter into the historical aspects of the language (usually
it does not), and it may or may not become part of the embodied
speaker (depending upon the importance[1] of the utterance).

Thus, it is that nature can be perceived as addressing me. However, because of the incongruity of personifying nature, it is possible to construe experiences of this sort as God speaking to man

---

[1] There are two dimensions in terms of which "importance may be gauged – syn-
chronic and diachronic. A particular utterance may or may not now have importance
for me. This specific sentence here and now is an example of synchronically important
sentences – it occurs in a context, performing just the function I intend it to do. The
bemused "Yes, dear," uttered while immersed in the newspaper can serve as the para-
digm of a synchronically unimportant sentence. But diachronically even the previously cited important sentence is unimportant. Next week or next year I may not recall
it, may not even accept it as having been my utterance. On the other hand, the significant conclusions of this paper, if any, would exemplify something diachronically
important – for even if I were to change my considered conclusions, they would, nonetheless, constitute a biographically relevant aspect of myself.

through nature. Among philosophers Bishop Berkeley has made much mileage from the notion that nature is the language of God. It might be worthwhile here to digress again to examine the transitive of the verb "hear" from an ordinary language point of view, to illuminate the approach to the problem of who speaks. When asking for the object of hearing, one may be referred to sounds. These are sometimes naively reduced to vibrations of the ear-drum, caused by compressions and rarefactions travelling as longitudinal waves. But, of course, sounds are phenomenally quite distinct from vibrations, and thus I for one would resist the notion that one hears air-vibrations or ear-drum resonances; although, I would assent to the claim that sounds can be heard. Perhaps the ordinary language philosopher may remark that the locution "I hear air-vibrations" is unusual and occurs at best only in a certain technical context. However, hearing sounds is in no way impermissible or unorthodox. On the other hand, sound is not the only possible object of hearing, one may hear words, or again, sentences. One may hear arguments. Notice that in each stage of the series – sounds, words, sentences, arguments – there is a progression of emphasis on the meaning complex, and the ultimate stage in this progression is, "I hear you," or more fully, "I hear you speaking." None of the lower levels of examination of the objects of hearing need be refuted or rejected. They each convey a fundamental truth, but as we progress from "sounds" to "you" in our constitution of the hearing event, we shift the focus of our being from the Buberian "I-It" relation toward "I-Thou" relation.

On careful thought we can see that the progression is in a sense asymmetric. To hear a word we must leave a sound or (its analogue); to hear a sound need not imply hearing a word. A sentence requires words; words do not necessitate a sentence. Arguments are couched in sentences, but sentences do not necessarily yield arguments. But in order to have especially the higher objects of "hearing" one must have two persons – the speaker and the hearer. These two may, under special circumstances, be in fact one, because of the possibility of reflexiveness. Thus, we see that in one sense (and only one sense) one can say that the object of the verb "to hear" is the other person. It is in that sense of this verb that hearing and speaking are inter-relevant. The speaker can be heard.

Now when the reflexive situation arises, when the speaker whom I listen to, whose speaking I hear is myself, then the process of speaking is no longer so called in language – it is called "thought." The trivial exception is the instance such as the present one, when what I hear is myself speaking but my speaking is tied to this previously written text. And so the "other" whom I now hear is that John Mayer of yesterday, who was writing a conclusion to this paper. To the degree that I can now correct or elaborate on the text is my present hearing myself, an instance of thinking as well.

But now to summarize. I have so far tried to show that in speaking, especially in the dialogue form, with encountering language as the first mode of dialogue, we lay the foundation of a philosophical psychology, a philosophical anthropology; I have hinted how it is possible to move toward a theology (in hearing God who uses the language of nature to intend moral and aesthetic addresses to which I am to respond creatively, freely in action), an ethics which combines the relativism of my personal situation with the absolutism of being addressed, an epistemology based on the encounter with language, and a metaphysic rooted in the experience of bridging the traditional subject-object, I–other, active-passive dichotomies by means of the fundamental fact of speaking.

WALTRAUT J. H. STEIN
West Georgia College

SYM-PHILOSOPHIZING IN AN ETHICS CLASS

> He who sings a true song joins in an antiphony and
> finds that his own voice does not simply die with his
> own last tones. To understand and to be understood,
> to love and to be loved, to create and to be the catalyst
> of creation – if these are the basic chords of life, then
> Herbert Spiegelberg is indeed singing a true song and
> this volume may be considered as part of his antiphony.

When I returned from Herbert Spiegelberg's Workshop in Phenomenology in the summer of 1967, I was quite upset about my
experiences. I had not gotten at all what I had expected to get.
To be sure, I had a pocketful of techniques, impressions of some
pleasant associations, visions of the St. Louis arch. But I did not
have any essences, and I had no clear idea of how I was ever
going to get any. It was not long before I began to wonder about
the whole idea of sym-philosophizing as working together to
grasp immutable essences on which everyone would agree. It was
this Platonic conception of philosophizing that I finally concluded
had been at the basis of the Workshop and that I now found it
incumbent on me to reject. If there was to be sym-philosophizing
at all, it must have a goal other than this.

In this paper, Herbert, I would like to share with you my reply
to the ideas I received in your Workshop. I also want to thank
you for arousing me to the kind of questioning in which I am
currently engaged. No, I do not agree with you, but I want you
to know that I am convinced that my disagreement has been most
important for my intellectual development. I view you as my
teacher, and I want to tell you what I have been learning.

Immediately upon returning from the Workshop, I began experimenting with the structure of my ethics class, which course

I have been teaching at least three times a year since then. At first I adhered fairly closely to your ideas of turn-taking and insisting that everyone take his turn. But I soon moved away from using these techniques exclusively, though I still use variations of them occasionally, as you will see.

At the same time as I began this experimenting in my classroom, I began to develop a theory of man and of education. Some of the results of my reflection appear in two papers.[1] Then, more recently, I became aware of therapeutic encounter groups and listened to the ideas of an existential psychiatrist in Atlanta, Georgia, Edward L. Askren III, who refused to make a theoretical distinction between psychotherapy and education.

Once more, I began to wonder about the educational process and its goals. Was I perhaps still conceiving of the goal of education too narrowly as "to equip the educated person with the means of realizing his own goals in the context of his cultural heritage in a way that at the same time creatively advances this heritage?"[2] Should the goal, for instance, be ecstasy, as Leonard suggests?[3] And what about the "relevance" about which students are clamoring so much? Surely the goal is not just to teach people to "relate"! Should education, and, in particular, courses in philosophy, have anything to do with "educating feelings"? Was the goal perhaps self-understanding? Or was it the case that when content was omitted, all that remained was "style" resulting in superficiality and eventual despair?[4] Perhaps it would then, after all, be better not to deal with students as persons with problems in living but as containers to be filled with information about their heritage. However, I refused to accept this conclusion, either and I continued my experiments, all the while reflecting on these questions, trying to hear what my students were really communicating to me, and evaluating the results of my efforts with them. Though today I have periods when I am most satisfied with what

---

[1] "Cosmopathy and Interpersonal Relations" in *Phenomenology in Perspective*, edited by F. J. Smith. (The Hague, Martinus Nijhoff, 1969).
"Exploiting Existential Tension in the Classroom," *The Record – Teachers College*. (May 1969, vol. 70, no. 8), pp. 747–753.
[2] "Exploiting Existential Tension . . .," *op. cit.*, p. 749.
[3] George B. Leonard, *Education and Ecstasy*. (New York, Delacorte Press, 1968).
[4] Seymour Halleck, "You can go to Hell with Style," *Psychology Today*. (November 1969, vol. 3, no. 6), p. 16 ff.

my students and I achieve together, I am also convinced that it is only now that I am really beginning to become an educator.

In fact, if you will pardon the audacity of the comparison, Herbert, it may be that continual beginning is integral to my truly being an educator, just as Husserl conceived of himself as a continual beginner in philosophy. I have discovered, for instance, that what informs all my work with my students is a radical openness. This openness is in three areas: epistemology, metaphysics, and ethics. I want to keep my theory of knowledge open and not permit it to congeal into rigid techniques. I want to keep open my idea of the proper subject matter of the course and of what this is that we want to learn. And, finally, I want to be open to every kind of communication on as many levels and in as many contexts as possible in all of my living. I do not hesitate at all to communicate these commitments to my students as soon in the course as I can in order to assist them in orienting themselves. I also acknowledge to them that I shall have great difficulty in working with people who do not share these commitments.

However, I must add that these commitments to openness have not prevented me from developing techniques to use in conducting my course nor from structuring learning situations for my students. It is just that I am continually developing my rationale for these techniques and the techniques themselves. In fact, I have discovered each of these techniques more or less spontaneously, sometimes at the suggestion of students, and worked out a rationale for it as I used it. I would like to describe a few of these techniques I am currently using and the rationales I am working out for them. This development is continuing, and I am only telling you where I am in it now. In fact, in the very telling, I am discovering for myself a little more clearly what I am doing. So in one more way you are acting as my teacher, Herbert, as I continue to reflect on the educational process and its goals.

In general, all my techniques revolve around balancing occasions for dialogue with the texts, the teacher, and fellow students with occasions for meditation alone and for independent thought. I present students with the following working definition of ethics: Ethics is seriously raising and attempting to answer the question of the proper way to live. I suggest that students consider the course like a cafeteria in which they are confronted with many differing selections. Their task is to consider their own needs, what each selection offers them, and then how or whether they can use it to fulfill their needs. I encourage independent and imaginative responses to the texts, but I also try to make sure that students are really listening to the texts and not just reading their own ideas into them. I point out to them that one gains no new insights from doing the latter, but only from really attempting to immerse oneself in another person's position. One can always reject the position later, though I also tell them that I have found that when I really make this attempt to grasp another's position, I almost always discover that he has *something* to say that I can use in developing my own ideas on how to live satisfactorily. I add that I find this to be true in my personal contacts, as well.

So now let me describe techniques I use under three general circumstances: (1) independent work outside of class, (2) in the classroom, and (3) for field trips.

The Notebook

To encourage independent work, the main technique I use is a notebook, which I ask each student to maintain throughout the course. His first entry is to be a "contract" with me and his fellow students, telling us as specifically as he can what he wants from us and from this course. To give him some idea of what he can reasonably expect to get, I present him with a detailed assignment sheet, textbook list, a few mineographed pages called "A Plan for Student Participation," and a copy of my paper on existential tension. I tell students that my plans are subject to revision and to be prepared to have their contracts read aloud in class. On the second day of class I read each contract aloud, giving each student my response in the presence of his fellow students and eliciting the response of other students. This technique immediately puts some responsibility for establishing educational goals in the hands of the students, it introduces them to one another and to me, it relieves some of their anxiety about not fitting in or not having the proper background to do the work when they discover that other students have these anxieties, too. Finally, it at once eliminates students who are completely unwilling to engage themselves actively. I encourage the last to drop out.

Students are further instructed to use their notebooks to record what they have learned that is in some way important to them in response to each class meeting. I emphasize that what I want is not just a record of what was said in class, either by me or by others, but of what impressed them, of what they can use in some way from the "cafeteria" presented and of how they can use this. If they got nothing they can use that day, they are simply to record this in their notebooks, and I assure them that I expect them not to get anything occasionally. I instruct them to use the first person in their writing and, in particular, to avoid the impersonal "you." My reason for giving this instruction is to help them to become aware of their ideas as their own and to recognize that everyone does not necessarily share them. Many of them find it quite difficult to use the first person, but usually admit later that this simple technique helps greatly in achieving the above goals. After I am convinced he understands what I want, I plan to read each student's notebook about once a week. My main goal in asking the students to record what they have learned in their notebooks is to let them develop the habit of noticing what they are learning and its "relevance" to them and their existence, actually defining "learning" as they do this. My goals are also to place some responsibility for getting something on them, to provide an opportunity for the expression of "second thoughts" or thoughts that they may have hesitated to present verbally in class, to encourage listening to what is going on, to give students an opportunity to correct mis-interpretations or errors they may have made in preparing for class. Finally, these responses provide very useful feedback for me in determining future content and techniques.

As students begin to understand what I expect of them, I encourage them to use their notebooks in imaginative ways. In fact, I even encourage students who present themselves more easily orally, to do less writing and more speaking, sometimes using a tape recorder.

I also ask students to record their preparations for class discussion in their notebooks. This usually means that they are to answer a few related questions on the text they have read, which questions they find on their assignment sheets. A typical set of questions might be: "In your own words explain what Kant means when he says that man is an end in himself and never a means only. What are the implications of this position for race relations and for business ethics? Do you think that people could or should live by this idea? Why or why not?" The question on Albert Camus' *Stranger*, with which I often begin the course, is this: "Does Camus' Stranger represent the proper way to live? Why or why not?" As you might expect, Herbert, this question raises a host of objections to its legitimacy and to the legitimacy of the enterprise of ethics at all. I encourage students to confront these questions seriously and not simply to dismiss them with "Who's to say?"

I ask students to answer these questions in writing to ensure preparation for class, telling them that the class will be little more than a bull session unless they make some preparation for it. I also want to give students an opportunity to make independent attempts to understand the text and to consider the implications of the problems involved in the views presented. I find that asking them to record their ideas in their notebooks lets them spend more time in thinking and less time in composing a formal paper.

As students get to know one another, I encourage them to exchange their notebooks and to make the same kind of marginal notes I make. This technique lets them assume the role of teacher in relation to one another, to communicate with one another in one more form, and to integrate their verbal communications with their written ones.

In about the middle of the course I ask each student to review his notebook, replying to any marginal comments that warrant reply and then to write a short essay on "What my notebook tells me about who I am." Following this, they are to revise their original contracts and the assignment sheet in the light of where they now want to go in the remainder of the course. I expect replies to be quite specific at this point, and I make actual revisions in the assignment sheet in response to them. I make this assignment to encourage "recollection," which I take to include serious turning inward and the attempt to synthesize one's own values. The revision of the contract and of the assignment sheet once more puts them in a position to take the course of their education actively into their own hands.

After the middle of the course, I introduce little new material but rather concentrate on repeating assignments to permit students to penetrate the texts more deeply and to relate varying views to one another. I point out to them that I consider much of learning in spiral terms: that the learner spends his life going over and over a limited number of themes on ever deeper levels. Students are occasionally asked to construct hypothetical dialogues on specified issues between two, and sometimes among three, thinkers in their notebooks. A typical such instruction might be: "Every person has the right to ask for and get whatever he wants. Construct a dialogue among Hobbes, Mill, and Epictetus, indicating their views on this statement. Conclude by presenting your own views in response to this dialogue." A variation of preparing for class by actually constructing a dialogue is to assign each student one thinker to defend orally in class and to elicit each student's own views at the end of the class.

The Classroom

So now perhaps I should leave the discussion of how I use the notebook and describe a few of my classroom techniques. Again, in using any of these techniques, I try to be responsive to what is going on in the classroom, and I do not hesitate completely to abandon any technique on the spot, if I become convinced that it is serving no useful purpose. In general, my goal in developing these classroom techniques is, of course, to create a situation in which optimal learning can take place, be it learning of what I am expecting the students to learn or of something quite unexpected. The main problem with which I find myself involved in developing all of these techniques, either in the classroom or in independent writing, is that of how much structure the students require for optimal achievement. I usually find that I can gradually reduce formal structure and very specific assignments as the course progresses at which time we can all more freely follow where our ideas lead us.

As you know, Herbert, I am working in the South with young people who have generally been exposed almost exclusively to a very authoritarian style of teaching. Consequently, they generally present a most passive front to me when I first encounter them. Many of them can see little intrinsic value in formal education at all. They lack spontaneity, independence, and a willingness to take responsibility for the course of their education. However, the brighter ones are seldom as passive as they seem, expressing their hostility to authoritarian procedures typically in passive-aggressive ways. Until they become convinced that I am not going to convert them to anything unless they want to be converted and am not going to force them to memorize material that they cannot understand or see any reason for memorizing, I find I have to deal with much passive-aggressive behavior. Thus, many of my techniques center around minimizing occasions for such behavior and protecting myself from being exploited by these manipulations.

As I have become aware of what my students are doing, I have observed an interesting process in our developing relationship. In the beginning I am clearly very active, stating my goals and trying to convince them that they should involve themselves in their education rather than just memorize and feed me back what I say. After the first few weeks, I usually begin to feel that many of them are exploiting my good will and manipulating me passive-aggressively. At this point, I confront them with my anger at being so manipulated, expressing my helplessness to make them do anything at all. At the same time, I also tell them that I will return to authoritarian methods if they insist on defining the situation in this way, because I refuse to be exploited by them. This confrontation makes many of them aware of their behavior and its effect, and they very often give it up. They then make some active attempts to convince me that they want to continue with what we have been doing. It is only after we have worked through this process, which I call "mutual seduction," that I feel we are really in a position to enter into a genuine collaborative effort to achieve the goals upon which we now all agree, rather than dissipating our energies in a power struggle. My guess is that this process of mutual seduction is also a part of developing a collaborative relationship with students who have other patterns of relating to teachers.

This means that at this time I include in my idea of e-ducation (with the etymology of "to lead out of") the idea of seduction (with the etymology of "to lead aside or away"). A teacher must lead her students "out of" their ignorances by taking them along a path they have not been following where they may see things that they have not seen.

I have also found that I can be most sure that learning is taking place in my students when learning is taking place in myself. If I am excited about what we are doing or saying and developing ideas or points of view actively myself in the classroom, students almost always "get" something and note that this was a good class. On the other hand, if I am simply expositing an idea that I am no longer involved with, no matter how great it may have appeared to me when I first developed it, I later discover in their notebooks that students very seldom record this idea as valuable to them. To put it into other words, I find that most learning occurs when I am most truly "with" myself and with my students. Thus, my main concern in the classroom has become to be as actively involved intellectually with what is going on as I can, no matter what the specific technique I am using at the time may be, and to abandon or adapt any technique or content when I find my own attention wandering.

Because my classroom techniques are so flexible, I will just indicate briefly, in general, how I proceed at the beginning of the course and then how I proceed after the middle of the course. I cannot describe to you how I proceed at the end of the course because I let students take the initiative almost entirely, sometimes even reversing the student-teacher relation completely. As a result, each class meeting is different. I might add that I have not used these techniques with more than twenty-five students, though I see no reason why, in principle, they cannot be adapted to any size group.

At the beginning of the course, I usually ask students to divide themselves into groups of from three to five (and occasionally two). They are to use the notes they have prepared for class to attempt to come to an agreement on the best possible answer to the questions on the assignment sheet. Or, if they cannot agree, they are to spell out clearly where their disagreement lies. Each group is to select a spokesman who is to report to the re-assembled class the results of the group's activities. I move in and out of the groups, making sure that the members are really working on the questions assigned. I may throw in further questions to discussion of issues involved. I do *not* tell them what the text "means" at this point, but show them how they can interpret it for themselves. For instance, I may point out key passages or concepts. If I find that a group has really gotten itself into a hopeless impasse, I try to indicate how it might extricate itself by raising questions that it may not have considered, suggesting a distinction, etc. I have even assigned such a group to write an essay on ways of getting out of an impasse in their notebooks after class. I also note problems in communication itself and handle them in various ways, according to the seriousness and nature of the problems. Since I expect students to be imaginative in their responses to the learning situation with which I present them, I try to be imaginative in handling the problems that arise and, once more, to be sensitive to the underlying group dynamics. I do not believe it would be useful to go into more detail on my ideas in this area here.

The goals of these small group discussions are to give each student an opportunity to share with some of his fellow students the results of his independent reflection, to receive views other than his own, to consider his own views further, to grasp the text better by attempting to come to an agreement on the interpretation of it and by making disagreements explicit. In their speaking, in addition to asking them to use the first person, I make the rule that they are to address the person to whom they are speaking directly as "you" and not to talk about him as "he." Just as in using the first person, this simple rule is sometimes very difficult for them to follow because so much of their communication is in the form of gossip in the third person. My goal in asking them to use these verbal patterns is to put them in a position to confront others directly with their own positions and so to discover where they actually are in relation to one another. Once more, they are to become aware of their own ideas as often different from those of others and to take responsibility for them as theirs.

Following the small group discussions, I ask students to form a large circle and place myself at an arbitrary place in it. Then I ask the spokesman for one group to report the results of his group's work. After his report, I first ask whether there is anything that other members of his group have to add. Then I ask whether the class noted any errors in the report or whether there was anything that they found particularly good, both in terms of the interpretation of the text or of interesting ideas. I myself also point out errors I note and support correct interpretations and ideas that interest me. Following this, the spokesman for a second group is asked whether he has anything to add to the report of the first group. In this way, I begin to correct errors and to elucidate the text more formally to present the thinker's central argument and conclusions and some problems I see that these involve. I use the lecture form, although, even now, I encourage interruptions and discussions at any point and I may abandon my lecture notes entirely to discuss a point that arises about ethics in general or about an important ethical problem. When I believe that the text is too difficult for a beginning student to understand without some help from me, such as in the cases of Kant and Aristotle, I reverse the order of lecture and discussion. However, I still expect the students to attempt to read the text before the lecture. As I have developed my techniques, I find I use fewer and fewer prepared formal lectures, although I still have definite ideas that I want to communicate about each thinker we study. When I do give lectures, it is usually in response to the students' expression of the real desire to understand what the author is saying and to clear up some of their own confusions.

One of my goals in this ethics class is to create a situation in which students can become aware of themselves and of their ethical commitments. For this reason, I soon begin very gradually to introduce some encounter techniques into the classroom. I have adapted these techniques from those I have observed Edward Askren using. The kind of thing I am doing is so well-described by William Schutz,[5] for instance, that I believe it unnecessary to do so further here. In using these techniques, I have become aware of their very real power and of how fragile the emotional integration is of many of my students. Thus, I now use them with great care and stop as soon as I begin to feel a great deal of anxiety about what is going on with me and with my students, for I believe that overwhelming anxiety is no more conducive

---

[5] William C. Schutz, *Joy*, (New York, Grove Press, Inc., 1967).

to the kind of education in which I am interested than no anxiety at all.[6] My more specific goals in using these encounter techniques at all are to let students become aware of their feelings, including the sensations in their bodies. They are also to become aware of how others feel. I suggest to them that their feelings, along with their conceptions of how others are feeling, are some most important materials they are using in developing their styles of life. Their value commitments, I continue, are largely based on what they feel and on what they take others to be feeling. Thus, insofar as they are interested in taking their lives deliberately into their own hands, they must become aware of this experiential base: They must notice their spontaneous emotional activity. We usually conclude these very short encounter experiments with a further exploration of the place of feelings in the moral life. I also give students an opportunity to ventilate their anxiety about what we have been doing. Though I realize that I do not have a contract to engage these students in psychotherapy nor the training to deal with what can result from using these encounter techniques with them, I continue to risk their becoming disturbed. I take this risk because I realize that any powerful tool, be it the knife of a surgeon or a psychological technique, can potentially do great harm as well as great good; and I have seen enough good result from using these encounter techniques with my students to be willing to risk an occasional student responding negatively to them. Also, as I have already noted, I stop as soon as I notice anyone becoming extremely anxious. I will, therefore, continue using these techniques because I believe it is so very important to give these young people an opportunity to awaken to their feelings along with awakening to their ideas.

In the realm of ethics at least, I believe that focusing on ideas alone to the exclusion of feelings makes for so much of the aridity of the subject matter, about which students are complaining. Since my formal training is in dealing with ideas, I do, in fact, concentrate the bulk of my attention on them. But I find, for instance, that students do not even distinguish between an idea and a feeling, often saying "I feel" when they clearly mean "I think" and vice versa. To become aware of their feelings and to distinguish them from their thoughts is, I believe, important for

---

[6] "Exploiting Existential Tension ...," *op. cit.*, p. 749.

them to learn. This is not to say that I believe that thoughts do not involve feelings nor feelings thoughts. It is precisely because I *do* believe the preceding that I am dealing with feelings in a philosophy class and with confusions surrounding both feelings and thoughts. The "love of wisdom" in the ethical realm, I am presently convinced, is a desire for a wisdom by which one can live fully and honestly, not having to lie to himself or others. This includes the "wisdom of one's body," of what to do with his love and anger, as well as the more abstract wisdom of the meaning of his human existence and of the principles that make his life livable.

This leads me to the idea that an ethics course should really be taught by someone with training in dealing with *both* feelings and ideas. But enough on this subject for now.

After the middle of the course, I use frequent hypothetical dialogues in which the class is divided into groups representing differing positions. The spokesmen for various positions shift as students assist each other in defending the views they have chosen to defend. Also students are free to change sides when they become convinced that the better arguments are on the other side. Such a class is usually concluded by a few moments of silence in which each person is asked to step out of his role and to consider his own views on the topic. Then we go around the room, giving each person a turn to express his views with responses from me and fellow students forthcoming as they will. I often give my own views at the end and possibly summarize very briefly what went on in that class period as far as I could see. Students' responses at the end of such a session are often quite imaginative and independent, which I encourage heartily. My goals in these group dialogues are generally the same as those I have in asking them to construct hypothetical dialogues in their notebooks with the addition that they deepen their understanding of the thinkers and the issues involved by speaking and listening to one another.

My own general classroom techniques are to support correct ideas strongly and to minimize errors, assuring students that it is O.K. to make mistakes and to change their minds. I tell them that I do not expect them to be able to find all the answers on their own, but just to make a serious effort to do so. Actually,

I have been quite pleasantly surprised at what even the so-called "average" student can accomplish on his own when his independent efforts are supported and encouraged and when he sees the value in making them.

The Field Trip

Once each quarter I take the class on a field trip. We have visited both the state mental hospital and a trappist monastery. Preparation for these trips includes relevant reading and some discussion of what they may expect to find. After the trip, students are to deal with an ethical question in their notebooks. For instance, in preparation for the trip to the monastery, they read *Siddhartha* by Hermann Hesse and were instructed to deal with these questions: "What are the values of the contemplative life as presented by Hesse and the trappist monks? What kind of a place, if any, is there for such a life in America today? Is it your place? Why or why not?" We spend at least two hours several days later discussing their conclusions and anything else they would like to discuss about the trip. We have met at my home for this discussion and occasionally had a party afterwards.

These field trips have had a result that I did not expect. Students have responded with great interest to the particular people they met. For instance, they were impressed by the altruistic, non-materialistic commitment of the social worker who talked with us at the state hospital. The monks we met impressed them as really "with it," in spite of their physical seclusion. These kinds of responses confirm my view, which is one I have heard widely expressed, that young people today are seeking models for a satisfactory style of life and are less concerned with formal principles or formulae for living. My goals in taking students on field trips are thus now mainly to let them observe a style of life that presumably they have not seen and hear how people who live this way justify themselves. I also find that these trips provide an opportunity for the class to develop further into a group of people who are interested in each other.

To conclude this rather detailed description, I would like to summarize how my educational goals appear to me at this time and to generalize about how I am trying to attain them with my students. First of all, I want my students to become aware of the values to which they are already committed and to examine them. Secondly, I want them to differentiate their own commitment from that of their fellow students and become aware of themselves as individuals with a unique view of the world. Thirdly, I want them to become aware of the sources of their commitments in the history of ethical thought, in their own experience, and in current cultural patterns. Fourthly, I want them to recognize that even though they have differing commitments, they have many ideas in common with one another because we all share the same heritage and have certain basic needs and desires as human beings. Thus, even though it is temporary, I want to engender in my students a sense of community as an answer to the alienation so many of them express continuously in a great variety of ways. I want to join with them in this community in order to feel more at home in the world myself. Finally, I want to give them the opportunity to experience themselves and their views, along with the views of others, as valuable, that they are worth being listened to and that it is worthwhile to listen to others. This is to say that I want to give them the opportunity to hear and to be heard, and, above all, to listen to themselves as they find their own voices.

Thus all that I do centers around exposing them to as many differing voices as I can, giving them frequent chances to speak, listening to what they have to say myself at the same time as I listen to my own voice. There are many times when I fail, which failure I recognize as a failure *between* me and my students. However, when I succeed, I sometimes have the rare privilege of watching someone change, and I know that I am beginning to become an educator.

WOLFE MAYS

University of Manchester

PHENOMENOLOGICAL ASPECTS OF PROBABILITY

I. Foundations of Probability: The Informal Linguistic Approach

Venn, in his preface to the *Logic of Chance* (*1866*), pointed out that the science of probability at present occupies a somewhat anomalous position. "By a small body of ardent students it has been cultivated with great assiduity, and the results they have obtained will always be reckoned among the most extraordinary products of mathematical genius."[1] However, he goes on, by the general body of thinking men its principles seem to be regarded with indifference or suspicion. Although one may admire the ingenuity displayed, there seems to be an unreality about the whole treatment. "To many persons the mention of Probability suggests little else than the notion of a set of rules ,. . . with which mathematicians amuse themselves by setting and solving problems."[2]

Venn thinks that a ground for this may be found in the dicing and card-playing examples used to illustrate the theory and the neglect of illustrations from the practical business of life. According to him, the real principles of the science have been meagrely discussed; writers have taken up the subject where their mathematics would best come into play, which has not been at the foundations.

Since Venn's time there has been a considerable amount of discussion of the logic of probability. Axiomatic systems have been constructed to deal with the foundations of the subject.

---

[1] J. Venn, *The Logic of Chance*, Preface to the first edition in the third edition, p. v.
[2] *Ibid.*, p. vi.

Nevertheless, in the 1950 Aristotelian Society and Mind Association Joint Session symposium on Probability, we find Toulmin making the same plaint as Venn did in 1866, except that he rather traces it as due to a failure to study ordinary linguistic usage. He believes that the puzzles of probability arise from a too great interest in abstract nouns such as "probability," "knowledge" and "belief."[3] The reason for this is that they fail to provide a satisfactory analysis of such phrases as "I shall probably come," "It seemed unlikely," "They believe," etc. He finds it difficult to see in concrete terms what one means when one uses the abstract noun "probability." The answer is probably very little, since it refers to a generalized situation, not always specifiable by concrete operations. For example, individuals are referred to a class of instances, as in the case of insurance, etc. Toulmin believes the answer to our probability problems will rather come from analyzing and expanding carefully all the uses of the word "probability" both inside and outside science.

One way of doing this is to see how we learn to use the adverb "probably." We are told a story about a little boy who, faced with a difficult decision whether to meet a friend the following week or to perform some other delectable task, was told by his mother to answer by using the magic word "probably." Toulmin's contribution, I may say, also starts with a quotation from a biography called *A Nursery in the Nineties* by Eleanor Farjeon. I think the appeal to the nursery is important, but in these matters I prefer the treatment of the child psychologist to that of the novelist.

In any case, such anecdotal descriptions of how the child learns to use the word "probably" retailed by proud parents must, I think, be counted among the Platonic myths. Below a certain age children have little conception of what is meant by "chance," a concept which has not yet swum into their intellectual horizon. Even if they do learn to use the word "probably," it has not for them the conceptual connotation it has for the adult (who needs abstract nouns to describe it) – it merely, at least in this example, seems to have a tension releasing effect.

I also think that Toulmin underestimates how much of our

[3] Aristotelian Society Supplementary Volume: *Psychical Research, Ethics and Logic*, 1950, cf. pp. 27 ff.

adult civilized thinking occurring on a common-sense plane has been permeated by technical notions derivative from gambling and games of chance, which form a characteristic feature of 20th century society. Indeed I have found myself that ordinary people are much more likely to make snap judgments of equipossibility than is usually supposed.

L. J. Russell, the other symposiast, strongly repudiated this approach.[4] He asked, is a scientific theory of dynamics to be tested by its ability to explain and justify our usages of words like "force," "motion," etc.? If ordinary usages are based on mistaken assumptions, it is the business of the scientist to reject them, and not to justify them. The scientist should have his eye on the development of his subject rather than on ordinary usage.

It might be objected that one prefers an empirical science to be based on solid foundations, and not be a purely "as if" structure without any concrete exemplification. And, further, even if one does not accept the view that the philosopher's task in probability is to clarify the meaning of probability statements made by the ordinary man, there is also another aspect to this question. In some situations it might be of value to note the differences between and vagaries of our private probability judgments. Even if we agree with L. J. Russell that it is wrong to tell the probability theorist what to do on the basis of everyday usage (which in our culture is permeated by scientific notions), there is no reason, even if everyday usage is highly illusory by objective (mathematical) standards of probability, to reject it out of hand. After all, we have the example of Freud, who took certain illusory experiences – namely dreams – and showed that not only were they subject to some sort of law, but that an analysis of them also helped to put our normal behaviour into its proper perspective. In the past the so-called illusions and fallacies of probability have either tended to be passed over or paraded as examples of the fallibility of the human mind. Both Laplace and Venn, however, recognized their importance by devoting chapters to them. It may be that it is unsound to base a theory of probability on such experiences, but they are interesting in themselves, and in the long run may not be entirely irrelevant to the foundations of the subject.

4 *Ibid.*, pp. 63–74.

As long as the applications of probability theory were restricted largely to the inorganic world, to molecules in gas chambers, to the disintegration of radium atoms, etc., the aberrations and illusions of our probability judgments remained curiosities, forms of subjective error. However, this theory is being progressively applied nowadays, either in its classical form or in its information theory derivatives, to human behaviour. It has been applied to learning theory in the guise of dependent probabilities. And in some cybernetic circles randomness has been taken as synonymous with free will.

What is clear is that when we apply probability methods to the study of individual psychological behaviour, instead of the study of group behaviour, we do need a preliminary investigation of how a person actually does make such judgments. There is an astonishing complacency in the way we apply questionable generalizations relating to chance and probability to our ordinary life situations. If human probability judgments follow different laws from that of the classical mathematical model, then it may be a misuse of this model to apply it uncorrected to human judgments.

II. Foundations of Probability: The Formal Logical Approach

Let us now turn to the views of Keynes as to the nature of probability. As he regards it as a purely logical relationship, his view would appear to differ from that of those philosophers who wish to base this notion on ordinary usage. For Keynes, probability seems not to admit of further analysis. "We cannot analyse the probability-relation in terms of simpler ideas."[5] It would thus seem to be taken as an unanalysable relation – something grasped by an intellectual intuition. This position could be reconciled with that of ordinary usage, since it might be said to be merely an appraisal of the common understanding of the word "probability."

Such an approach may be the simplest and most satisfactory, if we are merely interested in the formal development of the subject. However, on an epistemological level (which the practical worker in the field of probability may feel that he can ignore),

---

[5] J. M. Keynes, *A Treatise on Probability*, 1921, p. 8.

the logical concept of probability, satisfactory though it may be, lays itself open to the criticism that what it takes to be simple and unanalysable is really complex and further reducible to simpler terms. A similar criticism is made by Quine in the field of conceptual meaning, when he asks for the pragmatic counter-parts of such concepts as "synonymy" and "analyticity." I imagine Toulmin is really trying to do something on these lines, when he asks what in our ordinary linguistic usage corresponds to the "abstract nouns" used in probability theory.

In recent years Carnap, for example, has shown more sensitivity to pragmatic questions. He has gone out of his way to state a behaviourist operational procedure for the determination of the conceptual meaning of such intentional notions as "synonymy" and "analyticity." He has not as far as I know yet developed a pragmatics of probability.

In his *Logical Foundations of Probability*, Carnap seems only to have dealt with probability on a semantic level. He was concerned to point out there that in our language there is a multiplicity of phrases which express probability notions, such as "degrees of belief," "reasonable expectation," etc. For Carnap the problem of probability is the problem of finding an adequate explication of the word "probability" in its ordinary meaning. He therefore examines a number of phrases relating to probability notions taken from philosophical writings, and concludes that they are reducible to one of two forms:

(1) Probability as an objective logical relation;

(2) Probability as a relative frequency.

Although Carnap may be right in this analysis, his sample of phrases is a somewhat special one, taken from the vocabulary of professional writers on probability theory. This does not seem to be the same as giving an account of the ordinary meaning of the word, which presumably he is seeking.

Carnap does not attempt to exhibit to us all the multiplicity of correct and incorrect ways in which probability notions might be used. His approach seems rather to have been the *ad hoc* one of starting from the learned literature on the subject, to select phrases and expressions reducible to these two notions. As I have said Carnap may be right, but he seems to have gone the wrong way about demonstrating this, if the philosophical problem of probability is, as he says, to find adequate explicata of the technical notions of probability in our ordinary usage.

Philosophers of a linguistic persuasion interested in ordinary usage have, it is true, put forward programmes for the study and cataloguing of the diverse ways expressions function in probability situations. As far as I can see, however, their writings seem preliminaries for a journey rather than the journey itself. Nevertheless there is at least one piece of solid empirical research in this field. Arne Naess has interested himself, using the questionnaire method, in the way subjects (usually university students) discriminate between such expressions as "true," "equally likely," "probably," etc.[6]

One limitation of his experimental semantic enquiry, a field in which Naess is a pioneer, is that it remains largely peripheral. It does not get down to investigating what sort of concepts the subjects possess about probability situations, and their reasons for holding them. They are merely asked to discriminate between shades of meaning. Naess's investigation raises a well-worn question of principle: Can one have concepts in a vague way, though one may not possess a precise vocabulary for differentiating between them? One can give a subject a range of terms and expressions relating to probability situations, but few adults, let alone children, have a sufficiently fine linguistic sense, as well as an adequate conceptual apparatus, to distinguish between them. The sort of reply one gets from the less sophisticated is that these terms all mean the same.

III. The Psychological Approach to Probability

An approach to the pragmatic understanding of probability notions has in recent years been made by psychologists, who have attacked the problem from the standpoint (a) of scientific methodology and (b) concept formation.

As far as I can make out, the initial impulse came in the case of (a) from the attempts by Rhine and others to apply statistical techniques to E.S.P. experiments, where the subject's guesses appeared to be more than chance, which thus seemed to give

---

[6] Arne Naess, *An Empirical Study of the Expressions "True," "Perfectly Certain" and "Extremely Probable,"* (Oslo, 1953).

some evidence for precognition. Some psychologists attempted to spike Rhine's guns by questioning whether human beings really made choices according to the laws of mathematical probability. They distinguished between "subjective" and "objective" probabilities, where "subjective" is used in a rather special sense[7] to describe what one actually does believe, whether it is illusory or not. They attempted in their own experiments on card guessing to explain Rhine's results on the lines that our guessing patterns followed different (private) rules from those postulated by mathematical probability theory in terms of which these guesses were said to be extra-chance.

It was pointed out by them that different persons used different rules when guessing, and that only if we use a machine or a roulette wheel to do our guessing for us, could we eliminate the effect of such sets of private rules from the field of response. A situation involving a machine "guessing" according to a random pattern, might be considered as an example of a more objective probability than one involving a human respondent. Such a guessing machine would not seek to remember its calls or employ rational inference. Each response would be entirely independent of every other, providing, of course, the machine was a perfect one, which is already an ideal. The complete independence of previous selections which would be a feature of such a machine, is in any case seldom true of the human subject. The person does not necessarily behave like such a machine. In a set-up such as Rhine's the subject may be responding to a series which exists only in his imagination (and using private rules of prediction), as well as to the actual physical series. The probabilities may then be incomparable.

In judgments involving a chance situation, it is clear that the more closely the empirical series and the ideal series coincide, the more correct will the predictions be. I do not think that these arguments necessarily dispose of the E.S.P. position, I merely state them in order to sketch the background against which the psychologists' interests in subjective probability developed.

By far the clearest account of this sort of subjective probability

---

[7] This has been called by Frechet "irrational subjective probability" and is to be distinguished from the "rational subjective probability" of Ramsey, Savage, etc. which deals with what one ought to believe.

is to be found in Goodfellow's paper "The Human Element in Probability."[8] He argues there that human judgments are not necessarily distributed according to the laws of probability. The tossing of a coin, for example, is governed by certain physical factors remaining constant throughout the experiment. On the other hand, the calling of the coin is governed by the "mental set" of the caller, which changes from trial to trial. He goes on to assert that many of our statistical techniques for evaluating human judgments do not consider the effect on the data of the observer's "mental set."

He enumerates a number of important differences between physical chance and chance involving a psychological element. One of these is that an individual's response is influenced by his previous response, whereas the physical counterpart is independent of previous selections.

The interdependency of an observer's judgments is (1) due partly to his tendency to change his response because of his previous response (by way of compensation) – this we are told probably arises from a misconception of probability – and (2) one of the alternatives offered may be loaded in various ways. In the case of coin tossing, the verbal habit head-tails explains, he contends, why three-fourths of the population have a tendency to call heads rather than tails. He reports that the subjective expectancy of obtaining a head on the first toss of a coin is not .50 but .80; on the second toss it is close to .57, and close to .44 on the third toss.

The combined effect of these two factors is to produce decided preferences for certain patterns of response. As a result, only a small proportion of the possible sequences is used by the great majority of observers, although our statistical techniques assume that each possible order should occur an equal number of times.

In studying pattern preferences, Goodfellow made the interesting observation that the experimenter in selecting what he considers to be a random order of stimuli, actually uses only a few different sequences. And strangely enough these are the same sequences which are used most frequently by the observers.

Throughout subsequent psychological experiments of this sort

[8] Louis D. Goodfellow, "The Human Element in Probability" in *The Journal of General Psychology* (1940), pp. 201–05.

one finds the dependency-independency theme occurring time and again. In cases where series of random digits or letters are presented to subjects, they do not perceive them as truly random, whatever this might mean. They respond as though some parts of the series are dependable cues to its future behavior. Their judgment depends not just on the past history of the series, but is also contaminated by their previous predictions, their success, etc., which influence their expectations.

Although this field has been extensively studied by psychologists, Venn in his discussion of what he termed the "belief meter" had already noted the disturbing influences of emotions; that our convictions generally rest upon a sort of chaotic basis composed of an infinite number of inferences and analogies of every description. Our convictions are further distorted by our state of feeling at the time and dimmed by our degree of recollection of them afterwards. The amount of our belief depends upon a great variety of causes of which statistical frequency is merely one.

However, these descriptions ought not to be taken as guides to rational behavior, which presumably "rational subjective probabilities" are meant to be (i.e. as ethical norms). They are descriptions of how people do behave, which may, of course, not be the best way of behaving in games of chance, but are perhaps adequate for our day to day existence. It has, for example been pointed out that the rational subjective probabilities postulated by Ramsey, Savage, de Finetti and others, have the mathematical properties of objective probabilities.

Some psychologists, especially Piaget, have tried to work out this independency-dependency theme in the field of child behaviour. This field is basic if we are to see how the concept of chance develops, and whether it is an innate intellectual intuition. In these studies there seems to be no reference to Goodfellow's work, although the conclusions are substantially the same. In Piaget's case, however, the type of experiments performed seem substantially different from the American variety.

The main feature, or peculiarity, of this work of Piaget and others has been to take the abstract calculus of probabilities as an objective standard of mature behaviour. And deviations from it, the so-called illusions, have been taken as a mark of immaturity.

One writer, for example, starts by noting a strange phenomenon, also noted by Laplace in his *A Philosophical Essay on Probabilities*, that if a coin is tossed and appears head nine times in a run, people will regard the appearance of the tail on the tenth toss as having a very high likelihood and the appearance of the head as being extremely unlikely. They will not regard it as an independent event and assign a probability of 0.5. This tendency, we are told, to assign to a single member of a series a probability properly belonging to the entire series is a deep-seated one. It is apparently the root of fallacious "gambling" behaviour as seen, for example, in the belief in the maturity of chances. Incidentally, the maturity of chances policy arises from the justifiable belief that if the penny is a good randomiser, a run of ten heads is unlikely. This belief may be mistaken, but it is certainly not a sign of immaturity. If anything, it shows some sophistication.

The interesting thing is that Laplace, after noting this fact, goes on in his *Essay* to make a related point. "But the past indicating in the coin a greater propensity for heads than for tails renders the first of the events [i.e. heads] more probable than the second; it increases as one has seen the probability of throwing heads on the following throw.[9] Laplace himself therefore leaves open the possibility that there may be some dependency and does not reject it out of hand. In such a context this seems nothing else but a policy of common sense.

The main burden of the experiments described is to show that the child at the age of six, when faced with the task of predicting the outcome in a situation with two alternatives merely alternates from his previous choice (compensation). He also apparently tends to alternate from the side with the larger number of previous outcomes. Success on the previous choice leads him to change, failure to repeat it. At the age of twelve there is the first sign of the concept of independence expressed in the judgment either may happen. There is now an awareness that the outcome of any occasion is entirely unaffected by what has happened on other occasions.

Gamblers, we are told, behave as if they follow the principle of dependence, the fall of a die being based on past outcomes. Such

---

[9] Pierre Simon, Marquis de Laplace, *A Philosophical Essay on Probabilities*, Dover edition, 1951, p. 162.

a belief in dependence has therefore some of the characteristics of an optical illusion.

This sort of study which performs experiments to show that children do not use the calculus of probability in their judgments about chance situations (which should be obvious without much experimentation) makes little attempt to analyse why children's judgments have this character. Instead a special type of subjective probability is postulated to cover what is really an amalgam of emotional and intellectual attitudes. This approach reminds one of the Aristotelian inclined instinct psychologists who postulated a new type of instinct for every form of behaviour, in this case guessing behaviour. Further, such a view overlooks that a belief in abstract equipossibilities (or event independence) may in certain concrete circumstances be itself fallacious. After all, in some situations a belief in event dependency may be our best policy, or stategy, where the coin is biassed.

Further, the whole of our learning depends on a belief in event dependency, and it is doubtful whether one ought to describe behaviour of this sort as immature. This attitude taken to its logical conclusion would imply that a mature person cannot learn by experience.

IV. Piaget and the Child's Conception of Chance

I come next to consider the work of Piaget which is reported on in his book *La Genèse de l'idée de l'hasard chez l'enfant*. He makes a serious attempt to analyse why the child behaves the way he does in chance situations. I am not myself entirely happy about his analysis, and his use of the probability calculus as a criterion of intellectual excellence. However, he has certainly performed a number of ingenious experiments which show how a child behaves when confronted with a probability situation.

Piaget asks the question, is the concept of chance something innate in us or is it something acquired? The whole object of his experiments is to show that the concept of "chance" is not an intellectual intuition, but has to be learnt. He points out that a certain degree of intellectual maturity is required before the child can proceed to make probability judgments.

What Piaget tries to show in his analysis is that since the child endeavours to find a causal factor in everything he observes, he is unable to apply the notion of equipossibilities (or combinatorial notions) to probability situations. My own reaction to this is that the search for causal regularities in situations of this sort is not such a sign of immaturity as Piaget makes it out to be. It must be remembered that the vast mass of situations the child meets with in his day to day life follow a causal pattern, and random situations are most often the exception.

As a model of a physical chance situation Piaget takes Cournot's conception of it "as the inference of independent causal series." Such a notion, he says, can hardly be meaningful to a mind engrained in teleological explanation. When, for example, a gust of wind shuts the door, close to which the child may be standing, he thinks this has been done expressly to annoy him. He does not regard this coincidence as the crossing of two independent causal series of events.

This notion of a series of events at once independent and yet interfering with one another, is best seen in a physical mixture, for example, when we scramble coloured balls in a bag. Piaget takes such experimental mixtures as forming the essence of a chance situation. In such situations the child ceaselessly looks for a hidden order under this disorder, which he considers only as apparent.[10]

The order the child discovers may be based on either certain qualities the elements may have in common or on their arrangement before mixture. These experiments to which the children are subjected, are carried out with the aid of Galton Boards, pin-tables, magnetized roulette wheels, tricked counters, double headed pennies and bags containing different coloured balls. All in all the apparatus used is an exemplification of the sort of problems discussed in abstract probability theory. Its disadvantage is that it forces the child's answers into a predetermined mould.

---

[10] In one such experiment a child is shown an open rectangular box which contains a row of eight white beads followed by another row of eight red ones. The box is then shaken from side to side and the beads collide with one another, so that their positions are changed when they come to rest at the bottom of the box. Before the box is shaken, the child is asked what will happen to the order of the beads if the box is shaken. Between 4 and 7 years of age, he will tend to predict that the beads will return to their original order, that the reds will merely cross over to the positions of the white ones and *vice versa*, and then both proceed back to their original positions. The child is consequently surprised when he sees the actual outcome of the experiment.

As far as early judgments of probability are concerned, Piaget's conclusions are:

(1) In these experimental mixtures the child tries to discover a hidden order founded on their arrangement before mixing.

(2) The child often bases his predictions on the greatest frequencies observed until then. In the case of two possibilities A and B, the subject will bet on A if it has come out more often than B.

Probability arises at a later stage for the child because only when he has built up a system of logical operations so that he can contemplate possibilities (in terms of combinations and permutations) over and above the actual run of events, can he be said to possess the concept of chance. On this level probability consists in judging isolated cases in relation to a group of possible cases. In other words, there is a growth of generality. The child no longer emphasizes particular cases, he is now able to understand abstract nouns. Piaget concludes that psychologically as well as logically, the judgment of probability is closely connected with the elaboration of combinatorial operations.

It is clear that Piaget takes our probability judgments as being modelled on the notions of the mathematical calculus of chances. In this sense, he is no doubt right when he says the child can have no understanding of probability until he learns to manipulate possibilities logically. Nevertheless, in some ways this seems to be a strange doctrine. If children were not able to make day to day probability judgments of a sort in situations of uncertainty, they might soon come to an untimely end. They usually work as most of us do, on the principle of letting past experience be one's guide. Perhaps the child is less able than we adults to dissociate those parts of his experience to which the notion of causal dependency applies from those parts to which the notion of equipossibilities may be applied. He also seems to have difficulty in seeing individual experiences as belonging to a class of experiences. The child likes to treat them as individuals, as unique events.

What Piaget seems then to be really saying is that up to a certain age the child does not possess a conceptual apparatus in terms of which he may carry out intellectual experiments, and contemplate unrealized possibilities. However, the fact that the child, when put into highly artificial experimental situations, uses causal hypotheses instead of the calculus of chances, should not lead us to characterize this behaviour as immature, as many adults would also qualify. It is clear that such probability problem situations, the answers to which are dictated by the experimental set up, reflect sophisticated notions of probability. Such situations may confuse the young child, who looks for causal explanations everywhere. The reason for the child being unable to cope with them is because they are so different from the normal situations in which he finds himself.

V. A Questionnaire on Chance and Uncertainty

We have argued in the main body of this paper that much of our everyday thinking about probability, including the language in which it is expressed, is permeated by technical notions derivative from gambling and games of chance. If this is the case, the attempt to elucidate the puzzles of probability in terms of ordinary linguistic usage presupposes the very notions it set out to explain. Hence, we are faced with the following problem: How far do the technical notions of probability agree or diasagree with the ordinary person's attitudes towards situations involving chance and uncertainty?

In an attempt to answer this question, I devised a questionnaire containing twelve items. These were largely of two types. The first group, bearing in mind the two main theories as to the nature of probability, was concerned to discover whether people believed there were objective probabilities in nature (either as a random series or as equipossible alternatives) or whether they regarded probability as subjective: as a matter of belief. The second group of items dealt with attitudes to such questions as fate and coincidence, and we wanted to see whether these attitudes were consistent or inconsistent with the probability notions people held.[11]

---

[11] The items in the questionnaire covered such notions as randomness, maturity of chances, the principle of indifference and the use of past experience as a guide to future events. Our object was not to discover the precise meaning of the words used by the ordinary person in probability situations to which he has not devoted too much thought, but to map out his specific attitudes to them. Our main interest lay in the classification and description of probability attitudes as a pragmatic counterpart to logical discussions of probability.

The results reported on here are drawn from a small random sample (*20*) of the employees at the Atomic Energy Research Establishment, Harwell, England, who answered the questionnaire. Broadly similar results have been obtained from samples drawn from other sectors of industry and commerce. This investigation, however, claims to be no more than a pilot survey, and should merely be taken as a pointer to future research.

Question (*1*) asked whether it was fair to decide by the toss of a coin, which of the employees in a factory should work on a Saturday afternoon. Most people considered this method to be fair where no rota system was employed, since it makes certain no prejudice is involved. A minority held that it was a haphazard method of making decisions and that rational beings ought to decide by seeing who had the least need to be at home, the toss of a coin having no causal connections with this. The question then raised here is whether a random procedure is a fair, i.e., objective method to use in making certain decisions.

For most people the region of experience in which a person uses a random procedure to make a decision will vary with its importance. Although most of us would perhaps decide whether or not to go to the cinema by the toss of a coin, few would use this procedure to decide whether to get married.

Question (*2*) dealt with a maternity hospital where over the last 150 years, only once had ten boys been born in succession: a run of nine boy births had just occurred, and a donation had been promised to the hospital if the next birth was also a boy. What likelihood was there of the hospital receiving the donation?

Most people took the view that it was a 50–50 chance, and explained this by saying that each birth is a separate event having no connection with the other. Some, however, thought it unlikely, since the odds were very heavily against a second run of boys. But a small number pointed out that there may be factors, geographical or biological which might favour the birth of one particular sex in a community or district. Some people then believe that the births are independent of each other, others again in a minority – hold that there may be a principle of causal dependency between them.

Question (*3*) dealt with the nature of coincidence. One rather sophisticated subject defined it as "a linking up of two or more unlikely events which occur without planning." We found people who believe in some sort of direct objective relationship between the unlikely events. For example, someone has a dream that a certain event is happening and at the same time the event actually occurs. As against this, others regarded the correlation as purely subjective, surprise arising from what appears to us as an unlikely concatenation of events.

Question (4) dealt with a coin tossing situation where a run of ten heads has occurred, and asked whether the run was likely to continue. This question may seem identical with (2) (the maternity hospital example); the former, however, occurs in a context in which one would normally expect to find causal connections, the other is a randomized one. Most people in our sample took this distinction into account, and believed that the events in such contests can be regarded as independent of each other. They held that after a run of ten heads the likelihood of the next throw coming up heads is still *50–50*.

However, as the more sophisticated were quick to point out, "The evidence weighs strongly in favour of the likelihood of a bias and suggests that heads and tails are not in this case equally likely." Thus when we get such a run, a belief in a continuation of heads may be our best policy.[12] This does bring out the danger of applying the abstract notion of equilikelihoods regardless of the particular context.

Question (5) related to a belief in fate, and to whether or not our actions are determined. Some people believed that their destinies were governed by an outside influence, whether physical or supernatural, others that they were masters of their own fate. Some felt that fate is within limits controllable, as we can in a certain measure choose our occupations, etc. In most people's conception of fate there is a close interplay between chance and design.

Question (6) dealt with the nature of luck, and gave as an example someone winning a large prize in a lottery. "Luck," one reply said, "usually means getting what you want in a situation where neither skill, influence, looks or anything else can help you to get it." Another said, "Good luck is to win intelligently against the odds."

[12] As we have seen, Laplace himself made a similar point.

Question (7) enquired what was meant by "chance" and "design." Some replies related chance to the possibility of alternative happenings. Others denied the existence of chance, "there are known effects of every unknown cause, whether the cause is physical or due to God." Some connection between design and chance was seen by most people. Thus it was stated, "Whereas chance is not previously arranged or is accidental, design is planned beforehand, design being the opposite of chance." Very few clear definitions of these notions were given.

Question (8) dealt with a weight-lifter who had only been able to lift a weight ten times in succession in the past. On this occasion he had lifted it ten times and is trying again. What is likely to happen now? Unlike the coin tossing example, people readily admitted the influence of past events on future behaviour. A number said, he would not be able to lift it since the result of the next try is causally connected with the previous results. A minority believed, however, that if a man made up his mind he might be successful on the eleventh try, and also brought in the effect of training, comparing it to running a mile in under four minutes. Both these sets of replies may be contrasted with the replies to the coin tossing questions, where it was generally held that there was no causal connection between the throws.

Question (9) enquired what was meant by an equal chance, and whether in tossing a coin each side has an equal chance of coming up. Equal chances were both objectively and subjectively defined as, for example, when it was said, "The factors on either side influencing the outcome are equally balanced." "Equal chance is luck." "An equal chance is an equal level of mental expectation."

Question (10) dealt with the nature of risk and gave an example of someone placing a bet on a 100–1 outsider in the Derby. "Taking a risk," one reply went, "implies taking a course of action over which one has little or no control or which has an appreciable probability of failure." Some people asserted that the risk would vary with the amount of money put on, but one said, "I don't think the risk would vary – only the amount of money," and we also got the opinion: "The amount of money has nothing to do with the risk."

Question (11) enquired what would happen to the distribution of heads and tails if a coin was tossed a large number of times.

Most people thought that the number would be equally divided. A minority held that in some cases the thrower may develop the art of making the coin turn more on one side than the other. One reply pinpointed the abstract and somewhat *a priori* character of the majority view by saying, "Only if one assumes that the thrower and the coin are unbiassed will the number be equally divided: if not, all can be heads for all one can tell."

Question (*12*) required the writing down of a number and a colour at random. The colour and number most commonly selected were red and seven. We do not have to look for the reason for this, as one reply explained, "I cannot select at random a number for I shall have been influenced by previous experiences, conditioning if you will."

What conclusions can we draw from these results? Apart from a sophisticated minority who accept a subjectivist view that chance is due to our ignorance of the causal factors in play, most of our respondents believe that what are in effect the traditional concepts of Laplacean *a priori* probability have an objective character. In other words, they give an ontological significance to what are really abstract models. If these attitudes are fairly widespread in our culture, the claim that probability problems can be clarified by an analysis of ordinary linguistic usage, will need to be taken with more than the proverbial grain of salt.

Summary

Most discussions of the concept of probability in the past have been of a technical nature and have led to the belief that it has not much to do with the practical business of life. In recent years an attempt has been made by linguistic philosophers and others, to relate the abstract notion of probability to our everyday use of this concept.

Another approach to this problem has been made by psychologists. Their interest arose from a twofold source: (*a*) a study of guessing behaviour and (*b*) a study of the development of the concept of chance in the child. In the case of (*a*) this study originated in an attempt to explain the correlations found in experiments on extra-sensory perception, by the assumption that our guessing behaviour followed certain predetermined patterns.

As far as (b) is concerned it was noted that the probability judgments of the child took time to develop, that his judgments about questions of chance differed from that of the adult. For example, the child when confronted with a randomized experimental situation may seek for causal regularities where none are to be found. The Achilles heel of such experiments is that they put the child into artificial situations which reflect sophisticated notions of probability. They overlook that the vast mass of phenomena met with by the child in his daily life follow a causal pattern, and that gaming and betting problems rarely arise in his experience.

This brings out the danger of taking abstract models, in this case the mathematical theory of probability, and using them as criteria to evaluate our everyday behaviour. If the child is unable to cope with such randomized experimental situations, it is because they diverge so much from his normal experience. We have no reason to suppose that because he does not use the probability laws in his predictions that his behaviour is immature, or reflects some special kind of subjective probability. Children act as most of us do on the principle of "let past experience be your guide."

Finally, we tried to find out what the ordinary adult has in mind when he speaks of such notions as chance and uncertainty. This we did by means of a questionnaire. What our survey showed, among other things, was that the technical notions of probability have percolated down even to the non-mathematical man in the street. It became clear that quite often abstract models, which apply only to highly abstract situations are applied to concrete situations in our everyday life, without adequate realization that such models rarely apply precisely to the facts.

Appendix: Probability and Belief

We have noted that the two best known views held by probability theorists are:

(1) Objectivist views. These hold that some repetitive events, such as the throws of a penny prove to be in reasonably close agreement with the mathematical concept of independently repeated random events all with the same probability.

(2) Subjectivist views. Probability measures the confidence

that a particular individual (assuming he is reasonable) has in the truth of a particular proposition, for example, that it will rain tomorrow. Probability is simply the degree of belief we attach to propositions.

There are certain difficulties in trying to quantify degrees of belief. As Venn pointed out already, any strong emotion exerts a disturbing influence on our belief. It therefore has to be assumed that the mind is quite unimpassioned in weighing the evidence. In rational subjective probability we therefore deal with the behaviour of a highly idealized rational person, whose judgments can be quantified, at least in terms of degrees of belief. As opposed to this are the irrational subjective probabilities, the conscious or unconscious appreciation of probabilities which guide us in daily life, business, politics, war, etc., to the exclusion of the estimation of objective probabilities based directly on frequencies or symmetries.

PART III

BIBLIOGRAPHICAL PERSPECTIVES

HERBERT SPIEGELBERG
Washington University

APOLOGIA PRO BIBLIOGRAPHIA MEA

In acceding to the request for my updated bibliography as an appendix to this volume, I confess to considerable uneasiness at letting it stand as a valid record of my work thus far. What I would like to add on the following pages is some biographical clues which may make the seeming hodgepodge of my publications a little more intelligible. I don't apologize for it nor do I want to defend it. I merely want to provide a frame for some of the pieces, set a few accents, and deemphasize mere by-products from my present perspective.

At this stage it would be premature for me to talk about my ultimate objectives in philosophy which antedate my involvement in it and specifically in phenomenology. I shall begin with the record of my printed publications, to which I added specific annotations separately. But in addition to these, I would like to give some general hints as to my guiding interests and their shifts, without concealing the fact that I have let myself be diverted by incidental temptations such as solicitations for book reviews and historical detective work, the latter one of my chief hobbies and weaknesses in the interest of salvaging the perishable record of the recent past.

The basic fact about my bibliography is its bisection not only in terms of language but of topics by my transplantation from the German world of my accidental birth to the Anglo-American world of my choice. It also led to a complete disruption of my original literary plans, however tentative.

During my German life my first objective in preparing the apprentice piece of my dissertation (#1) was to investigate the strange role of what Plato had called Ideas in ontology and in phenomenological philosophy. Beyond the mere fact, established at the time to my satisfaction by Husserl in his *Logical Investigations*, of their indispensability, I had in mind a concrete exploration not only of their "essence" but of their mode of "existence" in order to determine their role in human life. I hoped that this would provide decisive evidence for freedom of "will", inasmuch as Ideas could not dispose of any power of their own but required "empowering" by the free acts of persons. I have never returned to this project and feel no longer sure that it is urgent and feasible. Such urgency led me to turn to the study of problems of ethics and "natural law" prepared by my preceding law studies, in which I had a much more direct interest, even before my over-ambitious start in phenomenological ontology. The immediate result of this seemingly unrelated enterprise was the book on law and moral law (#5), which was to serve as the basis for my admission to lectureship (*Privatdozentur*) at the University of Munich, with a systematic and an historical part, motivated partly by academic reasons. It was to supply the basis for asystematic deontological ethics without appeal to the concept of moral law, which is so much more prevalent in the German than in the Anglo-American tradition. I completed this manuscript under the title *Sollen und Dürfen* (Ought and May) before leaving Europe, where it could no longer be published.

My transition to the New World was prepared by a year in England with two months in Cambridge and Oxford used partly for the study of the new British moral philosophy and jurisprudence, with a view to finding out whether my German work could be relevant in the new setting. The adjustment to the American academic world required a complete reorientation especially since my first chance for teaching was on the introductory undergraduate level. For the first fifteen years the preparation of book manuscripts, especially in a language in which I was not yet at home, was out of the question. My first attempt to contribute to the discussion in ethics and philosophy of law (#10, 19, 29) seemed ineffective, although one piece, a new defense of human equality, recently re-emerged in John Rawls' *Theory of Justice*. Other attempts to contribute to such controversies as that of naturalism versus supernaturalism did not fare better. Even my attempt to use the first opening for phenomenology in the United States in the early forties for the clarification of some of its problematic concepts and for stating the case for a modified phenomenological realism did not help toward breaking out of the philosophical isolation in a small Wisconsin college for twenty-two years of my American life. In 1951 I had finally become so frustrated with my college uselessness that I took the gamble of an unpaid sabbatical leave for preparing a larger treatise on the ethics of self-transposal as a new foundation for a deepened and widened social and international ethics. It was at this point that the biggest and in a sense most fateful diversion in my literary life began. It consisted in an invitation to visit as a pinch hitter at the University of Michigan for my first graduate teaching, a temptation which I could not resist. Expecting to have a chance for trying out my new ideas on social philosophy, I found out that the main demand was for a seminar on contemporary continental philosophy, a demand which I could meet only by improvising a syllabus with the main emphasis on phenomenology. The result of this improvisation was the suggestion by my colleague friends, the late Paul Hene and William Frankena to prepare a brief historical introduction to the Phenomenological Movement, which soon developed into two volumes, on which I had never planned in this form. Thus in terms of my bibliography the time since 1951 has been on the surface one of doing nothing but history of phenomenology rather than phenomenology proper. This fateful trend has continued even after I came to Washington University in Saint Louis in 1963, when I was already started on the supplementary job of tracing the role of phenomenological philosophy in psychology and psychiatry, which turned out to be as demanding in terms of studying and writing time as had been its predecessor. In this connection I should also mention another diversion related to my one remaining ambition in Europe: that of awakening interest in the unfinished work of my main teacher, Alexander Pfänder, Husserl's early independent associate, not for sentimental reasons but because I believe that this posthumous work contains a valid alternative to Husserl's radical phenomenology without its idealistic conclusion. Now that this has been made accessible in German, it may even become relevant for Anglo-American philosophy.

Under these circumstances I have probably little chance of living down my questionable reputation of being the "definitive" historiographer of the Phenomenological Movement. But at least I would like to combine my protest with pointing out that since my coming to the graduate freedom of Saint Louis teaching I was able to resume work on some of the issues for whose sake I had turned to philosophy, and which I had had to shelve since coming to America. By this I mean chiefly my efforts to develop an ethics based on a deepened phenomenology of the self and its fundamental predicament, which I sketched out thus far only in my German lectures at the University of Munich in 1962. Instalments of this project in English can be found in # 36, 37, 45, 58, 60 and 67. How far shall I be able to carry out this plan?

But there is one other ambition which means to me more than history of phenomenology and "meta-phenomenology": that of promoting the doing of phenomenology by a combination of individual and group phenomenology. This idea has led to the pilot experiment of the five Washington University Workshops in Phenomenology, 1965, 1966, 1967, 1969, and 1972. The results have been encouraging but far from conclusive. I have hopes that this approach will bear more fruit once it can be emancipated from my personal leading strings. Considering all the help and inspiration I have enjoyed in this enterprise from so many friends, including contributors to this volume, the actual workshops certainly never belonged to me.

I realize that even this explanatory apologia cannot integrate my scattered enterprises into a convincing pattern. The fact remains that my actual publications represent a compromise between evolving plans and distorting circumstances. But a single-purpose system of philosophy was never my ambition. I have always been a piecemeal worker. I wanted to do what seemed urgent and manageable to me whenever I felt capable of doing it and therefore responsible for it. As to more basic concerns and motivations this is not the occasion to speak of them. They belong to a part of my biography not directly related to the inordinate number of publications for which I wanted to do some accounting here in a way which will help those looking for an Ariadne's thread through this maze.

CONTEXTUAL ANNOTATIONS TO ITEMS
OTHER THAN INCIDENTAL PIECES

such as most book reviews

1. An attempt to explore the concrete "essence" of Husserl's universals preparatory to an investigation of their comparative mode of existence.

3. A study of a concept basic in Alexander Pfänder's ethics and later in my unpublished manuscript on the grounds of moral rights and duties; some traces of it also occur in #22.

4. An attempt to buttress the epistemological foundations for ethics and for a non-relativistic theory of values, obligations and rights.

5. A study motivated in part by the desirability for academic use of presenting a systematic as well as historical piece of research, preparing the ground for a larger book on *Ought and May: The Philosophical Foundations of Moral Rights and Duties*.

6. An isolated piece inspired by the need to distinguish the modern conceptions of intentionality from their alleged foundations in scholastic philosophy, ending with some ideas on philosophical anthropology.

7. A by-product of my historical studies for #4, triggered by a chance discovery of a dialogue on conscientious objection in the 100 Year War, related to my stake in the philosophical foundations of pacifism.

9. A consideration of the consequences of overpopulation for man's consciousness of his own value.

10. A first attempt to present some ideas of my plan for a new value-based natural law in the setting of a Meeting of the Southern Society for Philosophy and Psychology in Knoxville, Tennessee, which I attended soon after my arrival in the States in 1938.

13 and 14. Originally one article cut in two because of a retroactive space limitation, in which I presented the case for a "critical" phenomenological realism; I also tried to assimilate some of the evidence presented by American philosophy into the realistic version of phenomenology given by Pfänder.

17. An attempt stimulated by an invitation to submit a paper to compete in a symposium on phenomenology arranged by the American Philosophical Association, Eastern Division in 1940, in which I tried to refine the concept of self-evidence phenomenologically with a view to meeting some of the major objections to its validity.

19. A first attempt, motivated by the totalitarian challenge to the "self-evident truth" of equality, to find existential foundations for the legitimate core of the demand for equalization.

22. An attempt to make an addition to the moral philosophy of W. D. Ross and C. D. Broad in line with Pfänder's unpublished ethics.

23. An attempt to establish a minimum Cartesian foundation for ethics in the spirit of Husserl's pure phenomenology.

26. An attempt motivated by the expectation I encountered in Wisconsin at the time of my arrival to take a stand in the controversy between naturalism and anti-naturalism, a disjunction whose validity I tried to contest by a phenomenological use of the tools of analytic philosophy.

27. An incidental attempt to condense some ideas on social philosophy which I had tried to develop in my lectures at the University of Michigan when reentering Continental philosophy at the Brussels International Congress.

28. An attempt to show the varieties of existentialism and its social philosophies, in partial refutation of generalizations about its alleged nihilism, prepared in response to an invitation by an editor of the Review.

30. A result of an invitation by the Peirce Society to speak about the relation of Peirce and Husserl.

31. A sample from my unpublished German manuscript mentioned under #5.

32. Sparked by an invitation to take part in a symposium on phenomenology arranged by the American Catholic Philosophical Association.

33. An attempt to combine the record of my encounters with Husserl with a case study in the phenomenology of constitution, allegedly rejected by phenomenologists with a Munich background.

34. Written between 1952 and 1959. Published in the Netherlands because of lack of interest of American presses.
35. Written for a symposium of the American Philosophical Association, Western Division in Madison, Wisconsin.
36. An attempt to utilize a historical observation on Mill's writings for the clarification of a concept basic to my defense of human equality, #19.
37. A first attempt to make sure of the basis for a fundamental experience at the root of my phenomenology and philosophy of the self by empirical methods.
39. An attempt to reintroduce the forgotten Pfänder as a phenomenologist to German philosophy as a basis for later editions of posthumous texts.
40. A partial reply to Marvin Farber's review of *The Phenomenological Movement*, mostly by presenting additional evidence.
41. The remainder of an attempt in the framework of President Nathan M. Pusey's Freshmen Studies course at Lawrence College to show the significance of Socrates not only by presenting the case against him (in a dramatic skit) but by assembling the testimony pro and con from intellectual history up to the present. This anthology, published fifteen years later, could be rationalized phenomenologically as a case study in perspectives on different facets of historical figure.
42. Written in response to an invitation of the Metaphysical Society of America for a symposium on "Experience."
43. Written for the first Lexington Conference on Phenomenology as an attempt to relate my studies in phenomenological psychiatry to phenomenology proper.
44. An attempt to show a convergence between Austin's linguistic analysis and Pfänder's phenomenology, motivated by the occasion of the International Philosophical Congress in Mexico City, in view of the special interest in Pfänder in Hispano-American countries.
45. Introductory paper for a symposium about philosophy and linguistic philosophy at Columbus, unsuccessful in my estimate since the idea of an independent exploration of the same topic by both approaches followed by a comparative evaluation was not taken up.

46. A paper first presented before the Acolyte Club at Ann Arbor in 1952 as an attempt to show the significance of phenomenology for a basic concept in Charles Stevenson's approach to ethics.

47. A first attempt to introduce Pfänder in the atmosphere of Saint Louis University as relevant to the new questions of philosophical anthropology.

48. Written when J. N. Findlay's replacement of Husserl's original telescoped article was to be replaced in turn by an article with a wider scope.

49. An attempt to develop a neglected dimension in the phenomenology of the self, motivated by Erwin Straus's interest in the lived body.

50. An attempt to use the occasion of an invitation for a contribution to the *Nomos* volume on "Equality" not only to explore the varieties of existentialist replies to the question but also to relate it to my own case for human equality in #19.

51. An attempt to formulate one of the lessons of my second historical book in advance of #63.

52. Uses an incidental discovery as an occasion for presenting a remarkable phenomenology of the self in line with my own ideas, especially those in #49.

53. A response to the first spontaneous interest for Pfänder in the States, partly inspired by Paul Ricoeur's pleas.

54. An attempt to introduce some ideas from the unpublished German manuscript mentioned under #5 and #31 in a context apparently ready for it.

55. An attempt to present new evidence about Wittgenstein's middle phase that had just become available in German, motivated by Ricoeur's thesis about parallel developments in Husserl and Wittgenstein in their early and late phases.

56 and 57. An attempt to salvage evidence about the beginnings of phenomenology in England on the occasion of its recent second chance.

58. An attempt at an existential vindication for the different types of phenomenology as distinguished in #34.

60. A first attempt to state an issue with existential implications posed by the increasing appeals to a vague and powerful idea

about which very little has been done thus far, written in connection with a symposium which I had suggested but which turned out very different from what I had in mind.

61. Written in connection with Richard Palmer's new unabridged translation of the German original of Husserl's Britannica article.

62. An incidental piece with the secondary purpose of showing the importance of salvaging correspondences as a particularly effective way of destroying historical legends.

63. Meant also as a model for tracing the impact of phenomenology on areas other than psychology and psychiatry.

65. An incidental piece honoring Dorion Cairns' role in introducing phenomenology to the United States.

66. An English version of a German paper on "Epoché und Reduktion bei Pfänder und Husserl" to be published in *Pfänder-Studien* (München, Wilhelm Fink Verlag).

67. An outline of an "existential" social ethics written in 1969 in response to an invitation by Professor Peter Bertocci for a statement on matters which I considered most urgent in my philosophy.

75. Volume of collected essays on and in phenomenology, tentatively called *Doing Phenomenology*, in which I want to integrate essays on crucial problems in phenomenology published during the past 32 years, such as #13, #14 and #17, supplemented by unpublished pieces, and by concrete demonstrations of such a phenomenology from different areas as the best antidote to metaphenomenology, as represented in mere history or methodology.

BIBLIOGRAPHY
OF
HERBERT SPIEGELBERG'S
PUBLISHED WORKS
1930–1974

1. "Ueber das Wesen der Idee." Munich Dissertation, published in *Jahrbuch für Philosophie und Phänomenologische Forschung*, ed. by E. Husserl, 11 (1930), 1–228.
2. Review of Roman Ingarden, *Das literarische Kunstwerk, Zeitschrift für Ästhetik und allgemeine Kunstwissenschaft* 75 (1930), 380–87.
3. "Sinn und Recht der Begründung in der axiologischen und praktischen Philosophie" in *Neue Münchner Philosophische Abhandlungen*, ed. by E. Heller and F. Loew, (Leipzig, 1933) 100–42.
4. *Antirelativismus.* Kritik des Relativismus und Skeptizismus der Werte und des Sollens. (Zürich, Max Niehans Verlag, 1935) 100 pp.
5. *Gesetz und Sittengesetz.* Strukturanalytische und historische Vorstudien zu einer gesetzesfreien Ethik. (Zürich, Max Niehans Verlag, 1935) 380 pp.
6. "Der Begriff der Intentionalität in der Scholastik, bei Brentano und Husserl" in *Philosophische Hefte*, 5 (1936, 74–91; reprinted with additions in *Studia Philosophica*, XXIX (1970), 189–216.
7. "Johannes Gerson und die christliche Friedensidee." Four articles, published in *Friedenswarte* (Geneva, 1934) pp. 156–168; 1936, pp. 221–35; 1937, pp. 70–81, 106–18.
8. "Zur Rehabilitierung der philosophischen Tradition" (Review of Maximilian Beck, *Philosophische Hefte*) *Neue Zürcher Zeitung*, October 22, 1934.
9. "Entwertung des Menschen" (Review of Victor Monod, *La Dévalorisation de l'homme*) *Ibid.* August 12, 1937.
10. "Justice Presupposes Natural Law," *Ethics* 49 (1939) 343–348.
11. Rev. of Peter Kamm, *Philosophie und Pädagogik Paul Häberlins.* *Ethics* 49 (1939), 245.
12. Rev. of William Ebenstein, *Die rechtsphilosophische Schule der reinen Rechtslehre. Ibid.* 49 (1939) 495 f.
13. "The 'Reality-Phenomenon' and Reality," *Philosophical Essays in Memory of Edmund Husserl*, ed. by Marvin Farber. (Cambridge, Harvard University Press 1940) pp. 84–105.
14. "Critical Phenomenological Realism," *Philosophy and Phenomenological Research* 1 (1941), 154–76.
15. Rev. of Wolfgang Köhler, *The Place of Value in a World of Facts. Ibid.* 1 (1941), 337–86.

16. "Alexander Pfänder (1870–1941)," *Ibid.* 2 (1941), 263–65.
17. "Phenomenology of Direct Evidence," *Ibid.* 2 (1942), 427–56.
18. Rev. of E. Parl Welch, *The Philosophy of Edmund Husserl. Ibid.* 3 (1942), 219–32.
19. "A Defense of Human Equality," *The Philosophical Review* 53 (1944), 101–24; reprinted in Blackstone, W. T., ed. *The Concept of Equality,* (Minneapolis, Burgess, 1969) pp. 144–164.
20. Rev. of Curt J. Ducasse, *Art, the Critics, and You, Philos. and Phen. Res.* 6 (1946), 445–49.
21. Rev. of Kurt F. Reinhardt, *A Realistic Philosophy. Ibid.* 6 (1946), 648–50.
22. "What Makes Good Things Good? An Inquiry into the Grounds of Value," *Ibid.* 7 (1947), 578–611.
23. "Indubitables in Ethics: A Cartesian Meditation," *Ethics* 58 (1947), 35–50.
24. Rev. of Jean-Paul Sartre, *The Psychology of the Imagination, Philos. and Phen. Res.* 10 (1949), 274–78.
25. Rev. of Alexander Pfänder, *Philosophie der Lebensziele, Ibid.,* 10 (1949), 438–42.
26. "Supernaturalism or Naturalism? A Study in Meaning and Verifiability," *Philosophy of Science* 18 (1951), 339–68.
27. "Toward a Phenomenology of Imaginative Understanding of Others." *Proceedings of the XIth International Congress of Philosophy* (Brussels, 1953), 7, 235–39.
28. "French Existentialism: Its Social Philosophies, *Kenyon Review* 16, (1954), 446–62.
29. Rev. of Maurice Mandelbaum, *Phenomenology of Moral Experience, Social Research* 23 (1956), 117–20.
30. "Husserl's and Peirce's Phenomenologies: Coincidence or Interaction." *Philosophy and Phenomenological Research* 17 (1957), 164–85.
31. "Zur Ontologie des idealen Sollens." *Philosophisches Jahrbuch der Görres-Gesellschaft* 66 (1958), 243–53.
32. "How Subjective is Phenomenology?" *Proceedings of the American Catholic Philosophical Association* 33 (1959), 28–36. Also, abridged in Natanson, Maurice, ed. *Essays in Phenomenology* (The Hague, Nijhoff, 1966) pp. 137–143.
33. "Perspektivenwandel: Konstitution eines Husserl-bildes." *Edmund Husserl,* 1859–1959 *(Phaenomenologica* IV) (1959), 56–63.
34. *The Phenomenological Movement: A Historical Introduction.* 2 vols. (The Hague, Martinus Nijhoff) (Phaenomenologica V and VI) 1960; second revised edition (1965) XXII, 735 pp. – Separate edition of Ch. XIV (*The Essentials of the Phenomenological Method* with new preface) 1966.
35. "Husserl's Phenomenology and Existentialism," *Journal of Philosophy* 57 (1960) 762–74.
36. "'Accident of Birth': A Non-utilitarian Motif in Mill's Philosophy," *Journal of the History of Ideas* 22 (1961), 475–592.
37. "On the 'I-am-me' Experience in Childhood and Adolescence." *Psychologia* (Kyoto) 4 (1961), 135–146; republished in *Review of Existential Psychology and Psychiatry* 4 (1964) 3–21.
38. Review of Wilhelm Szilasi, *Einführung in die Phänomenologie Edmund Husserls. Philos. Review* 70 (1961), 267–269.

39. *Alexander Pfänders Phänomenologie*, (Den Haag, Martinus Nijhoff, 1963) VIII, 72 pp.
40. "Concerning 'The Phenomenological Tendency,'" *Journal of Philosophy* 9 (1963), 583–588.
41. *The Socratic Enigma*. A Collection of Testimonies through Twenty-Four Centuries. In collaboration with Bayard Quincy Morgan. The Bobbs-Merrill Company (Library of Liberal Arts) 1964, 334 pp.
42. "Toward a Phenomenology of Experience." *American Philosophical Quarterly* 1 (1964), 325–32.
43. "Phenomenology through Vicarious Experience," in *Phenomenology: Pure and Applied*, ed. by Erwin Straus, (Pittsburgh, Duquesne University Press, 1964) pp. 105–126.
44. "Linguistic Phenomenology: John L. Austin and Alexander Pfänder," *Proceedings of the XIIIth International Congress Comunicaciones libres* IX (1964), 509–17; reprinted in #53, pp. 86–92.
45. "A Phenomenological Approach to the Ego." *The Monist* 49 (1965), 1–17, 38–43.
46. "A Phenomenological Analysis of Approval," Edie, James E., ed., *Invitation to Phenomenology*. (Chicago, Quadrangle Club, 1965) 183–210.
47. "The Idea of a Phenomenological Anthropology and Alexander Pfänder's Psychology of Man," *Review of Existential Psychology and Psychiatry* 5 (1965) 122–136; reprinted in #53, pp. 75–85.
48. Article "Phenomenology" in *Encyclopaedia Britannica*. Edition 1966. vol. 17, pp. 810–812.
49. "The Motility of the Ego," *Conditio humana*. Festschrift für Erwin Straus. (Heidelberg, Springer, 1966) pp. 289–306.
50. "Equality in Existentialism," *Nomos* IX (1967), 193–213.
51. "The Relevance of Phenomenological Philosophy for Psychology," in Mandelbaum, Maurice, ed., *Phenomenology and Existentialism*. (Baltimore, 1967) pp. 219–241.
52. Amiel's 'New Phenomenology,'" *Archiv für Geschichte der Philosophie*, 49 (1967), 201–214.
53. *Alexander Pfänder, Phenomenology of Willing and Motivation*. Translated with an introduction. (Northwestern University Press, 1967).
54. "Rules and Order," in Kuntz, Paul, ed., The *Grinnell Symposium*, (University of Washington Press, 1968) pp. 290–308.
55. "The Puzzle of Ludwig Wittgenstein's Phänomenologie (1929–?)," *American Philosophical Quarterly*, V (1968), 244–256.
56. "Husserl in England: Facts and Lessons," *Journal of the British Society for Phenomenology*, I (1970), pp. 4–15.
57. Notes on Husserl's Syllabus for the London Lectures, *ibid.*, pp. 16–17.
58. "Some Human Uses of Phenomenology" in Smith, F. J., ed., *Perspectives in Phenomenology*, (The Hague, Martinus Nijhoff, 1970).
59. "Brentano on Husserl: The Lost Portrait of Edmund Husserl by Ida and Franz Brentano" in Memorial Volume for Philip Merlan (The Hague, Martinus Nijhoff, 1971). *Philomathes*. Studies and Essays in the Humanities in Memory of Philip Merlan, ed. by R. B. Palmer, (The Hague, Martinus Nijhoff, 1971), 341–345.
60. "Human Dignity: A Challenge to Contemporary Philosophy," in Gotesky, R. and Laszlo, E., ed. *Human Dignity*. (New York, Gordon & Breach, 1971). The Philosophy Forum IX (1971) 39–64.

61. "On the Misfortunes of Edmund Husserl's Encyclopaedia Britannica Article 'Phenomenology,'" *Journal of the British Society for Phenomenology* II (1971) 74–76.
62. "What William James Knew about Edmund Husserl. On the Credibility of Pitkin's Testimony" in Embree, Lester, ed., *Consciousness and Lifeworld; Essays for Aron Gurwitsch*. (Evanston, Northwestern University Press, 1972), pp. 407–424.
63. *Phenomenology in Psychology and Psychiatry. A Historical Introduction*. (Evanston, Northwestern University Press, 1972).
64. "Remarks on J. N. Findlay's Translation of Husserl's *Logical Investigations*," *Journal of the British Society for Phenomenology III* (1972), pp. 195–96.
65. "Husserl's Way into Phenomenology for Americans: A Letter and Its Sequel," in Kersten, F. and Zaner, R., eds., *Phenomenology: Continuation and Criticism, Essays in Memory of Dorion Cairns*, (The Hague, Martinus Nijhoff, 1973), pp. 168–191.
66. "Is the Reduction Necessary for Phenomenology? Husserl's and Pfänder's Replies," *Journal of the British Society for Phenomenology IV* (1973), pp. 3–15.
67. "Ethics for Fellows in the Fate of Existence," in Bertocci, P. ed., *Mid-Century American Philosophy: Personal Statements*, (New York, Humanities Press, 1974).
68. *Alexander Pfaender, Philosophie auf phänomenologischer Grundlage* and *Einleitung in die Philosophie und Phänomenologie*, edited and introduced by Herbert Spiegelberg, (München, Wilhelm Fink Verlag, 1973).
69. "Albert Schweitzer's 'Other Thought': Fortune Obligates" in Africa: Thought and Practice (Nairobi, Kenya), I (1974, 11–17). German translation in *Universitas* (Tübingen), October 1974.
70. "Has Man a 'Human Right' to His Native Soil?" (mistitled as "A Question of Rights") in *Friends Journal*, September 15, 1974, pp. 458–9.
71. "Epoché Without Reduction: Some Replies to My Critics," *Journal of the British Society for Phenomenology* V (1974), pp. 256–261.
72. Review of Karl Schuhmann, *Die Dialektik der Phänomenologie, Journal of the British Society for Phenomenology* V (1974), pp. 273–276.
73. "Neues Licht auf die Beziehungen zwischen Husserl und Pfänder" in *Tijdschrift voor Philosophie* XXXVI (1974), pp. 565–573.
74. "Husserl's Syllabus for the Paris Lectures "Introduction to Transcendental Phenomenology" translated and introduced by H. Spiegelberg, *Journal of the British Society for Phenomenology*.
75. *Doing Phenomenology. Essays on and in Phenomenology* (The Hague: Martinus Nijhoff, 1975).
76. "Good Fortune Obligates: Albert Schweitzer's Second Ethical Principle" *Ethics*.